# PRAISE FOR *DO YOU HAVE*

# DO YOU
# HAVE KIDS?

# LIFE WHEN
# THE ANSWER
# IS NO

# DO YOU HAVE KIDS?

# LIFE WHEN THE ANSWER IS NO

KATE KAUFMANN

SHE WRITES PRESS

Published April 2, 2019
Printed in the United States of America
Print ISBN: 978-1-63152-581-0
E-ISBN: 978-1-63152-582-7
Library of Congress Control Number: 2018954595

For information, address:
She Writes Press
1563 Solano Ave #546
Berkeley, CA 94707

Interior design by Tabitha Lahr

She Writes Press is a division of SparkPoint Studio, LLC.

Names and identifying characteristics have been changed to protect the privacy of certain individuals.

## THIS BOOK IS DEDICATED TO:

Anne, mother of my heart, for her support since the first time I spoke in public about not having children,

Deb, who accompanied me on the beach walk that initiated my quest and has become one of my most cherished dear friends,

Jenny, who urged me to take my writing seriously and continually champions me and my work,

And the hundreds of women who shared their stories about what it's like creating life without having children.

 **CONTENTS**

# INTRODUCTION

A new friend and I walk along a near-deserted beach, kicking sand, talking as women do when getting better acquainted. I inhale, then pose the question I always dread hearing and never ask. Simply to get it over with.

"Do you have kids?"

"No, I don't," she answers. "You?"

"No."

We stroll in silence for a while, drifting through the expanse of sand that engulfs us. I've wanted to talk about life without kids for a long time. So I ask if she's okay discussing the subject. She is.

We talk about how we define our lives, what matters to us, how we are different than our sisters and friends with children of their own. It is fascinating. Neither of us has ever talked like this before.

As the years pass our friendship grows, and we keep talking. Sometimes we include another childless friend or two in the conversation.

Nowadays, every once in a while, we host small gatherings of women who likewise don't have kids. We talk about how our lives are impacted in many ways by the absence of offspring, including health, spirituality, and how we define family. Money, end-of-life planning, how we spend holidays. Like us, these women rarely talk about these topics with other people, even with women they know who also don't have children.

Some of us failed to conceive. Others opted out or chose not to risk passing on genetic conditions. Bottom line: no one has sprung from our loins. That's not bad or good, just different.

There are things we non-moms know little about, like labor pains, imposing teen curfews, what it feels like when a daughter becomes a mother herself.

There are other things we often know quite a lot about—continuous learning or personal independence or donating to a college fund for a child we may never meet. Such things are not off-limits to mothers, of course, we simply have more capacity in our lives to pursue them.

Why does this matter? For one, because women without kids are everywhere—a sister, an aunt, a child's favorite teacher. Depending on when they were born, one of every five or six women over age forty-five will never have children. That's double the ratio just one generation ago. Today's younger daughters and granddaughters may well grow up to join us. Childlessness could double again as Gen X and millennial women consider their partnering options, the economics of raising a family, and the impact of population growth on our planet.

As today's young women contemplate motherhood, who do they turn to with their questions if they're considering a path that doesn't include making babies? Or learn they might not have them because of infertility or lack of a viable partner? I wish I'd had older non-moms to confide in and seek guidance from.

But after my husband and I moved away from the city in which we met—first to the suburbs, then to a small rural community—I rarely met other childless women. When I did I was unsure how to broach the subject without feeling like I was prying. If I spoke up, and mothers were in the group, they'd quickly console me or point out all the kids I have in my life—nieces and nephews and my friends' kids. Or talk about pets. That was nice, but the women I wanted to hear from, the ones like me, mostly kept mum.

———————

Now my days of timidity are over. I've become sensitively unabashed about asking the same question I balked at posing that day on the beach. Not to get it over with anymore, but so we can get into the nitty-gritty. I've had a chance to learn from women of all ages who don't have children. Exploring others' lives has opened up options for living I never knew existed.

I know many parents and grandparents are interested in what their children's and grandchildren's lives without their own kids are like, but they're reluctant to approach the topic for fear of hurting feelings. In *Do You Have Kids? Life When the Answer is No* those of us who have been without children for years share our stories in hopes of building broader understanding and encouraging conversation.

What's nowhere in these pages is criticism of mothers for having children, nor are there value judgments of any woman for her reproductive choices or circumstances. Not because these comments were edited out, but because no woman I spoke with expressed any such sentiment.

Life without kids can be as interesting and rewarding as raising a family. Our impact in the world is enormous, but often understated. At work we earn money and wield power. In relationships with friends, family, and other peoples' kids, our interests and contributions change lives. While our reproductive systems may be susceptible to malady, we bring a diverse presence to the communities in which we live. And after our time on Earth is done, we leave behind something other than the footsteps of our children.

Mothers regularly help other expectant women navigate pregnancy, and after their babies are born, they guide new mothers in their unfamiliar new role. It's a beautiful intergenerational connection.

But your mom can't describe what it's like not having kids, and there's no *What to Expect When You're Expecting* when you're not and never will be. Who mentors a non-mom? In *Do You Have Kids?* women without children are candid, often funny, and always insightful about what our lives are like—the good, the bad, the unexpected.

CHAPTER 1

----------

# WHO WE ARE

**F**idgety girls file into the school multipurpose room, giggling, self-conscious. Breast buds chafe against cotton, a few already buxom. Some of the popular girls vamp for the boys, who pass by gawking on their way to an extra-long recess. Inside, girls sit on bleachers, not really ready to talk women's business: menstruation, sex, and babies. How girls become women. Most know something of sex from movies, siblings, and slumber parties, but today's talk is mainly about periods and the bloody show that will soon appear in their panties. This happens to every girl in the room, the health teacher announces, except for a few athletes, whose high level of physical activity might delay their monthly cycles. Once you get your period, she says, watch out. It's easy to get pregnant.

It's a delicate line that teacher walks—providing useful information without too much shock, scare, or sexuality. But the blaring message is clear: be careful, because with your first period comes fertility, and with fertility comes the risk of getting pregnant. A planned baby is a gift to your future marriage, but bearing a baby too soon is tragic. It's up to you girls to keep the boys at bay until you're ready to become a mother.

Most of these girls will grow up to be mothers. It's been that way forever. A woman gets pregnant and delivers her baby. On that day, she becomes a mom. Her life is now linked to the new life she created. She'll never be the same.

But what about those who don't. Who are we? And why don't we have kids?

———·———·———

First, a word or two about words. The words we use when referring to each other matter. So it grieves me to say there's no good word in the English language for a woman who hasn't had children. Every term invokes what we're not, not who we are.

Barren. Childfree. Childless.

Judgment oozes out of those words.

Non-mom. Woman without children. Nobody's mother.

There's no way to describe the woman without the negative. We're simply left being the opposite of what a mother is.

Even a nationwide network of women and gender studies professors was stumped over what to call us. In an email exchange, they debated the fuzzy frontier that differentiates the *childless* from the *childfree*. *Childless* typically refers to women who wanted kids but never had them, childfree to those who chose not to have children. A few advocated for the acronym "PANK" (for Professional Aunt, No Kids). "Non-breeder" was mentioned, I believe in jest. Then, in a slick professorial bait-and-switch, they shifted the discussion to one's right to be referred to by her preferred term, racialization of language, and class realities of motherhood. Fascinating topics, to be sure, but finding a neutral, easy-to-say term eluded even them.

For now we're stuck with terms like *childless* and *childfree*, both of which suggest there's some fixed boundary between the seemingly sorrowful and the giddily free.

*Nullipara*, medical-speak for a woman who has never given birth, comes closest. But it's a mouthful, and the term is also used for a woman who doesn't have a child *yet*.

Without a proper title, referring to us is cumbersome and clumsy. Surely though, as our numbers increase, an appropriate term will come into common usage. Until then, imperfect words will have to suffice. With apologies to all who may feel slighted by my word choices, in *Do You Have Kids?* the terms *childless*, *childfree*, *non-mom*, *not-mom*, *nullipara* are all used in context and with care and respect.

———————

You can't watch an hour of television without seeing ads starring babies, vibrant families, glowing grandparents cuddling adorable wee ones. The United States is one of the most pronatal countries in the world, and it's still a cultural expectation that women make babies. But there is always some percentage that doesn't. At the start of the twenty-first century it was about 20 percent, twice what it was back in 1980. In 2016 overall childlessness, according to the Pew Research Center, has fallen to around 14 percent.

Demographers in the United States define childlessness as the share of women aged forty to forty-four who have not given birth to a living child and assume these women will remain childless for the rest of their lives. Despite cover photos of aging celebrity baby bumps and breakthroughs in reproductive technologies, the number of births to women age forty-five or older is still minuscule (<0.2 percent in 2016 according to Pew's analysis of US Census Bureau data).

We still don't know how the Great Recession will affect the rate of childlessness, but during the Great Depression and both World Wars it was about 20 percent. In those days poverty, poor nutrition, and a paucity of men spiked the birth dearth. Today it's largely healthy females who are foregoing motherhood, and most of our men are not active military.

An oddsmaker might say today's women without children are more likely to be well-educated, urban dwelling, and Caucasian. That would be so, except that childless Caucasian, African-American, and Asian women are now similarly represented in their ethnic pie charts (respectively 17, 15, and 14 percent). At 10 percent, childless Hispanic women are not far behind demographically. A woman without kids is also more likely to be single, employed in a professional or managerial occupation, own her own home (often in a city), and be the only child in her family of origin.

Some of us try to have kids and are unsuccessful. Twelve or more months of unprotected sex that fails to yield a pregnancy earns the notation "fecundity impaired" on medical charts (yet another unpleasant term). Approximately 18 percent of all childless women in the forty to forty-four age bracket fall into that category, which means having a baby someday is unlikely. As childbearing is delayed in favor of schooling and careers, eggs get older. And older eggs are not only more difficult to fertilize, the percentage with genetic and physical abnormalities increases with age.

Some of us—the childfree—try not to get pregnant. Strides in contraceptive drugs and devices support the effort. But do we *decide* against having children or do we simply remain childless?

Studies suggest that being childfree is not so much a single big decision as it is the result of many smaller choices. Instead of choosing explicitly *not to have* children, many simply don't make the affirmative decision *to have them*. In other words, *remaining* childless is the logical outcome of putting off the decision to focus on other endeavors. Then nature makes the decision for us when menopause ends our fertility.

Blame it on school. And work. And commitment.

Study after study confirms that women with higher levels of education are more likely to remain childless or delay childbearing. According to one, with each academic level a woman completes (bachelor's, master's, doctorate) her odds of remaining childless go up 14 percent.

Higher levels of education often result in greater employment opportunities, and continuously employed women (with no period of unemployment exceeding one month) are much less likely to become mothers. Ironically, continuously employed men are much *more* likely to become fathers. Since 2010 women have held more than half of all managerial and professional jobs, and more managerial and professional women are childless.

Then there's commitment. Today many young Americans put off marriage or shun it altogether. The median age in 2010 was twenty-eight for grooms and twenty-six for brides; in 1960, twenty-three for grooms and twenty for brides. During her period of fertility, every year a woman is without a committed partner increases her odds of remaining childless by 15 percent, though there is mounting evidence that single women are willing to have kids without tying the marital knot. In fact, as of 2014, the majority of never-married women are mothers.

Schooling, career, and delayed marriage decisions can add up to years of fruitless fertility. With the stubborn cultural bias that men often partner with younger women, as the window of fertile time narrows, so does the pool of possible partners.

Behind all these trends and statistics, of course, are the individual non-moms we all know and love. A woman becomes a mother the moment she has a baby. But for most women without kids, there is no specific time when childlessness happens. Motivations and circumstances of how we come to remain non-moms can blend into one another, creating more nuanced story lines than definitive explanations.

---

October 2015, Cleveland, Ohio. Over a hundred women, me included, file into a Marriott Hotel banquet room for the first-ever NotMom Summit. Ranging in age from twenty-four to sixty-nine, we hail from fourteen American states, three Canadian provinces, England, Iceland, and China. We're here to spend two days listening to keynote speeches and participating in workshops, all of them focused on life without kids.

Karen Malone Wright, an energetic sixty-year-old, is the summit organizer and founder of the event-sponsoring website theNotMom.com. After welcoming us all to Cleveland, Wright poses a question, "Are you a NotMom [a term she coined] by choice or by chance?" She suggests we ask each other this question as a way to break the ice, share our stories, and find common ground, regardless if we're child*less* or child*free*.

Over the next two days about half the women I meet characterize themselves as not-moms by chance, the other half say they're by choice.

At age fourteen Catherine learned she was physically unable to have a child. Today she's in her late twenties, still struggling with this reality.

Gladys blew out a fallopian tube with an ectopic pregnancy (where the embryo implants not in the lining of the uterus where it belongs, but in one of the fallopian tubes that connect ovaries to the womb). It's a life-threatening emergency that can make future pregnancies unwise or impossible.

Beth is married to a great guy, but she hasn't been able to conceive after years trying, even with infertility treatments. Now in her forties, she fears her time has expired.

Kim wants kids but hasn't found a steady guy who would be a good daddy.

Several women have partners with kids from prior unions who don't want or can't have any more (often due to unsuccessful attempts to reverse their vasectomies).

Heidi was diagnosed bipolar and manages her condition

with a variety of prescription drugs. She's unwilling to risk the birth defects she'd face were she to become pregnant, nor is she willing to go off her meds.

Another woman I meet tells me her partner is female, too, and they couldn't agree on who, how, and when to get pregnant.

On the choice side, I hear a similarly wide range of reasons why women chose not to have kids.

More than one says she can't afford to raise a child.

Another can't reconcile adding to the world's overpopulation.

Debbie postponed deciding whether to become a mom until nature took over and an early menopause made the decision for her.

Jenny comes from a family lineage with a poor parenting track record, and she's breaking the cycle of dysfunction.

I meet several firstborns who say they were designated caregivers in their families of origin and feel they've raised enough kids already.

Amy is happy with her work and her family of two. She chose against adding a child to her already satisfying home and professional life.

A few women express discomfort with children.

One or two say they simply don't like them.

———————

Counterintuitively, the state of non-motherhood can be full of kids. Some women become stepmothers to their mates' children or grandkids. Some gather other people's children into a hybrid sort of family. Some mother school kids or young neighbors.

Then there are women who give birth and release their babies to adoption. Women whose children are taken from them in court proceedings. Women whose children die after birth. Physically all these women count in statistics as mothers, but with no children now they may have much in common with women who never had them. There are women who adopted children or raised younger relatives without birthing children themselves. Especially in physical matters, they may resonate with experiences of non-moms. Some moms may be estranged from their children. They, too, may identify with aspects of life without kids.

Mothers may wonder what their lives might have been like had they not given birth or what their daughters' lives will be like if they don't have kids. There's no point in getting specific about who "counts" as a non-mom. It's like trying to lasso hummingbirds.

———————-

Sooner or later, regardless why we didn't have kids, we focus not on growing a bio-family, but on composing our own lives. Not having children becomes as much a part of who we are as having them does for parents. If circumstances precluded childbearing, we grieve that, along with other losses life deals. If we opted out, the need to justify ourselves fades. Regret for the path not taken may surface from time to time, just like it probably does for those raising families.

There are no common blueprints for how we structure our lives, where we live, who we befriend. Without child-rearing responsibilities we lack well-defined paths and readily apparent role models. Without responsibility for young lives or a genetic trajectory into future generations, our lifetimes have genetic finish lines. Our limb on the family tree does not branch or bear fruit. So we fashion and form our own lives differently than mothers do.

Who guides the non-mom through this vast sea of possibility from young womanhood to old age?

Until I started researching *Do You Have Kids?*, I never heard another non-mom's story, nor had I shared much of my own. Perhaps we're hesitant to talk because we come to be childless from such diverse paths. Some of us have been accused of being selfish because we're childfree and are weary of justifying our reality. Some still carry soft sorrow for the children we didn't have and cringe at the discomfort and pity our disclosure can elicit. And some rarely think about kids at all. With silence, however, comes stigma, marginalization, and misunderstanding of our situation. With silence, younger women who may forego motherhood are denied access to the possibilities of a future without kids and navigate their life choices solo.

Like any truth, there's power in the telling.

Since that day on the beach years ago, I've hosted many small gatherings of women who haven't had kids. Sometimes with strangers, sometimes with women I know. Regardless of venue or makeup of the group, it doesn't take long to get the conversation underway.

———————

After the NotMom Summit, I drive three-plus hours southwest to Dayton. A dozen women I've never met responded to a Women's & Gender Studies Department posting about a discussion I'm facilitating entitled, "'Do you have children?' Life when the answer is 'No'" at the University of Dayton. This ethnically diverse group includes both faculty and staff, ranging in age from early thirties to late sixties.

After quick introductions, I describe how we'll broach the subject that brings us together.

"Pick a card that resonates with your experience of not having kids," I say, as I scatter multicolored index cards on the conference room table. Written on them are questions about how not having children can affect women's lives. Questions like: *When people learn you don't have kids, what do they say? How does not having kids impact your friendships? What might your friends or family find surprising about your life?*

The women scramble to choose cards. A bit of bartering ensues. Then we're ready to talk, each woman leading the discussion about her question. Each topic leads naturally to the next. With nary a moment's lull in the conversation, our allotted ninety minutes together fly by. Just like mothers nod knowingly when another describes her experiences raising a child, these women share understanding about what life can be like without them.

Snippets from conversations with various groups of women open each chapter, followed by more in-depth exploration of individual women's experiences, research findings, and my own story.

Welcome to the world of women without children.

—————

My story of non-motherhood begins with a mummy.

I met my future husband standing in line for the King Tut exhibit in San Francisco. He was respectable and responsible—very different from the ever-unemployed dreamers I'd hooked up with previously. I was thirty when we married, Dan thirty-seven.

My tiny San Francisco apartment was home for the first year of our marriage. Then we bought a house in the suburbs in an excellent school district, keeping our parenthood options open as we stabilized our corporate careers. As the eldest of four daughters in a dysfunctional household, I felt in some ways like I'd already raised a family. Then a couple we loved said they were trying to have a baby, so we joined them. Once my IUD was removed, I started standing on my head after sex, focused intently on getting pregnant. I wanted to feel a baby growing inside me.

Months passed, then years. Our friends got pregnant. We went to the doctor.

Infertility treatment was still relatively new in the mid-1980s. Month after month brought testing, invasive procedures, ever more potent drug concoctions. I was the issue, not Dan. My cycle was too short, so even had we conceived, it was unlikely the embryo would be able to attach to my uterine wall. In the recovery room after laparoscopic surgery, I learned I had endometriosis, too.

"I cleaned it all out," said the surgeon. "This next year is your best chance to get pregnant."

Shortly after the doctor flipped that fertility hourglass, I pulled sweatpants over my surgery-bloated stomach and was discharged. Halfway to the car I threw up in the shrubs. I'll never know if it was an anesthetic hangover or the looming deadline that twisted my gut.

## CHAPTER 2

# MAKING A LIVING

*In my workplace when we need you, we need you. It doesn't matter if you have kids. I don't feel taken advantage of.*

*All the parties at work are related to weddings and baby showers. I'm never going to have a celebration like that.*

*I am a mother. I'm a mother to my work. I give life to my work and to my relationships.*

Coworkers later confessed they thought I had cancer, because I went to the doctor so much. In those days I worked as a recruiter for Wells Fargo Bank, flitting around the nation's top business schools trying to lure MBAs aboard the stagecoach. No one knew Dan and I were trying to have kids, not even our parents. The last thing I wanted was everybody checking how things were going with my period each month. Besides, work was my haven from never-ending procedures, ovulation calendars, and counting days between disappointments. I was pursuing motherhood and career with equal vigor.

————————

Not having children is a boon to a woman's career. And if she never marries, so much the better for her success at work. Paradoxically, it's better for a man if he has some, according to data from the National Longitudinal Survey of Youth. Have a baby, dad's lifetime earnings get a 6 percent pay bump. Mom, by contrast, takes a 4 percent hit with each child she delivers.

The gist of the dichotomy probably boils down to persistent cultural presumptions about gender and jobs. Fathers are perceived as more stable, committed employees with young families to support, while mothers need time off to take care of their tykes, according to traditional gender roles. So if a woman has no children, isn't she more inclined to work longer hours than a woman with a passel of them that need to be picked up from day care by six? And since a non-mom never takes maternity leave, no job has to be guaranteed for her postpartum return; she simply stays on the clock.

————————

Adrienne Casey walked the streets with a badge and a gun before she put on plain clothes to catch bigger bad guys. She pays close attention as we talk, speaking calmly and with assurance. I feel a touch squirmy, like she's sizing me up. I bet that's automatic once you've been in law enforcement.

"I went to work as a clerk for the San Diego Police Department in 1958," she says, "when I was eighteen, and started taking criminal justice classes at school at night. The SDPD had five women detectives who were very big shots. It was unusual for them to be in these positions of authority and make as much as the men. They were bigger, stronger, and a lot more gutsy than your average person. That sounded like something I wanted to do."

Those jobs didn't turn over often. They're also on Kiplinger's list of the Top Ten most risky professions, regardless what sex you are. But Adrienne wanted to be a cop, so she moved to Los Angeles on her own. She got her Deputy Sheriff's badge as soon as she turned twenty-one. A few years later one of the women detectives in San Diego finally quit, and Adrienne went back to her hometown.

"Yes, I carried a gun," she says, "and if I was ever in fear of great bodily injury or death, I would have shot somebody. But my gun was in my purse. We had to carry them that way then. Getting to it when I was really in trouble wasn't easy."

Adrienne is a small-framed woman, now seventy-five, with fine-boned hands that would look elegant on a piano. She tells me about a sergeant she once worked for who didn't approve of policewomen. He looked down his nose at her every time she asked for backup on what she knew would be a tough arrest.

"So I stopped doing it," she recalls. "I would take on anyone by myself, big monsters. I relied on bluff an awful lot. My best line was, 'Don't make me embarrass you in front of your friends.'" She chuckles and says the ploy worked equally well with all kinds of perps—men, women, and youth. "I remember telling a huge woman who looked like a Sumo wrestler that she should behave like a lady. I knew if she felt my little tiny hands on her, she was going to get an inkling of how little strength I really had, so I didn't handcuff her before I put her in the car. I didn't have a partner for that one."

Adrienne stayed with the SDPD for five years. Her first duty was in the juvenile division. "You deal with all the saddest situations," she says. "Women. Kids. Later I worked in forgery and homicide. Intelligence and fraud. I was assigned to sex crimes. Rapes." She drops her voice and talks about how challenging it was for victims to come forward in the late 1960s.

"That was a grim time for rape victims. If you were not a nun who was clubbed on the street and dragged into an alley, your reputation was likely to end up more beaten than your assailant. That was hard.

"But the cases that caused me the most sleepless nights," she says, "were the child abuse cases. When a child is abused badly enough that they have to be hospitalized, you go to talk to them, if they can talk. Take pictures if you can. But the hospital won't just let you in. You have to get permission from the parents. Of course, the parents are the people who usually did it. So I would sneak around the hospital, buffalo the nurses. The pediatrician wouldn't see you. You track them down at their houses and try to get them to talk."

I clutch my pencil as I listen to Adrienne tell grisly stories of her everyday work life. I struggle to string questions together, trying to take in what she's saying. Adrienne, on the other hand, seems relaxed, animated, like she's telling me about misbehaving schoolmates. I wonder aloud how a loving mother could handle being assigned cases like these. Adrienne's answer surprises me.

"Nowadays there's probably a difference between women who have kids and women who don't," she says. "I think the dangerous part wouldn't be as big a consideration as the hours, the unreliability." She's not sure, though, because she worked with so few women over the years. She's certainly worked with more than her share of men, however.

"People talk these days about the glass ceiling. Back then it was black and white—if you were hired as a policewoman, you could not be promoted. I didn't think that would bother me. But as more and more men would come in to supervise me who knew less and less about my job than I did, it began to get on my nerves."

So Adrienne quit the police force and went to work for the District Attorney as a criminal investigator, where women were few as well. She was responsible for bringing homicide, rape, child abuse, and organized crime cases through trial, hoping to put the really bad guys behind bars. Twelve-hour days and irregular work schedules were routine. Soon she was promoted to supervising investigator.

"I wouldn't be surprised if they didn't promote me simply because I was a woman," she says. "When I was a supervisor, if somebody had to go pick up their kids, I would definitely try to work around what they had to do. They knew, though, they couldn't use that as a permanent excuse with me. By the time I left, there were still only four women investigators out of sixty-some-odd men in the DA's office."

Even as supervisor, Adrienne worked cases. "The child abuse cases, I felt so responsible," she remembers. "I laid awake nights wondering if there was some other person I could talk to to make the case, because most of these kids would end up back with the abusing parent." She shakes her head. "That was so distressful. I got an overdose of sad situations. I try not to think about the icky stories still. When I was really young, they didn't bother me. They seem to grow heavier over time."

Adrienne was thirty-one when she married a reporter who came to do a story about her job; they've now been wed over forty-five years. "I think we talked about having kids but decided we weren't ready yet," she recalls. "Steve would have been a great father, but I think we would have fought over a child. He would have been overindulgent, I absolutely know. Today our dog is the most spoiled animal on the face of the planet."

She says she never really felt the urge to be a mother, and she thinks she knows why. "When I was a sophomore in high school," Adrienne recalls, "they showed all the girls a film of an actual childbirth, with an episiotomy and long needles and forceps—the whole thing. It was rather brutal. We all left the room saying, 'I'm never going to have children, or if I have them, they're going to be adopted.' That really stuck with me. I'm sure most who saw the film went on to have as many children as they would otherwise have had. But it made pregnancy a pretty frightening thing to me, and I was a very fearful person then. It scared me out of pregnancy for a lifetime."

———————

Bobbi Hartwell looks much younger than her forty-five years, perhaps because she's sculpted her work-life balance so purposefully. She and her husband Ken ooze energy and good health, and no wonder. They recently returned from a two-year trek through Europe, Africa, and Southeast Asia. Two years.

Trained as a nuclear engineer, Bobbi used to clean up bombsites for the Department of Energy. Then she volunteered for layoff so she would qualify for government-paid retraining. That covered her first year of law school, where she met Ken. Between them they amassed over $200,000 in education loans. So after graduation she briefly practiced family law. "I hated it," she says. "But because of the connections I'd made, I joined a legal software firm and stayed in that field for fifteen years. If we'd had kids, we would've been stuck with the legal careers we hated, just to support a family and pay down that debt."

She's now worked for three different software companies—sometimes at an office, sometimes from home, and always on the road—anywhere from 50 to 90 percent of the time. "The career is largely female," she says, "with lots of project management and software training. Most people couldn't keep up that kind of schedule for more than three years. Maybe a few women had kids, but I think they were mostly grown. The ones with young kids were men.

"My mom says that when I was as young as five years old I told her I didn't want kids. In my twenties I used to say, 'Never say never,' because you hear that maternal instinct can hit people sometimes. But it never did."

Bobbi's resolve was put to the test, and she made a tough decision. "I was seriously involved for many years with a wonderful man," she says. "But he really wanted children, and that's not something you compromise about. We had to break it off." A few years later she met Ken, who was relieved to find a partner who didn't want kids.

Besides, Ken had a yen to be his own boss. So the couple bought an old gas station in Carlton, Oregon, population 2,000, and turned it into a delicatessen. "For me it was a sort of ride-along," says Bobbi, "because I thought it would be enjoyable and a new thing to learn. It was. I learned bookkeeping and market-ing, things like that." She also stayed on as a part-time software consultant to pay the bills when sandwich sales were slow.

Six years later they sold the deli, and Ken joined Bobbi in the legal software consulting business. They soon realized that as long as they had their laptops and internet access they could work from anywhere in the world. Within a year, they sold all their possessions, rented out their little house, and hit the road.

"We decided where to go by setting priorities and indulg-ing our fantasies," she says. "For example, Ken is a mountain climber, and he had always wanted to climb in the Dolomites. I have always wanted to see Africa. We went to the most expensive locations at the beginning, because we never knew when our work contract would end." That meant Europe and Africa were first, which was ideal as far as the weather was concerned. When their contracted hours were reduced, they headed to Southeast Asia, because it was cheaper to live there. Their contract finally ended for good shortly after they returned home.

"Exactly what we anticipated might happen, did happen," she tells me. "We Gen Xers are known for hopping around and having lots of different careers. I've embraced that and thor-oughly enjoyed it with no apologies. It would have been much more difficult had I had the financial obligations of children."

Bobbi's current job in utility regulatory compliance com-bines her law and engineering background. "I make a lot less money today than I could," she notes, "because I've opted to follow career paths that are interesting, rather than getting sucked into following a certain career path. If I had kids to put through college, I would not feel that was an option. The person I am today could not have had kids and been as successful in my jobs as I have been."

————————

A quarter of a million dollars.

That's what the US Food and Drug Administration estimates it costs the average family to raise one child from birth to high school graduation. College is extra.

With such a hefty price tag on rearing kids, it seems fair to say that by foregoing motherhood a woman might choose work options that a mother might find more challenging to manage. Lower paying, but otherwise rewarding careers, like work in the arts or nonprofit organizations. High-stress, well-compensated jobs—doctor, lawyer, corporate executive. Work with long or irregular hours and/or significant safety risk—law enforcement, construction, the military. It's not that mothers don't work in all of these jobs; they do. Women without children at home, though, often have more time to devote to work and less to caretaking.

————————

Chris Clarke was in graduate school at the University of Florida in the late 1960s when she heard someone speak on behalf of the United Farm Workers. Moved by what she heard, as well as by what she'd seen firsthand at some agricultural sites in Florida, she took time off from writing her thesis and joined up, hoping to help organize Florida's farm workers. She was paid twenty dollars a week—ten for food, ten for necessities—and the UFW provided housing. Those were the days of the iconic Cesar Chavez, cofounder with Delores Huerta of the United

Farm Workers and proponent of nonviolent resistance. Chris met Chavez when she was sent to California for a few weeks to work and learn organizing from the pros.

"I spent several years with the United Farm Workers," says Chris, speaking with just a hint of soothing drawl that bespeaks her Southern roots. "They taught me organizing skills, and I ran their boycotts in Virginia, Maryland, and North Carolina. Then I left them and went into political work for several years."

She managed some election campaigns, then did political organizing. She was even a clown for a while.

"I had all these Big Bird and clown outfits and a whole alter ego," she remembers. "I was a big hit with the kids." Her laughter is quick to erupt as she recalls the time she showed up at a friend's child's party. "The little birthday girl started sobbing. I was trying to take everything off quickly. 'Lizzie, it's Chris. It's me,' I said. She was terrified."

Clowning, politics, and campaigns weren't her cup of tea. But nonprofit management was.

"It was interesting," she says, "because I got to work with different populations—the mentally ill, their families. I worked with different community boards, training them how to throw a fit, basically. How to go in and agitate for state budget money. I also worked with breast cancer, seniors, LGBT youth. I've used the UFW training all through my life and took it into different arenas. That training laid the foundation for the rest of my career. It's all about finding voice, helping people find common ground, and working towards achieving that."

Chris is now sixty-seven and lives in the capital of the Confederacy—Richmond, Virginia—with Kathy, her partner of nearly thirty years. They went to Vermont and entered into a civil union in 2000, the first year it was legal there. "In my generation lesbians weren't expected to have children," says Chris. "That was a foregone conclusion. But actually it was my generation that did have kids. This Mother's Day on Facebook it was so tender for me to see so many of my lesbian friends whose kids are now grown up and how much those kids are grateful—'I love my moms' they posted."

Growing up, Chris thought she'd have kids someday, and she was the one in their partnership who really wanted them. "Kathy would have gone along with it," she recalls, "but it would have had to be my decision. For me there was financial fear, because I worked mostly for nonprofits. I think it's totally possible to raise children without a lot of money in a loving home—that's more important—but it was of concern to me."

Money worries weren't her only concerns. "I traveled all the time," she says, "and going into the nonprofit world was pretty consuming. For two workaholic people it would have been challenging. Add to that the layer of being lesbians and dealing with that piece. And my family. It's not like they ever came to me and asked if I was going to have children. It would have been more like me saying, 'Sit down. I have even more news for you. Not only am I lesbian, I'm pregnant.' I approached the idea of having kids with more trepidation than my friends who had their kids when they were nineteen, twenty, twenty-one."

At times Chris thinks about what it would have been like having a son or daughter. "I guess we all have a vision of this child who wasn't," she says. "They might not have turned out that way. It probably helped my career, though, because I was able to devote my attention to my work life. Trust me, I've had jobs where I had no life. I don't think I could have done that and also been a good parent, a primary parent."

———————

Statistics specific to childless and childfree women are difficult to come by. But back in 2002 Sylvia Hewitt, in partnership with market research company Harris Interactive and the National Parenting Association, conducted a survey of successful career women. Results exposed a double standard that, more than two decades later, persists. Ambitious women still take career hits for having kids, while being a dad is the norm for high-achieving men. As she wrote in the *Harvard Business Review*, "The research shows that, generally speaking, the more successful the man, the more likely he will find a spouse and become a father. The opposite holds true for women, and the disparity is particularly striking among corporate ultra-achievers. In fact, 49 percent of these women are childless. But a mere 19 percent of their male colleagues are."

Women's earnings overall have been stalled at eighty-one cents per man's dollar since 2003, found Dr. Michelle Budig, Professor of Sociology at University of Massachusetts, Amherst. But as a subset, childless women bring in a whopping ninety-six cents to the man's dollar. If there's a minor child living at home, married mothers make seventy-six cents to the married fathers' dollar.

Spending more time in school is one of the key factors researchers have found that may tip a woman away from becoming a mother, or at least delay her trying. Dr. Budig cited US Department of Education statistics that show women earned more bachelor's and master's degrees than men beginning in the early 1980s, and the trend continues. "By 2016," she said, "women are projected to earn 60 percent of bachelor's, 63 percent of master's, and 54 percent of doctorate and professional degrees."

As if to make the point, when I looked for childless women to interview, I noticed that college professors were by far the easiest to find and also among the most willing to talk.

———·———

Una Cadegan crossed the academic finish line with a PhD in American Studies. I talk to her on the eve of her fifty-fifth birthday. Her "speed limit" birthday, she calls it.

She's small-town Ohio raised and has never married. Not necessarily on purpose, she says. "In my twenties all my friends were getting married. I was very anxious myself to get married at that point. I hoped I'd have children, if I met somebody I wanted to marry. I never did, for whatever reason." Coming from a large Irish family, though, she always assumed she'd have kids, but it never occurred to her to adopt or foster children to raise on her own. "I didn't want children for their own sake," she says.

Today Una is a tenured professor at the University of Dayton, her undergraduate alma mater. She's also the author of *All Good Books Are Catholic Books: Print Culture, Censorship, and Modernity in Twentieth-Century America*, as well as numerous scholarly articles. Dayton has always been her home. The only time she left was to get her PhD in Philadelphia.

"I'm really lucky," she says, "because I got a good tenure-track job just when those were becoming harder and harder to find. Working in the same place for a long time, I have savings and good insurance. I do feel some sadness about not having children, but I don't feel regret. Maybe that will come later on. But if I never wrote a book, now that would be really bad."

————————

A generation ahead of Una, Jane Zembaty taught at the same university. Today she's a striking, soft-spoken eighty-four-year-old who lives in an assisted living community just outside Dayton. She grew up Catholic in a Polish neighborhood in Buffalo, New York, second of three sisters in a row, then a younger brother. Married at nineteen, Jane assumed she would have children. "It was in the hands of God, as far as I was concerned," she tells me. "I was desperate to have children, but it didn't happen. During that period not having children was like not having a part of yourself. You've been through that, so you understand." I nod.

Jane's husband died of a heart attack at forty-six. She was ten years younger than he. "The saddest thing was there was nothing left of my love," she says. "I had no children, so there was nothing left of him. For me at that point, it was a tragedy."

Her brother Bob was the only one in the family who had gone to college. "'You've always wanted to go,'" she recalls him saying, "'and that's what you should do.' I said to myself, 'Okay, I cannot live a self-centric life. I have to focus my life some way. Maybe he's right.'"

Back when her brother was in school, Jane typed all his papers. "He hated philosophy and gave me all his books," she recalls. "I tried to read Plato's *Republic*, and I was completely lost. So I had two goals when I went into college: become an elementary teacher and find out about Plato."

She took all the philosophy courses her school offered. "I fell totally, completely in love with philosophy," she says. "It was a passion. Whatever my mind is like, philosophy fit it. I wanted to understand Plato's arguments. I was very theoretical."

She was also practical. Before he died, Jane's husband had run a small machine shop. She took over for a year and a half after his death while also attending college. "I kept getting colds and flus," she remembers, "and the doctor finally told me I had to give up either school or the shop. I gave up the shop."

At the end of her junior year, in 1970, Jane told her philosophy instructor she felt compelled to go into philosophy, not elementary education. "I know it's impractical," she told him. "There are no jobs for women in philosophy." He agreed it was impractical, then tutored her one-on-one at 6:00 a.m. every day for an entire year. He mobilized the whole philosophy department to help pull strings. "Thanks to John Carbonara," she says, "I was able to go to graduate school at Georgetown University and get a fellowship. I wasn't thinking about children at that time. Not even slightly. I was so into philosophy, that was my whole world. Children became totally irrelevant."

After receiving her PhD, Jane was hired by the University of Dayton. It was 1971, and she knows the then newly-enacted Affirmative Action program played a role in her hiring. Four years later she was Chair of the Philosophy Department. Then she went to Cambridge on sabbatical.

"I have to tell you the backstory," she says. "I told you my parents were Polish immigrants. My father was a steelworker. My mother considered herself an intellectual. At a time when Polish women didn't get jobs, she insisted on getting a job at a newspaper—a Polish newspaper in New York. My father hated it, because he didn't like the whole intellectual thing. My mother became mentally ill and spent the rest of her life in a mental hospital from the time I was about ten until she died, when I was eighteen. When I decided to go to college after my husband died, my father did not think it was a good idea, because he blamed my mother's intellectual interests for her illness. 'You can't do that,' he said. 'You're going to end up like your mother.'"

Jane takes me into her bedroom, where just inside the door there's a large framed photograph of Cambridge. I follow the path she makes with her finger. "This is what they call 'The Back,'" she explains. "It's all green, and there's the river beyond. I'm walking across the fields from my apartment to my college thinking about a paper I'm writing on Plato. Suddenly I thought of my mother, who I'd always blamed for not giving us a good childhood. *This is exactly what my mother would have wanted*, I thought. *She didn't want four kids and a husband.*

"That's when I realized that not having children was probably the best thing that ever happened to me. Had I had children when my husband died, they would have been young, and all my energies would have gone into them. Instead, because my husband died, which was very sad, I had this whole new life. It fit me much better, like a tailored suit of clothes."

---

30

Fate intervened, and Jane ended up with her well-tailored life. Biology also intervenes to make getting pregnant more difficult with the passage of time. With every year a woman spends educating herself without starting a family, her supply of eggs that could become babies dwindles. Before seriously considering the mommy track, however, ambitious women often feel pressure to stall motherhood, if not forego it altogether. After graduation some find it wise to kick-start careers while their schooling is still fresh.

But their eggs aren't. Especially if women continue their education beyond the bachelor's degree.

A baby girl is born with a lifetime supply of one to two million eggs. By the time of her first period, however, she's down to 300,000-400,000 eggs; at age thirty, 39,000-52,000; by age forty she has about 9,000-12,000 eggs left, up to 90 percent of them with genetic abnormalities.

Hence the employee benefit first offered to women employees at Facebook and Apple in 2014—freezing a female employee's eggs for fertilization and implantation later. For around $10,000 per harvest (and typically a woman undergoes three or four sessions to gather enough viable eggs for insemination at a later date), these companies must figure it's a good investment in terms of employee productivity and retention. Women workers can benefit by putting off decision-making and hedge against the potential infertility that goes along with aging. Why not cover all the bases, continuing an upward career trajectory until some future time when having a family might be more convenient for woman and company alike?

———————

Eggs. Harvest. There's something Orwellian about the barnyard language we use to describe women and fertility. On the other hand, men "collect" sperm and deposit it in a "bank." How come they don't "milk" semen and "silo" it?

Had she been born three decades later, Cheryl Katen might have considered the freezer. "In my forties I went through a period when my body was screeching at me, 'Have a baby.' My uterus was saying, 'Use me. Use me.' But by then my mind was strong enough that I could counteract those stupid tendencies."

Cheryl is now seventy, her short silver hair braided into a tight rattail that peeks out of her collar. Her bachelor's degree is in plastics engineering.

I can't help it. I have to ask. "So in *The Graduate*, when Mr. McGuire tells Ben, 'Just one word—plastics,' did you hoot and holler?

"Exactly," she replies with a laugh. Cheryl also earned a Masters in industrial engineering and an MBA.

Cheryl didn't start out plucky. She was the eldest of four children—three girls and a boy—and grew up in Pennsylvania's coal country. "I can't picture how my life would have gone had I had kids," she says, "because I've been so sure for so long. My mother wasn't the best example of mothering. She was a worrier and a nag. She had my brother when I was sixteen, and she was in her forties. He was too much for her. So my sisters and I took him on like he was a doll. I'd come home after school and get him. By then my mother couldn't take another moment of this kid. I'd put him in his carriage and walk like five miles with him. I loved him dearly. I still love him dearly. But this kid was impossible. How do you cope with this?"

At twenty-three, Cheryl broke her leg on a weekend skiing trip in Northern Vermont with the man who would become her husband. It was a nasty fall—spiral fractures of the tibia and fibula—then she got a staph infection and spent two and a half months in isolation at the hospital. Fearing contamination, everything she touched was thrown away, and her sheets had to be sterilized. "I had five operations trying to fix that fracture," she recalls. "The little bone healed, but there was a big gap in the big bone. I had to put my life on hold for a couple years, then

I said, 'Nope, life's not staying on hold.' Up to this point I was pretty uptight. I had no poise, no sense of the world. I came out of that experience an entirely different person."

In 1972 Cheryl and her husband Paul moved from Massachusetts to Colorado, where he started his PhD. Cheryl went to work at Hewlett-Packard, the first woman engineer they'd ever hired in the state. Her career took off. She was promoted to a job in the San Francisco Bay Area. Paul stayed in Colorado to finish his doctorate. Cheryl transferred to Corvallis, Oregon and stayed put for eleven years. After graduation Paul landed a job at Oregon State University in Corvallis, and they lived together for about four years. Then he took his sabbatical in Australia, and Cheryl was transferred to San Diego. Paul found a job and an apartment in Los Angeles. "We would meet at different places in the world," says Cheryl. "In our thirty-year work life, I'd say we lived together about 30 percent of the time. It was terrific. Dating [my husband] was for me."

Along with promotions, the number of predominantly male engineers she managed increased. "I was known as being a manager of off-the-wall, creative people," she says. "Other managers wanted conformity. I believed everyone was different. Being childless never came up at work, so I did fit in from that point of view. But I also had very maternal instincts. I called them 'My Boys,' and they called me 'Ma Katen.' People would say, 'Don't you miss not having kids?' I'd say, 'What are you talking about? I have 250 kids.'"

―――――――

After four years trying with medical assistance to conceive, I was still trying to have just one. But I was also a nervous wreck—waking extra early to take my temperature, tapping Dan on the shoulder to perform on demand, sucking foul-tasting progesterone lozenges to plump up my uterus, giving myself shots in the butt to release drug-generated eggs. I was nearing forty, Dan forty-eight.

Success at work lessened my feelings of failure at fecundity. My career was going fine, even though the country was in a period of high inflation and economic downturn. I was promoted a few times and developed expertise in the growing field of workforce reduction. I became a pro at laying people off just as Dan's career tanked with the economy. He found himself among the unemployed ranks of middle-aged financial professionals, and I found myself the family breadwinner. Supporting my family of two by eliminating coworkers' jobs was a cruel irony and a heavy burden.

We stopped trying to have a baby when the doctors said our next step was in vitro fertilization. That crossed a personal boundary I hadn't even known I had. Earlier I'd grudgingly taken the potent fertility drugs. But a technician mixing our sperm and eggs in a petri dish in some stainless steel lab was pushing nature too far. To me it was unnatural, not to mention prohibitively expensive. We'll be fine, we told each other.

But I wasn't. I felt like a failure and began to isolate myself from friends and family, particularly those who had children. I knew that wasn't emotionally healthy and soon found a therapist who specialized in infertility. She helped me start grieving the children I would never have. Adoption was a possibility, but Dan and I were both scared. Plus, I figured we were now so old no teenager would choose us to raise her baby. He was fearful we might get a child with fetal alcohol syndrome or drug addiction.

Workwise, Dan briefly tried brokering home mortgages, but his analytic temperament was ill-suited for such fierce competitiveness. He got interim jobs with real estate developers of tract neighborhoods and retirement communities, but nothing lasted. Meanwhile, I toiled long hours figuring out how to shrink the workforce and training managers how to lay people off sensitively. When I had doubts they would be able to do so, we delivered the dismal news together. Telling employees their jobs were being eliminated should always feel wrenching, I believed then and still do. If it ever becomes easy, you shouldn't be the one conveying the news. Nights after pink-slip days, I drove home in tears.

It all seemed pointless now—working like a maniac only to upend people's livelihoods, living in a family-centric suburb, Dan's unstable work life. We fantasized about moving to the country someday, shedding our gabardines, and maybe growing stuff in dirt.

Then Dan lost his job again. It's time, we decided. Let's go.

We sold the suburban house, I quit work, and we bought fifteen acres in rural Oregon. We were soon raising sheep instead of babies.

------------------

## CHAPTER 3

# BORROWED FROM THE BEGINNING

*Children are important to me. When I found out I couldn't have kids, I knew I needed other ways to build them into my life.*

*When I'm playing with someone's child, sometimes Mom throws the mother card, "Come here, honey. I can calm you down. She doesn't know how." Like hell I don't.*

*I didn't know you could volunteer in a school classroom if you didn't have kids.*

W hen you have no children of your own, every child you encounter "belongs" to someone else. You simply borrow them, whether for a lifetime or for the moment. While some women dedicate their working life to other people's children, there are myriad ways women without kids engage with them, even from the very start of life.

You might think women who don't have kids wouldn't be that interested in childbirth. But that's not necessarily so. I'd always been curious about the physical experience of gestation and giving birth. As a kid, one of my favorite scientific playthings was the Invisible Woman. You could see inside her clear plastic body, and she had a snap-on in utero baby attachment that kept my eleven-year-old attention for months.

When I attended my first birth, I was still in the throes of infertility treatment. I'd rented a beeper, which in those days was the only way to be sure someone could reach you anytime, anywhere. Fathers-to-be I worked with often sported them in meetings. I liked being on call for a baby. At 2:00 a.m. one October morning I woke to the ring of my bedside telephone.

"Come quick," said the father. "We're at the hospital."

I arrived just as my friend was barfing into a trash basket and cussing out her husband. I took her hand, while he went out for a walk. Her contractions were coming more and more quickly. I got right up in her face and breathed along with her. Somehow I knew what to do, and her acrid breath didn't repel me. I have no recollection of the passage of time. Everything was immediate. The father came back just as the pushing started. I relinquished my position and moved down by my friend's foot, a front-row seat for the wonder to come. My godson's crowning head looked like a shriveled up walnut; his glistening body followed soon after. Thirty years later the beauty of that moment still moves me to tears.

Once I'd witnessed birth from the outside, I ached to know how it felt from the inside.

———·———

About a third of the women I interviewed have witnessed the birth of a child. I wasn't prepared for that. I thought I was odd and figured most women would shy away from that particular life passage, regardless of why they hadn't become mothers themselves. Here's what several women had to say about the experience:

"If I had stayed in England, I'd probably be a midwife now," says Annie Eastap. Before immigrating to the United States in her midtwenties, she prepared to enter a three-year midwifery course. She attended quite a few births, all of them without complications, all of them at home. "It was such an intense experience," she recalls. "You either love it or hate it. It's always a circle of women; the men seem to hover on the periphery. Hours go by, but it doesn't seem like hours. It's such an incredible blessing to be invited by somebody to be present for something like that. It's a magical, supportive experience. Watching the little head emerge. Watching a woman go back to being almost completely animal. I love it. I love seeing what the human body can do. It's always been a really peaceful, magical experience, not scary at all."

Poet Suzanne Sigafoos was twenty-five when a friend asked her to come take photographs of her first birth. Suzanne didn't yet know she would want children of her own someday. "We'd been housemates," she remembers. "She had this tribal thing going on out in the woods and wanted her medicine woman there. She wanted our friend Adrianne and me there. Her partner was really clueless." That night Suzanne got in the hot tub with her expectant friend in the hours before the baby was born, because her friend was more comfortable in the warm water. Over the long labor, her three friends did breathing with the soon-to-be mother, walked with her, and massaged her feet. "It took her until dawn to have the baby," Suzanne recalls. "It's the great mandala—I got to be on the great mandala. Talk about cosmic. I'm terribly grateful I had that experience."

A yoga teacher I'll call Marie Erickson didn't regret not experiencing birth until she was sixty-one and witnessed her stepdaughter's delivery. "On the spot she let my husband and me stay while she gave birth," she says. "I cried through the whole thing. I never in a million years thought that I would ever see a baby being born. It was a peak moment of my life." As she speaks, seven years after the birth, she still looks awestruck. "What a universally female experience," she says. "It was everything, part of the cycle of life. So primal. So universal. Such a miracle. A human being comes out of a body? We see it with animals, but we humans are so complex. It's the mystery. We can't know it."

Canadian writer and former high school teacher Leslie Hill moved to the Findhorn community in Scotland after her husband died. She was forty-six. Shortly before she returned to Canada well into her fifties, Monica, a thirty-two-year-old woman she worked with and was quite fond of, partnered with a man Leslie's age. "She got pregnant, much to her delight and his dismay.

"I was her support person," she recalls, "and I was to be present at the birth. She'd been a midwife herself, and she had a couple midwives there through her labor. She really wanted children.

"The birth was a miracle. It was very, very moving. The baby was emerging, and he had the cord around his neck. The midwife said, 'Stop pushing, Monica,' and she stopped." Leslie goes quiet at the memory. "They cut the cord and eased the baby out. He was very blue. They took him over to the oxygen. He took a couple of breaths and emitted a sort of little squeak. Seeing the three of them together on the bed, it was just an incredible moment." Leslie pauses, as if savoring the memory. "I got to go into the lunchroom after the baby was born and make the announcement to the rest of the community. I almost could not speak, I was so emotional. The relationship didn't last, but that baby was fabulous."

Virginia activist Chris Clarke and one of her best friends used to go see their friends' newborns in the hospital. They'd compliment the mothers and tell them how cute their offspring was, then walk out and marvel to each other how ugly new babies can be. Then her friend asked Chris to be present for the birth of her first son. "I was grossed out," she remembers. "I told her 'I do not want to do that,' and I didn't. I was probably thirty-five, thirty-six. I was really horrified at the idea. She had a home birth—two days struggling to have this child. You can imagine what he looked like. I went over to her house to see him. I said, 'Oh my God, Mel, he's so ugly.' She was so hurt, and I was shocked she was hurt."

A more tenuous friendship may not have survived the slight. "I ended up being really close to that child," Chris says, "and the mother and I are still best friends. When she got pregnant again, she asked me to be at the birth with Cody, who was six by then. He really wanted to be there." So Chris reluctantly agreed. To prepare, she and Cody had to watch a film of a real birth. "The poor thing was sitting on my lap. After the movie I held him tightly. But he was so calm, cool, and collected. He still wanted to be at the real birth. I was hoping he wouldn't."

Cody's mom was planning to have her second baby at home, too. Chris picked Cody up in the morning, shortly after his mom went into labor. "We spent the day playing," she remembers, "went to the science museum, then the children's museum. We had a great time." Back at Chris's house, she prepared his dinner and thought maybe he'd forgotten about the birth. "I was in heaven," she recalls. "Suddenly he said, 'We need to go now.' I asked if he was sure he wanted to do this. He said, 'I know Mommy is going to be screaming and yelling.' I cannot believe this. I'm a wreck." So right away they went to Cody's house. His mother was in hard labor. "We were right there. It was a beautiful moment. He was six years old, and he was more prepared than I was."

Today Chris feels more connected to those two boys, who are now young men, than she does her nephew and niece.

————————

World traveler Bobbi Hartwell tried to participate in a stranger's birth experience. On the flip side of freezing eggs to fertilize later, she offered hers to someone she never met.

Back when she was in law school, Bobbi spied an ad in the campus newspaper seeking egg donors. "I was about twenty-eight," she says. "This was what people did when they needed eggs, because they figured people in law school would be smarter. It was also a pretty lucrative thing to do, and I was planning my wedding."

The idea of helping a couple, making them happy, appealed to her. She also thought she'd be a good donor. "I'm a pretty smart person," she says. "I wouldn't mind passing on my genes without the responsibility that goes along with having kids."

But the couple posting the ad wanted the donor to stay involved in the child's life. Attend birthday parties. Babysit, maybe.

"I think they were going to pay me $5,000 if it was a successful transplant," she remembers. "I thought, *Wow, it would be really cool to see what my kid might look like*, but I didn't want anything beyond that. It quickly became apparent we were not on the same page, so we agreed to part ways. I'm sure they found someone eventually."

Bobbi discovered that fertility clinics keep rosters of potential egg donors, just like they do for men who give sperm. "They put you in their little book," she says, "I guess so people can go through and look at their qualifications. I signed up."

But before she could be included in the fertility clinic's donor roster, Bobbi had to complete a thorough medical profile. "I'd had no contact with my biological father since I was about four years old and my parents divorced," she says. "I had questions I needed to answer on my father's side of my biology. I had to have a conversation with my mother about what she knew."

Bobbi was surprised to hear her mom link the eggs she was donating with grandchildren. "My mother got very emotional," she says. "When I told her I was going to donate my eggs, she was hurt that I was willing to give my eggs to somebody else. Like I was giving away her grandchildren.

"That's an issue she's got to work through," Bobbi remembers thinking. "I can't control that. It's not going to keep me from proceeding with my egg donor program, and it's not going to convince me I should have kids. She has never, ever given me any pressure to have kids of my own."

Bobbi went ahead with the process and was selected by a couple she never met. There was always a doctor in the middle.

Timing and preparation of both egg donor and hopeful mother-to-be are crucial to the process. That means injecting fertility drugs. For Bobbi the drugs were supposed to stimulate development of multiple follicles—six to twelve is the goal—many of which would ideally mature into viable eggs. After aspirating these eggs from her ovaries, testing them for genetic abnormalities, and fertilizing them with the father's sperm, the plan was to transfer at least one into the mother's uterus. Her womb had to be ripe enough to receive and implant an egg, so the women's cycles were synchronized. "We were both having our partners give us shots every day," Bobbi remembers.

"The day before we were all supposed to go to Seattle for the transfer, they called the whole thing off." Despite the ovary-stimulating drugs, Bobbi developed only three or four follicles. "We never went through the harvest process at all. I remember feeling really badly for the mom. To be called hours before and told, 'Don't go. You've got to start over with another donor or try adoption.' I felt terrible.

"Then the specialist told me, 'Look, I'm not your gynecologist, but you need to know that if you think you want kids someday, you need to make that happen in the next year or two, or you're not having them. That's how infertile you are.' I had to go home and tell Ken if any biological clocks were going to start ticking, they just started today. When I hit thirty, we made mention of it. That was it."

Bobbi is silent a moment, then she continues, "Until you and I started talking about this, it never occurred to me all that woman had gone through to get to this point. That this was her last shot before they decided whether they were going for adoption. For me it was just something I saw in the newspaper."

————————

Despite reproductive technologies, in developed countries worldwide the numbers of babies being born is fewer than the number of people involved in making them. In other words, we are failing to replace ourselves. Without immigration filling the birth dearth, that spells trouble for how to support aging populations in future years.

Trying to figure out why fewer babies are being born, a 2015 study tracked the well-being of German soon-to-be parents for two-plus years before and after the birth of their first child. As reported by Ariana Eunjung Cha in *The Washington Post*, more than two-thirds of the study's participants said their happiness decreased during the first two years after birth. Using a ten point scale, zero being completely dissatisfied and ten completely satisfied, the drop was considerable—1.4 "happiness" units. In comparison, that same happiness scale gauges divorce as a 0.6 drop; unemployment and death of a partner are each one unit. "The larger the loss in well-being," writes Cha, "the lower the likelihood of a second baby. The effect was especially strong in mothers and fathers who are older than age thirty and with higher education." Such a drop in well-being, the study postulates, may help explain why many parents are stopping at one child, instead of having the projected two.

There was some blowback on that German study. Sure, parents said, their happiness dropped during the first two years—they were pooped. But then the kids grew up and settled down a bit. They said it gets better.

I was left wondering how well-being and caring for others differs, if at all, between parents and non-parents over the entire life span. Developmental psychologists call this "generativity." This term was coined by psychologist Erik Erikson in his eight-stage theory of personality, based on social and cultural development. "Generativity versus stagnation" is his seventh stage and spans ages thirty-five to sixty-four. During this period of life, he proposed, we make contributions to the world that will outlive us, or we will fail to connect with a larger community. How we engage with our larger community contributes significantly to our sense of well-being.

Well-being and generativity are most commonly linked with the experience of parenthood. But two PhDs at the University of Missouri, Tanja Rothrauff and Teresa M. Cooney, examined previous studies and found the link wasn't limited to those with kids of their own.

They figured out a way to study differences between parents and non-parents specifically related to generativity. The 4,242 participants in their initial study were interviewed, then they completed a mail-back questionnaire. A subsample of 2,507 adults (respondents aged thirty-five to seventy-four) was divided into groups of parents and childless adults. When Rothrauff and Cooney analyzed questionnaire responses, they concluded that parenthood is not the only way to develop generativity, nor is it even the best way. "Childless adults, like parents," they found, "may be interested in giving back to the next generation by participating in the lives of children, providing care and assistance to family members, passing on knowledge and skills through teaching, and taking on active roles in their communities. Such activities are no more, or less, important to their well-being than they are to that of their peers who are parents."

———————

Cheryl Katen, the Hewlett-Packard engineer also known as "Ma Katen," took over coaching an American Youth Soccer Organization (AYSO) team when she was at the height of her career. It happened one day when she went to a friend's daughter's game. "The coach was browbeating her terribly," she recalls. "I thought, *This is not the right environment for a girl to get involved in sports.* So I volunteered to coach the girl's team the next year." As luck would have it, that year the AYSO integrated the teams, so Cheryl was soon coaching both girls and boys. "At first I tried to use a male co-coach," she says, "but the kids would listen to him and not me, so finally I got another young woman engineer to go with me. Then they all settled down."

She coached those kids for another five or six years, until they went to middle school and wanted to learn fancy kicks and moves that Cheryl knew nothing about. "We weren't cutthroat killers," she says, "but we would come in a decent second almost every year."

———————

A few years after moving to the country, I took a turn off the main road and ended up in the elementary school parking lot. Painted on the side of the building was the school mascot, a huge snarling cougar. *Must be a sign,* I thought. "Cougar" was my childhood nickname.

I pulled open the heavy front door. The hallway was quiet. Children's drawings and writings were stapled onto multicolored, construction-paper-covered bulletin boards edged with bright, corrugated borders. By my calculations it had been decades since I last stood outside the principal's office.

As I reached for the doorknob, I heard my name called out from down the hall. A woman I knew from my yoga class greeted me.

"Kate, what are you doing here?" she asked.

"I want to help kids learn to read and write," I told her. "I'd like to volunteer."

"You're welcome in my class," she said.

The following week I went back to third grade.

For the next ten years, at the beginning of each school year, I'd introduce myself the same way: "Hi, I'm Kate. I like it when you call me by my first name. I'm here to help you with reading and writing. This is my nth [whatever the correct number was] time in third grade."

About year three a little boy jumped out of his chair, grabbed my hand, and looked up at me with blue wide-eyed earnestness. "I'll help you, Miss Kate," he said. "I promise."

———————

Years after she tried unsuccessfully to give her eggs to a stranger, Bobbi Hartwell and her husband took their troubled teenage niece into their home. This was while they were running the deli, and Bobbi was working her full-time consulting job.

"She was seventeen," Bobbi recalls, "so it was her senior year of high school. She didn't have a driver's license when she came to us, so I'm driving her to school, places for activities. Having regular meals planned was one of the biggest shocks to my system from having a kid in the house."

Their niece had some issues with structure, and she'd gotten into some trouble. "It's not that her mom didn't care," Bobbi recalls. "Mom was just so busy trying to keep food on the table that she didn't have any energy for her daughter. There wasn't much discipline at home, and our niece knew given that kind of leeway she was about to hang herself with that much rope."

The girl instigated the move, asking Uncle Kenneth if she could come stay. "She's a pretty perceptive kid," says Bobbi, "and she knew we would give her the structure and discipline she didn't have at home. She also knew she would hate it, and she did, but it was the one chance she had to actually get her life organized. If it hadn't been for us, I don't think she would have graduated high school. It was a really hard year for all of us."

If Bobbi had any nagging questions about the idea of becoming a mom herself, that year put them to rest. "I saw and really understood for the first time what it means to work a lot of hours running a small business, working another full-time job, and doing lots of volunteer work," she says. "All of a sudden I tried to add a seventeen-year-old into the mix. It made me appreciate my friends who are mothers a lot more."

Bobbi refers to this time as her *cheater year.* "I can tell you exactly what it would have been like if I had had kids," she says. "It was like an exchange program. I feel like I had a little glimpse into how I would have reacted and responded. I got to see motherhood, and I did not like it. Not one bit. I couldn't wait for it to be over."

She knows now how life would have been different had she and Ken had a child from the beginning. "I never would have been willing to start the deli," she says. "I think my marriage would have been a lot less happy, because Ken would have been forced to be a person that really isn't in his nature. He's a much freer spirit than I am. He wouldn't have been the same person that he is.

"Boy, are we glad we didn't have children. This was confirmation we hadn't made a mistake."

———————

Sometimes borrowing children doesn't sit so well with their mothers. Sometimes it's a great blessing. Sometimes it's tough to know how a particular mother feels about your involvement with their child until she tells you.

Nanny Susan Gianotti has cared for the two boys in her charge for more than ten years. She sees no dividing line between her job and her love for the now ten- and thirteen-year-olds. They belong to their parents, sure, but Susan is the one who helps in their classrooms, cheers for them at swim meets, does homework with them. Even the thirteen-year-old still calls her by the name he gave her as a toddler, "Sue-Sue."

Susan grew up in a Catholic family of ten kids, half boys and half girls. "There are the first five and the second five," she says. "I'm the start of the second five. I was called 'Midget Mother,' because I was the one who planned things. If we were going on a long car trip, I would bring water and cups for everyone. I had aspirin and treats to pass out. They still call me Midget Mother, even though I don't have children."

When in her midforties Susan was diagnosed with ovarian cancer. Forty-eight hours after the diagnosis, her entire reproductive system was excised and with it her hopes of getting pregnant someday. "I'm not married," she says, "I'm single. I knew I was past my prime. But there are still moments when I think *now I'll never have a baby.*"

Three weeks after her surgery, Susan convinced one of her sisters to drive her over to visit the children she loves so much. "The boys just wanted me back," she recalls. Before she left the day of her visit, their parents met with her privately. "The mother says, 'We just want to let you know, if you don't work, you don't get paid. We're not going to help you out.'"

Susan was stunned. "I was so sick, but I had to work to make a living and pay for insurance," she says. "They have their issues, but I love those children dearly." Susan went back to work. "I do everything with them. I pick them up from school. I go on field trips, parties, plan snacks. Everything. The parents know that. The mother has often said, 'You've raised my kids.'"

A few months later, the parents told the children they were separating. "You'll still be here, right Sue-Sue?" the children later asked her.

"'Yes,' I said. 'I'm not going to leave.' It's heartbreaking. I don't have my own children. I've already told them I'll know them for the rest of my life. The parents have children, two beautiful children, but they're not there much. That's what makes me the saddest. I'd trade places in a heartbeat, because those boys could be gone, just like that."

A year after her surgery, Susan is feeling stronger and healthier. "I need to quit that job," she says, "but I'm still there. Those special little boys are the main reason I stay."

———————

*Alloparenting* sounds like what Susan is doing for those boys. The term means "other parenting" or "sharing child-rearing with other trusted adults or older children," says Daniel J. Siegel, MD, Executive Director of the Mindsight Institute and clinical professor of psychiatry at UCLA. Siegel has written extensively about attachment and the neuropsychology of children's, teenage, and adult brains.

"Human attachment can be understood as involving four S's," he explains. "We need to be *seen, safe,* and *soothed* in order to feel *secure.*"

Security is derived from, among other things, being noticed and attended to, protected from harm, and comforted by reliable others. According to Siegel, "We can have attachments to more than just our mother. We can form attachments to a few older, stronger, and hopefully wiser individuals to whom we can turn for protection and comfort."

———————

Sometimes sources of security live across the street. Barbara Hanna and her husband John were in their early fifties, living in Canton, Ohio, when new neighbors moved in—a couple a good twenty years younger. The four quickly bonded over a shared passion for biking. Their age difference didn't faze formation of strong friendships. In some ways it helped.

"Both couples were DINKs," Barbara, now seventy, tells me. "Do you know what that means?"

"Yup," I say. "Double income, no kids." The term was coined back in the 1980s.

The two couples didn't share DINK status for long. At lunch one day several months after moving in, her young neighbor told Barbara she was expecting. Right after she gave birth, the Hannas were the first people the new parents summoned to the hospital.

Today their eldest daughter is thirteen, her twin sisters twelve. When she was two years old, the big girl christened Barbara as "Ammie," husband John is called "Ampa," and the Hannas refer to the kids as their "grandgirls." Though the Hannas tried unsuccessfully to have children of their own, "one of the pluses," she says, "is it left us open when these three little grandgirls came into our lives. We've been there for them their whole lives."

With biological grandparents strewn across Florida, West Virginia, and Wisconsin, the Hannas fulfilled the role of local family, celebrating birthdays and holidays together, attending piano and ballet recitals, and hosting sleepovers. The grandparents didn't seem to feel slighted. "They say they're just glad their grandchildren are getting attention," says Barbara.

Last April the young family moved to Texas. When the parents got the call her father had died, they asked the Hannas to come care for the girls. They'd also watched them for three weeks while the parents were house hunting. A former schoolteacher, Barbara easily honchoed the girls' homeschooling, while John managed meal planning and preparation. "I called him the Cafeteria Lady," Barbara says, "because he would cook while I supervised the kids. We were more like parents, and the girls didn't like it. 'We like you better as Ammie and Ampa,' they said."

Barbara has been surprised by how family and friends react to the Hanna's special relationship with these youngsters, both pleasantly and not so much. When her aging mother was dividing up her Christmas ornaments among the grandchildren last year, she told Barbara, "Make sure you put your three on the list, because they're my grandgirls, too." The girls were thrilled to receive such special gifts.

"I find that when I'm with groups of friends, everybody asks about each others' kids," Barbara says. "They all know I have these girls in my life, but nobody asks me anything. I'm just kind of there. It's like they just don't see it, or they wouldn't be like that."

————–-

I, too, have some special young people in my life. They know about each other, but until a couple years ago they'd never met. I used to refer to them as "son- and daughter-of-my-heart." But not anymore.

The young woman's mother took me aside at a large family gathering one Easter to open her heart and share her hurt. She felt my using the term "daughter" somehow diminished her own relationship with her child. We were spending too much time together. I was struck dumb. I didn't know what to say, so I said nothing. Later I learned the mother also shared her feelings with her daughter. The daughter and I agreed to settle on some other term, maybe "special friend" or something. We still don't know what to call each other. Sometimes I feel the need to keep my expressions of love in check.

When he was a teenager, the son-of-my-heart told me he liked the honorific. Then he had children of his own. One day his knee-high girl called me "Grandma Kate." I savored the sound of that for a moment, then thought, *Oh no, here we go again*. I told her parents what happened and asked how they wanted to handle it. "Tia Kate," they said. That's "Aunt Kate" in Spanish—what their many sisters were called. I casually knew both grandmothers, and I wondered if they might welcome me into their special circle, but I didn't ask to be admitted.

Again I failed to share how I felt for fear of adding to the awkwardness or putting my loved ones in a position to feel they needed to choose. I agreed with the choice I'm sure they would have made.

Yet what, I wonder, is the risk of including us all in these matters of the heart? Is it because we lack our own terminology? Or does it have something to do with who owns children?

I heard once that in the Crow Nation, when a woman has no children she is considered mother to every child in the tribe. When she moves to the grandmother lodge after menopause, she becomes mother to every child in the entire world.

Imagine growing up in a community where every household contained an array of mothers a youngster could run to, particularly if their "real" mom was absent or it was dangerous at home. Imagine how adolescents with a problem could benefit from openly seeking counsel of others in the clan, weighing their advice alongside what their "own" mother thinks without fear of offending or minimizing anyone. Imagine every woman having the opportunity to feel and express a sense of kinship with every child in the whole world.

## CHAPTER 4

---------------------

# ABIDING FRIENDSHIP

*I feel like there's a barrier between me and my friends who have kids. Kids complicate friendships.*

*Some friends assume that our lives are empty without kids. It's just the opposite.*

*I know a lot of people whose friendships develop because their kids are in the same sports. It's more difficult outside of that realm.*

She was the queen of the swim-for-lunch bunch, a multi-generational crowd who swam laps at noon every day—the confident, curly-haired clothier everybody loved. I was a college student then, and I longed to be her friend. Every day after we each crawled our requisite daily mile, we bonded as we lay side-by-side on sun-heated concrete, burnishing our skin and etching deep lines into our future complexions.

Even after I graduated and moved a couple hours away, we stayed tight. One night my new husband Dan and I invited her and her new husband over for dinner.

"We've decided to try and get pregnant," she announced. Her proclamation came as a surprise, even though I knew she was from a large Catholic family and liked kids. I'd counted on having a bit more time to make adventures together. We toasted their fertility.

For days afterward, Dan and I debated whether to join in on their endeavor. He was decidedly iffy. Where before I'd been ambivalent about kids, now I warmed to the idea of making a mini-me or mini-he. Two, even. I remember wondering what else we were going to do with our lives anyway. What finally tilted me positive was a vision of raising our families together, a tumbling mass of comingled kids.

Always the trendsetter, my friend was pregnant in less than a year. Dan and I kept trying.

———————

The moment a child is born, he or she requires intense attention, care, and engagement. Everyone knows that the period of bonding between mother and child is a very special time of life, when attachments begun in utero deepen, and the mother's attention is crucial.

So friendships change. They have to for baby's sake.

*You'll never understand the meaning of love until you look into the eyes of your child* is said so ubiquitously as to be cliché. The galvanizing power of that gaze may be the first step in forming a chasm between those who are parents and those who aren't. In her book *Best Friends Forever*, Irene S. Levine, PhD writes about how babies affect women's friendships. "The childless friend may feel like she has been knocked down a notch—and in reality, she has been," Dr. Levine observes. "If the childless mom [sic] is having difficulty conceiving, it can be particularly painful for her to spend time with someone who had no fertility problems."

—————

Poet Suzanne Sigafoos is a redhead, who wants what she will never have.

"I want to be a mother out having lunch with my ten-year-old son or daughter," she says, "just talking and talking. At that age they talk in a way that is charming and beautiful. Ten-year-olds are the sophisticates of childhood in my fantasy life."

Suzanne, now sixty-seven, wanted kids. She married the first time at thirty-eight and felt optimistic when actress Ursula Andress and singer Bette Midler had their first babies at her age.

"My age is nothing," she recalls thinking about her chances. "It's going to be fine."

Two years passed. No babies. Her doctor told her she was perimenopausal.

"That was like throwing down the gauntlet," she remembers thinking. "No. We're going to find the best fertility doctor in San Francisco. We did, and we paid him a fortune."

She took all the drugs her doctor prescribed. An ultrasound found that even with drugs, she had developed only a few follicles, all of them too small to become viable eggs.

"That was the day I was found to be inadequate," she says. Suzanne and her husband talked about trying more aggressive procedures, maybe even surrogacy.

"But I was done. I was nearly forty-one. I was emotionally done, energetically done, and my marriage was falling apart."

At the same time Suzanne was trying to conceive, the close friend who introduced the two got pregnant twice with her lover and had abortions both times.

"I was in the midst of infertility treatment and crazy as a loon from the drugs," she recalls. "My friend's pregnancies happened during the most difficult time of my life. She wanted comfort from me, and I had nothing for her. The conflict between us was horrible, and we broke up as friends. I'd never felt like that in my life. The gravity of that is with me always—that I had nothing for a friend who needed me."

Years later, instigated by her friend, the two went through therapy together and have now renewed their friendship.

Later, in a new town and a new marriage, Suzanne embarked on what would soon develop into another deep friendship. When Suzanne disclosed she had no children, her new friend's reply came as a surprise. "I've had children," she said, "and I'm somewhat ambivalent about motherhood."

Ambivalent. Suzanne had never heard anyone say that about motherhood.

"My friend's candor has been a gift beyond measure," says Suzanne. "A loving mother, she has shared hard times with me, some of them to do with her grown children, their challenges and struggles.

"We connect deeply without her mother-self or my non-mother-self leading the way," she continues." Somehow, the full humanity of her 'ambivalence' has allowed me room to move toward accepting and appreciating my life as it stands. She and I are honest about jealousy, too. If envy shows up, we tell each other."

Suzanne wrote a poem about these important relationships:

### Still & All

My friend is staring at her black-eyed teen:
*where have you been?* Gone for days, the girl
gets high and hangs out with her dealer,
has a knack for living minus rules and clocks.

Another friend is pregnant, doesn't want
to be. She turns to me, the one who *wants*

a baby, can't conceive, who's treading loss,
who's shocked and done with *maybe next month.*

I had nothing for her; nothing
for the mother of the teen. There is no pretty
word: I turned my back, let silence pool.
In silence, purpled bruises heal, they fade;

older now, we're friends again, re-made:
tender, somber, loving, still and all.

Friendships between mothers and non-moms are different than those between similarly situated friends. Suzanne says she's never really had the opportunity to befriend another woman without children, and today many of Suzanne's friends are becoming enthusiastic grandmothers. "It's such a beautiful blooming," she says, "such a wonderful new identity for them. They want to talk about it. After ten minutes I just want to call a cab." She takes a breath. "There's loss in that. I can't go out to lunch with a bunch of women and feel part of this."

---

Do we really need friends? Myriad studies confirm that we do if we want to be physically and emotionally healthy. Confiding in a friend can reduce stress and release oxytocin, the feel-good hormone. The ongoing, decades-long Nurses' Health Study, which over the years has gathered data from over 200,000 women, found that the more friends a woman has, the fewer physical ailments she'll report as she ages. And relatives are second to friends when it comes to influencing our happiness and positive attitudes.

True friendships, the ones that last, have consistent elements—companionship, mutual support, reciprocity, and affection—say the experts. Given the stresses and changes of life, at times one friend may be more needy or distant, but the friendship rebalances over time. *Best Friends Forever* author Irene Levine coined the term "friendship coma" to describe the state of a friendship where communication has waned, and the relationship is in limbo. "When friendships reach this state," says Levine, "they usually wither away and die, sometimes beneath the radar of conscious awareness."

—————

"When my closest friend told me she was pregnant, I cried," recalls a woman I'll call Laura Johnson. "Not in front of her, but I knew our friendship was never going to be what it was. Just knowing how women often disappear into motherhood, I thought *I'm losing my friend.*"

Laura was quite sure she'd have children herself one day. "But when I was thirty," she says, "I was in an abusive relationship. After that was over I was totally freaked out about dating and men, so there was a good period of time—years—where I didn't date at all." Today she's forty-six and teaches English at a college in the Midwest. She's never married.

Turns out Laura didn't lose her closest friend. They've worked around breastfeeding and bedtimes and see each other on a regular basis.

"When we get together," she says, "we can have a conversation that does not revolve around her child. Not that I don't want to hear about him, but I don't want to spend two hours talking about her kid."

Instead they talk about areas of overlapping interests.

"She's still interested in what's going on in my life," says Laura. "She can get beyond the baby. There are people who can't. I think she shares baby-related things with other parents and negotiates our relationship in a way that keeps our friendship intact. I suspect she gave a lot of thought to her friendships before the baby was born."

Laura can think of only one friend who doesn't have kids. The others are moms ranging in age from their midthirties to midfifties. Two of them now have children who are older. She rarely saw these women when the kids were little.

"But now that the kids are old enough to not need so much supervision," she says, "my friends are ready to come back. I went out to coffee with one of them last weekend. She was saying that now that her girls don't need her as much, she's got more free time. We need to go to a movie. She's looking for someone to hang out with.

"As regards my other friend, it'll take patience on my part. Eventually she'll have more free time, and I'll get to see her a bit more often than I do. I look forward to that."

———————

Beverly Williams, another forty-six-year-old, is a writer and a teacher and a knitter. She's Connecticut-born and raised, the youngest of five kids. Two older brothers, followed by three girls. Everyone but Beverly has children. When she was a child she wanted to be a mom and a writer and a nun. She didn't know then that being both a mom and a nun was verboten.

"Today I vacillate between regret and relief," she says. "There are days when I think, *What did I do wrong that I didn't have a kid when I could have?* Between that and feeling *Thank God I don't have kids.* Mostly it's relief. The regret I feel today has more to do with my relationship with my current husband."

Her first marriage was at twenty-one to her high school sweetheart. Fourteen years later they divorced. "We grew up together," she says, "and then we grew apart. In hindsight, I'm glad we didn't try to have kids. It seems like when my friends who are parents split, they have really messy divorces. When you don't have kids, it's a parting of the ways and that's the end of it."

Beverly remarried when she was thirty-eight. "When Neal and I were dating," she recalls, "I was the person who didn't want children. He didn't really care one way or the other. Then on my thirty-ninth birthday we had this moment when we looked at each other—we should have a baby."

So Beverly talked to her doctor. Turns out she has health issues that may one day morph into something serious. "I freaked out and said to Neal, 'What if this is cancer, and I leave you with a baby that you were glad to parent with me but didn't really want to have on your own?' That nixed it. Having a child felt very irresponsible to me. I feel regret that we're not parents together more than the fact that I'm not a mom, if that makes sense. We would have functioned well together as parents."

Beverly remembers a time that a group of her friends sat knitting in a corner at their local Starbucks. Beverly is the only one of this band without children. That particular day, seven or eight years ago, a woman they didn't know approached the group.

"Hi, I'm Sarah. I knit. Can I join you guys?"

Beverly liked Sarah's moxie, and the two quickly became fast friends. Sarah's children are now nine and eleven. "She's an interesting person," says Beverly. "She was a doula, and now she's going back to school to become a nurse and midwife. She looks at her friendships as self-care. If she's happy, she feels, everybody's going to be happy. She takes care of the adult part of her life, which includes having meaningful activities with her friends without her kids."

On Beverly's side of the equation, she's flexible and understands that with kids in the mix things can change at the last minute. "I'm really low key if a kid gets sick and somebody has to break a date. I don't get riled up about that. I completely understand that her kids come first."

Beverly and her husband are also knit into Sarah's family structure. "We have a lot of different arrangements of how our friendship gets expressed," says Beverly. "We've done stuff with our husbands. I also really enjoy her kids a lot." That's because Beverly has worked hard to get to know them. "Her daughter is getting to the age where she really loves going to see musicals," she continues. "She feels like quite the young lady to be asked out to dinner and a play. So this spring I invited Sarah and her daughter to come over for dinner, then we went to a show. It felt terrific for the three of us to go out and for Ella to see this is what grownup friendship looks like. By getting to know her kids and enjoying them, it makes our friendship very easy. It's so satisfying."

Babies don't always simply strain friendships. Sometimes they precipitate their demise. Beverly had another friend she knew before kids came along. Now that friend has two children. "I really don't see her anymore," she says, "because she only wants friends who have kids the same age as hers. Without me having a child, she wasn't as interested in our friendship."

One night Beverly went out to dinner with a colleague. At the end of the evening her coworker put her hand on Beverly's arm and said, "I have something to tell you." Beverly's first thought was that someone they knew was dying. Instead she learned her coworker was pregnant.

"She was so apologetic," Beverly recalls. "We enjoy each other, but she's not like a sister to me. I was genuinely happy for her, because that's what she wanted. But I don't need to be comforted just because I don't have kids.

"My friendships change after they become moms," she continues. "Part of it is they get busy with their babies and are on different schedules. Another part is I'm not really tolerant of 'Well, you don't have kids, so you don't understand text or subtext that comes with that change.' I agree, I don't have kids. But I'm an imaginative person. I find that very tough on friendships."

Beverly has thought a lot about how her life differs from those of her friends who are mothers. "For women who have had kids, no matter how old they are, that birth story is very much an important part of their identity. We don't have the equivalent of a birth story to tell."

———-——-

Michelle Callahan, PhD is a psychologist who contributes regularly to *Women's Health* magazine. She appeared on the *CBS Early Show* in 2010 and talked with coanchor Maggie Rodriguez about ways women's friendships can weather life changes, like when one friend has a child and the other doesn't. "We're often drawn to people based on common interests and circumstances, and when life changes, the friendship can become vulnerable," Callahan observed.

For the friendship to last, she said, making time for each other is crucial. Instead of stating a general desire to get together, commit to a specific date. "Facebook is a way to stay close, but it can't be your primary way of contact. It's the icing on the cake." Finally, Callahan stressed the importance of being available to each other at key times of need. "Make sure whatever significant life events happen with your friend, you're in contact at that time, even if you're not in touch all the time."

———-——-

"When you're single, you depend on your friends for your basic nourishment," says Una Cadegan, who lives by herself in Dayton, Ohio. "Most married people depend on their friends for dessert and snacks."

The elder sister of two younger brothers, Una learned early how to care for kids. She's kept those skills honed by helping friends when they become new mothers, especially her friend whose mother died when the two of them were in college. "Her husband worked nights, so I would go out there a lot," she remembers. "We would fix dinner, feed the kids, and put them to bed, then watch TV together. There were several years when they were small that I put them to bed more often than their father did."

Una's competence with children means a lot to her. "It's important to me that others know I know how to take care of them," she says. "I learned things about myself and about parenting, mothering. I can make babies go to sleep in my arms, and I can do it without nursing them, which I think is a really valuable life skill. I admit there's a lot that I don't know and will never know, but I do know how to be present in their lives, know them well, and take care of them."

Two young families she was closest to moved away when their children were still in grade school. "I was lonely," she recalls, "and they were so overwhelmed with new jobs and having young kids that they told me, 'Look, we can't keep up with you, and you're going to have to live with that.' It was one of the hardest things that ever happened to me.

"Now I get invited for graduations and weddings," she says, "and I'm glad to go. They probably think our connection is thicker than I do, because I've been so conscious over the years about not having had ongoing contact. Being single, you have a choice about whether you try to make people feel bad about those kinds of things. You can decide the tie is broken and I'm never going to have anything to do with you again. Or you can just be patient and let them do what they can."

Una still gets lonely sometimes, but she's built a rich network of friends, some with kids, others not. "They're the people I rely on and the people that sustain me day-to-day," she says. "They think I'm exaggerating. But there's an imbalance you have to be careful about, because relationships can get out of whack in ways that can be destructive to the friendship and to your own personal concept.

"People will say, 'You have so many friends.' When I'm struggling I want to say, 'Well, I have to, because I only get little teeny bits and pieces. If you've got x number of friends and each of them can only see you a few times a year," she continues, "that may not be enough for a basic level of human contact."

She knows in some ways her relationships aren't reciprocal. "I need to call on people for things they don't need to call on me for. Like when I need more than two hands. There aren't that many times. I can do an awful lot by myself." But when the pilot light on her old furnace blew out a few years back, she called a friend. He came over with his wife and daughter. "So we're going to blow up the house," she recalls asking, "and you're going to take the whole family with you?" In the end, he and Una successfully relit the pilot light while his wife and little girl sat on the basement stairs watching.

Certain attitudes raise Una's hackles. Like when people say she can't understand something simply because she's not a parent. "I get really angry about that," she says. "Especially when it's associated with not understanding a certain kind of sympathy that people who are parents understand. They don't have any idea what kind of person they would be if they hadn't had children. Sometimes there's a kind of selfishness that parents can have about the world, because what matters is what protects their child. But not always poor children or children they don't know. Just because it took you having a child to give you a heart, it doesn't mean that's true of everybody else.

"You're expected to be an infinitely patient audience for something that for me ends up being really boring. I don't find it painful, but especially when they're talking about kids' sports I'm like, 'Can I have another glass of wine, please?'"

———————

Not having kids has made me a good listener when my friends talk. Because most of them have children and grandchildren, and they talk about them. A lot. Sometimes I think they don't know me as well as I know them. I've tried to describe how things are different for me, but only rarely does that conversation get traction.

The sweet spot of friendship was the time after my friends' kids went away to college and before grandchildren entered the scene. In a buddy bonanza, women I enjoyed spending time with were interested in weekend yoga retreats, lunch dates, day hikes. Times together were even more abundant once we all started retiring, and time became more plentiful than it was scarce. I finally felt like a full member of the friendship club.

I was blindsided when the first of my close friends had a grandchild. Subconsciously I think my reaction might have been primed by baby showers. Never my favorite ritual, now there were two generations of birth stories to hear. And quandaries at the cash register about whether onesies needed to be organic cotton or not (they do, I later was told). I was about to boot myself out the back door of the clubhouse.

Babies come in bunches. It's been that way for years now. Friends whose kids are local often have as little time after grandchildren are born as they did when their own children were young. They babysit and run errands and shuttle the kids to and from school. When my mother lived in a retirement community, I was astonished at the amount of table talk devoted to grandchildren, great-grandchildren, and their photographs. Not that any of these activities are inappropriate. Those of us without children would simply like to switch subjects sometimes.

—————

I just picked up my friend Susan at the airport. She's returning from a monthlong visit with her daughter's young family in Nicaragua. Susan is a good friend. We play music together, even go to ukulele camps a couple times a year. We yak. We kayak.

It's late when her plane lands, but she bubbles with energy, stories, and the healthy mien of someone who's just spent time in the sun. We toss her busting-at-the-seams backpack in the trunk. As I slam the lid shut, I get just a whiff of moist tropical must.

"I did exactly what I wanted on this trip," she tells me. "I was grandmother all day every day for a month. It was perfect."

Now Susan is a very considerate friend. She reaches over and puts her hand on my forearm. I wait for whatever bad news is coming. Instead she says, "Are you okay if I talk to you about this grandmothering thing? I was thinking as I came down the jetway—*I'm going to see Kate in a few moments. Should I talk about my grandmother time? Will it make her uncomfortable?*"

I return the solemn hand-on-the-forearm gesture. "Of course it's okay to talk about being a grandmother," I say. "I want to hear all about Nicaragua and the grandkids, too."

"But tell me if it's not okay, and we can talk about something else."

"I'll tell you," I say, patting her arm then returning my hand to the steering wheel. "Thanks for checking. That was nice."

And also slightly screwy. I love that my friend relishes her grandmother role. I love that she cares about my feelings, but it's the emotion behind the arm-patting that's slightly off base. Today I don't need soothing. Were I still a thirty-something in the throes of infertility treatments, it would be different. But I'm not. That was a long time ago. What I need now is the companionship, support, and affection that come with well-balanced friendships. Like I enjoy with Susan.

———————

I'd like to say my old poolside-born friendship survived. As she raised her two little boys, I continued fertility treatments. I kept my distance to save my sanity, while she focused on family. She invited us to holidays and birthday parties when the boys were small. After we moved to the country, their family visited a time or two. I remember we went to the rodeo together and bought fudge. The dad even helped us wrangle our sheep to the ground to give them their annual worming shots. "I'll never complain again about taking out the garbage," he said, sweat dripping from his chin.

As teenagers, each boy spent a week with us on the farm—turning compost heaps, mucking sheep shit out of barn stalls, laying down new straw. As reward, they rode the little green John Deere all over our land, shearing acres of grass, gleefully reducing our workload. I loved their clumsy boy-man personas and the pungent aromas that encircled them at day's end. I gladly cooked them mountains of nourishment.

Years passed, and our friendship petered. We had so little in common anymore. She tried to stay in touch, but I felt like an add-on to their family-centric system, when what I wanted was the closeness of mutual give and take. It's been years since we last spoke.

------------------

## CHAPTER 5

# FAMILY MATTERS

*Being single, you learn to create family in different ways.*

*People ask, "When will you start a family?" We already are a family. A family of two.*

*On the holidays I open up my house, so nobody's alone. This Easter I had thirty-four people over for dinner.*

W ho counts as family when you don't have kids? The answer can be ambiguous. We can look back from the end of our branch on the family tree to our parents and sideways to siblings—we all belong to a family of origin. With the birth of children, though, siblings bud their branches into new nuclear families, and dynamics in the family of origin shift. As aunties, we may fill new roles we embrace or become a once-removed part of a secondary circle of family.

Some of us stay single, while others add mates and become families of two. If our mate already has children, we might call ourselves stepmothers, maybe step-grandmas, and try to attach to that family.

It's a delicate dance sometimes, finding our family roles and places of belonging with parents and siblings and mates. That delicate dance can get intricate in families fraught with dysfunction, whether within the family of origin or a family acquired through marriage, choice, or domestic partnership. Women without children don't figure into idealized images of doting grown-ups cuddling the next generation. We can choose how we fill our roles, or we can try to fulfill someone else's vision of how we're supposed to be. Our challenge is to become clear about who we are in this jellylike substance called Family.

—————

Indiana University's Brian Powell, Chair of the Department of Sociology, wrote about family in his book *Counted Out*. He surveyed fifteen hundred people and found a range of opinions about what respondents believed constitutes a family:

| INDIVIDUALS IN A HOUSEHOLD | PERCENTAGE OF RESPONDENTS WHO CONSIDER THE HOUSEHOLD A FAMILY |
|---|---|
| Married heterosexual couple, with children | 100% |
| Umarried heterosexual couple, with children | 83% |
| Same-sex couple, with children* | 64% |
| Married heterosexual couple, without children | 92% |
| Umarried heterosexual couple, without children | 40% |
| Same-sex couple, without children* | 33% |

*Powell's survey was conducted prior to the Supreme Court's June 26, 2015 decision that legalized same-sex marriage.*

According to the US Census Bureau, "A family consists of two or more people (one of whom is the householder) related by birth, marriage, or adoption residing in the same housing unit."

————————

Sometimes family looks more like a lopsided Venn diagram, with its circles overlapping. When a childless woman partners with someone who has kids, the big circle of parent and children dwarfs the small circle—the person without them. I imagine becoming a stepparent with no children of your own in the mix might feel something like the first day of school when you're the new kid, and everyone else has known each other for ages.

Aziza Cunin (not her real name) is an artist. Her mixed-media pieces are what get people's attention. Her studio is strewn with bins of found objects and things people are constantly giving her. She never knows what might spark a new idea.

Growing up, her Midwestern household consisted of working father, stay-at-home mom, and a brother five years younger. While her mother took care of the home front, Aziza earned money babysitting neighborhood kids most every day. She didn't understand when her girlfriends cooed over the youngsters in her charge. "You have to change diapers, you have to wash out those diapers, then the baby spits up," she'd tell them. "Yuck. I didn't really like it." By the time she was a teenager, Aziza was positive she didn't want kids.

After watching two of her friends get pregnant at sixteen and seventeen, Aziza went on birth control, even though she wasn't having sex yet. She never quit taking the pill. She soon ended up with kids anyway.

When her mom died of ovarian cancer, Aziza's dad urged her to stay home and take care of him and her brother. Instead, Aziza got married. She was twenty-one. Her new husband was five years her senior, and he already had a couple of kids, ages five and seven. They lived with their mom and visited the newly-weds on weekends.

One weekday about six months into their marriage, her husband came home with the kids in tow. "Congratulations," she remembers him saying, "you're a mother now. I got temporary custody." Aziza was dumbfounded. That day she took on the responsibility of caring for them, because she felt she had to. She also thought it was temporary.

Turns out her husband had been talking to his lawyer about custody all along. The only way he'd get it was if his ex screwed up, and she did. A drunk-driving conviction landed her in jail. Aziza's husband and his attorney pounced. "We had not even discussed it," Aziza recalls. "I felt sorry for the kids and their situation. I stepped into the role as if I were my own mother. I identify as a person who accepts responsibility."

She quit her bank job immediately. She had to, because her husband was a long-distance truck driver at the time. Other times he worked selling insurance. She became room mother and den mother, and chauffeured the kids to school and activities. He'd switch jobs depending on his whim. "He couldn't decide whether he wanted to be the truck-driver type," she remembers, "or the guy in a suit and tie."

The good thing about selling insurance was it brought him home nights. Aziza's dad lent them money to buy a little house, and the family settled into a bit of routine. "He did things with the kids," she says. "We did things as a family. They were definitely happier when he was there. It was more normal. That was the best period.

"I don't know what they thought of me, except that I wasn't their mom. They were still so young and had lived in a dramatic environment before that, but they still missed her." After their mother got out of jail she'd call them on birthdays, saying she was going to come by with a present. The two would sit on the front porch waiting. "She'd never show up," Aziza recalls. "She was always letting them down."

A promotion sent her husband back on the road for short spurts, this time pitching employee insurance coverage to big-shot executives. He and his work friends pumped themselves up for presentations by snorting cocaine.

"He managed to keep it together for a while," she says, "but looking back I can see his behaviors were consistent with an addict's, especially of that type of drug, because he was volatile. He hadn't been before. I didn't know how to deal with it. I did my best. I tried to live with it for about six months. At that point of my life I didn't know myself well enough to articulate what I needed." Aziza was then twenty-six.

One day when the kids were at school she packed some things, left a note, and went to a friend's house. That night there was a knock on the door. Aziza found the kids outside on the doorstep crying, "Dad dropped us off, and he's going to commit suicide." She brought them into the house. "My friend gave them something to eat and plopped them in front of the television. At that point they would have been ten and thirteen.

"Then he shows up at the door," she says. "He didn't commit suicide, he just wanted to get me back. I don't remember the conversation, but I went back."

The kids never really cottoned to Aziza, nor she to them. "I felt sorry for them. I had compassion for them, but did I love them? That is a difficult question." She pauses a moment. "There was no bond. You would think there would be some small amount of bonding that would happen if this woman takes care of you and feeds you and makes you cupcakes. But the bond did not happen. I was going through the motions. Everybody was blocked. We were all damaged people doing the best we could."

Aziza spent the next two years planning her escape. She got a job, squirreled away some money, bought a car she put in her own name. It all came to a head one day when the school called to say they'd found marijuana in the daughter's locker. They said both Aziza and her husband needed to come to the school. "He flipped out and said he wasn't going. 'They're your responsibility,' he said. 'It's your fault this happened.' Earlier that evening I'd listened to both of the kids saying, 'Fuck you, you're not my mom,' then he's telling me I created this? Enough.

"'They're right, I'm not their mom,' I told him. 'This is not my fault, and you can deal with the repercussions of not going to talk to the school.' That's when I left."

She saw the kids only twice more, right after the divorce.

"I don't say I wish it never happened," she says. "I don't say 'poor me.' I don't feel victimized. I went into that relationship as a person who didn't have strong enough boundaries or a strong enough sense of self to say what I want, what I don't want. Looking back on it, I think the whole marriage was an opportunity to set boundaries. Having the kids increased that necessity. If I hadn't had all that animosity and conflict with the kids there, would I have had the courage to stand up and say I'm not going to live this way anymore? I don't know. I hope I would have. I think that whole part of my life was really necessary for me to be who I am today."

She's never seen nor heard from the kids again, though she does look for them periodically on Facebook.

———————

Had Aziza hung in there, it's unlikely the kids' chill would have warmed. Less than twenty percent of young adult stepchildren feel close to their stepmothers, found Dr. Mavis T. Hethrington, professor emeritus of psychology from University of Virginia. As she told Karen S. Peterson of *USA Today*, "If children are in marriages with parents who are contemptuous of each other, not even with overt conflict, but just sneering and subtle putdowns that erode the partner's self-esteem, that is very bad for kids."

On the HuffPost Divorce blog, Mary T. Kelly, a psychotherapist specializing in stepfamily issues, offers tips to women without children who are married to mates with kids.

"You are an 'outsider,'" she writes. "There is a ready-made biological system already in place—a system that came into existence years before you made your entrance. I've yet to meet a stepchild who felt the same way about their stepmother as they did their biological parents."

Kelly's suggestions for women joining a household of another's youngsters:

1. Accept that feeling like an outsider when your partner is with their children is normal and natural.
2. Make sure that your partner understands your feelings.
3. Don't take it personally.
4. Stay connected to yourself.
5. Focus on your partnership.

----------

McMinnville, Oregon is a rural town of thirty thousand. Jenny Berg, forty-five, is its public library director. Jenny busts the frumpy librarian stereotype with flair, energy, and élan. Two years ago she married a man with two teenaged daughters. This is her first marriage.

As a teen Jenny knew kids were not part of her life plan. "I thought there was a real lack of fairness in my mom's role versus my dad's role," she says. "Also, I was always interested in doing what I'm interested in doing and not ashamed of being selfish."

Jenny chose not to have children, even ended a number of relationships because of her decision.

Then she met John and soon learned he was a dad. "My first reaction was, *Oh, this is going to be a fun fling.* Had his kids been younger, there would have been warning flags for me. Because they were a little older, I thought they were reasonable ages for me to think about, I guess.

"I remember telling John that I didn't want to be a mom. He said, 'That's good, because they already have a mom.' I loved that. Both John and the girls' mother are really great parents. That helped me be okay with my role."

Jenny can readily articulate what her role is not, as well as what it is. "I don't try and act towards them any way that I don't feel," she says. "I'm not a confidante. I'm maybe a bit of a buddy, but not a lot of a buddy. I'm as much in charge of the household and the money and the car as their dad is, sometimes more. They go to John first, unless they want to use my car, or if they need a check and their dad's not there. It's definitely not like a mom role; I'm another adult that lives in the house that can be a caretaker of sorts."

The girls call her by her first name and refer to her as their stepmom. But Jenny's still not sure what familial term to use for them. "A friend of mine recently referred to them as my 'bonus children.' I like that terminology better than 'stepchild.' It sounds more happy and fun." She gets an impish gleam in her eye, "But 'bonus' can also be like that little packet of conditioner you get with your shampoo—the tiny one, the bonus. The girls are not the primary purchase or prize of having John as my husband, but they're the bonus. I thought it was a sweet way to refer to them."

After two years, she still doesn't know what to say when people ask her if she has kids. "It's basically you're a mom or you're not a mom. I feel like if I say, 'Yes, I have kids,' they put me into this mom quadrant that I don't think is accurate for me. That's kind of unfair anyway, because every mom is a different mom. I have a hard time just answering yes."

In the early days of family life Jenny, as might be expected, brought home a pile of library books about stepparenting, but after opening the first one she returned them all. "I checked out a book called *Step Monster*," she says. "It must have been for stepmothers having troubles, because it talked about different struggles and how to deal with them, like difficulties with a father's guilt or lack of discipline or an overprotective biomom."

She noticed she began looking at their home life with more negativity and questioned how to effectively fill her new role. "It made me less sure of what I wanted and who I wanted to be in relationship to them," she says. "That caused stress for me, and it caused stress for John. What I figured out, with John's help, is I need to be just me and not take somebody else's advice about what my role is supposed to be or what to watch out for."

That realization made a small but impactful change in her home life. John's a contractor and completely renovated the 1860s era house they bought shortly before their wedding. Jenny wanted her new kitchen kept clean.

"I was regularly frustrated that John wasn't doing anything to get the girls to clean the kitchen," she says, "probably because he didn't care about it either. I took a stance that I'm not going to be the person who tells them what to do. He disagreed. I'm a member of the household, he said, and if I have an issue, I should do something about it. So I started asking them to clean the kitchen, and they mostly did it. It was easy."

Jenny says everyone is now quite genuine with each other. "Rude or gross or happy or cranky or funny or whatever, there's no artifice. John talks about them getting to see us having a good relationship, but they also get to see us fighting and how we work it through. They get to see me as a professional woman and what that means, also me as a community member."

Thanks to her state's requirement that every divorcing couple with children creates a parenting plan detailing custody arrangements, Jenny knows the kids will be with them every other week, as well as the Fourth of July and Christmas Eve. "The first year we spent Christmas Eve together John and I sat down with the girls and said, 'This is new, we can create our own traditions. What traditions do you want to create? We can do whatever we want.' It was a neat exercise to do as a group. Everybody got input and had a little of what they wanted to have as a tradition brought into our Christmas together."

She interacts with the girls' mother only sporadically, typically at drop-offs or pickups. "It's very friendly, easy, casual, not a problem," says Jenny. "There's not any sort of competition or ill will. I don't try to take any sort of role I think would threaten her in any way. She's treated me with respect as well. I have occasionally thanked her for that. She acts like it's no big deal. But it is a big deal."

The amount of family togetherness can sometimes be challenging for Jenny. "John and I have really busy lives," she says, "with our own meetings and classes that we want to take in the evenings. Add two more people on top of that who need rides and have events to attend—that can be tiring for me and rough for John as well."

Jenny can take care of herself. She shares an example. "Tonight the younger girl has a track meet, and I said 'I'm not going.' I don't feel the need to be a soccer mom. I don't feel the need to join the ranks of the other parents watching their kids. Maybe some of them think I'm standoffish, but I have to be true to myself and how I feel about things."

She's pretty sure sometime in the next ten years or so there will be grandchildren. "I'll probably operate the same way as I do now. It's not really my thing," she says. "One of the things I have really enjoyed is watching John be a dad. He is a great dad. I imagine the same thing will be the case when he's a granddad. He'll have such a good time with those grandkids. I really love thinking of that."

—————-

Taking on the role of quasimom seems like it would feel less daunting with the kids nearly grown and some maturity about who you are as a woman. Having lived self-directed for years, options and possibilities abound.

Deb Fischer was forty-two when her marriage ended, at least in part because she didn't want to be a traditional wife and mother. After the divorce she dated for quite a while before meeting Paul, now her partner for fourteen years.

"I assumed the odds were if I was with someone, they would have children," she says. "I didn't want to be a stepparent with active kids at home, and I was old enough that that was probably not likely." Paul has three grown kids—one in Atlanta, one in Chicago, and one in Seattle. All of them were in college when Deb and Paul met.

Deb was forty-nine, Paul fifty-four. He lived in Chicago, she in Vancouver, Washington. After a two-year commuting relationship, he moved west to her place.

"Early on we picked up his youngest daughter at the train station," she recalls. "Paul was out visiting; she was coming to visit, too. When they saw each other, she jumped up into his arms, wrapped her legs around his waist, and they had this incredibly long, big papa hug. It touched my heart in a way that said, 'Whoa, there's something to this guy. I would never have done that with my dad.' That was one of my first memories of meeting any of his kids."

She took a wait-and-see approach about what her role in their lives might be; they'd discover it as they went along. Stepping into a mothering role was never part of Deb's vision, rather she hoped she'd become a friend.

"I wanted to be integrated into their lives and thought that might be a really cool experience," she says. "I didn't have the sense of being mentoring. I didn't have the sense of being parental. Probably because I was so independent when I was their age, I expected them to be independent, too. These young people were going to be a part of my life. What's that going to be like? Are they going to like me?

"I also knew that when dad is happy, his relationship with his kids is better. So I saw my role as encouraging healthy father-child relationships. How could I augment that? How could I play a supportive role? I knew the father-child relationship is a big dynamic in a kid's life that lasts until death."

The kids call her Deb or Debbie. She usually refers to them as "Paul's kids."

"I'm really sensitive to their mom," she says, "even though we have very little communication and interact only at weddings, births, visits. I respect what it takes to be a mother, and I was not their mother. I have a pretty, maybe too strong sense of that differential.

"It's been much easier, because I was never a parent living in the household with them. If I had, it would have been totally different. That could be really awkward and weird. I can't even fathom being called anything even close to 'Mom.'"

A few years ago the eldest daughter married and gave birth to a son, followed by a daughter, then another son. What should they call her, the new parents wanted to know.

"I would feel like I was tripping into something that wasn't true if I were Nana, Grandma, Grammy, or any of the typical grandma names," she says. "Yet the kids really wanted a name they could use consistently with their kids. I chose 'Debma.' It's perfect. It stuck because I'm Deb, and I'm not trying to be anything other than that. The 'ma' is in relationship with the grandchildren, and they want me to have a relationship with their kids."

Paul's younger daughter and her husband now have a young son and infant daughter. They call her "Debma" too.

"To an extent, it's all about the grandchildren," says Deb. "I think because I am not a super little baby person, where I get my real joy is watching them as parents and noticing my own wows—what is it like to have a relationship with a baby or a one-year-old or a two-year-old. Grandchildren change everything in everybody's life."

Like where Deb and Paul might choose to live out their retirement years. Let's just say, hints were dropped.

"I said, 'Okay, Elizabeth, let's talk about this further. Tell me more.' She wanted to have a grandparent down the street. It wasn't an expectation, but more 'Wouldn't that be cool?'

"I allowed myself to play around with the idea. It was clear to me I didn't want to be a babysitter. And I didn't have any desire to do the one-day-a-week, three-days-a-week, drop-the-kids-off arrangement.

"There are times when I feel like I'm being a bad Debma because I don't want that. Paul seems to be fine, and we really do look for times to go and support them. They welcome whatever we can do and know they're responsible to get their own childcare. That's hard, and getting harder."

She and Paul are open to what happens, but it's pretty settled that they won't live down the street from Elizabeth and her young family. At least for now.

I ask her how she thinks she's doing in her role as a grand.

"Word from the outside is I'm doing marvelously," she says. "Word from the inside is, *Oh my god, there's so much I don't know.* Part of it is because I was the youngest of five growing up. Part of it is because the kids are used to certain routines and where things are. It's a discovery every time—their habits, how they do things, what this little cry and whimper means, what's dangerous, what isn't.

"I'm getting better at it, but because I don't spend enough time, I'm not at ease. I'm afraid for their safety. I'm afraid they'll be bored. I'm afraid they don't like me. I approach it with much less confidence, and yet I'm playful. I'm probably doing a ton better than I think I am.

"I get to have an experience that I never thought I would have. I'm lucky. But I won't say, 'Oh man, I can't wait to see them.' Isn't that terrible? I'm not avoiding them either.

"As the kids get older," she says, "I would love if they thought, 'I can't wait to go and spend a weekend with Debma and Grandpa.'"

———————

While there are challenges and unclear roles as one blends into an already-established clan, take out the presence of children, and is what's left really a family?

Amy Blackstone knows a thing or two about the morphing definition of family. She's chair of the University of Maine's Sociology Department and an expert on childlessness and the childfree choice. On April Fool's Day 2013, she and her husband, Lance, launched the arrival of their website "We're {Not} Having a Baby" by sending out a non–birth announcement. Blackstone was the opening speaker at Cleveland's 2015 NotMom Summit and participant in the two-day conference.

From the podium, Blackstone told us that "family scholars recognize four major functions that families fulfill in our society:

- Fulfilling the sexual and emotional companionship needs of members;
- Providing economically for members;
- Providing a home to members;
- Engaging in reproduction, which can be biological and/or social."

Those of us without kids form lasting relationships, nurture ourselves, our mates, our parents, and our pets, explains

Blackstone, adding that research confirms non-parents' marital satisfaction and emotional wellbeing are on par or greater than that of parents.

Even though we don't typically provide economically for children, women without them often provide for partners and sometimes other family members. We can share our homes with mates, other people's children, and families of the heart.

While parents birth children, thus fulfilling the biological reproductive function, Blackstone notes that social reproduction—how children become contributing members of society—is often fulfilled by activities outside the nuclear family at school, church, and in the greater community. Those guiding these activities may not be parents themselves, but they play a crucial role in supporting the development of a healthy society. "It is precisely because they are childfree," Blackstone says, "that they can serve in these capacities.

"When we talk about families, be it in politics, in the workplace, or in our popular culture, the childfree often get left out of the conversation," she continues.

"Yet the reality is that the childfree do form families just as those with children do. Recognizing that the childfree form families—and how they do so—is an important step toward destigmatizing the choice not to have kids."

————————

Blood family. Chosen family. That's how Elsa Stavney, forty-five, differentiates family. Her blood relatives—parents, brother, his wife and kids, aunts, uncles, cousins—are important to her, and she loves them. Chosen family includes her husband, a couple she knows who have two young children, a single woman friend, and another couple who don't have kids. Some members of this chosen family have known each other for decades, others have been added along the way. These are the people she relies on.

The nine of them often spend holidays together, even big-ticket ones, like Thanksgiving and Christmas. "We joke that holidays with each other are so much easier, relaxing, and enjoyable than when we're with our blood families," she says. "We get to do kid stuff with the two kids, which is great. They get all excited about Christmas, so we decorate the tree when they're here for Thanksgiving. Time creates family."

Elsa was a special-education teacher for years before she went back to school to get her MBA at age forty. She managed her classroom of constantly erupting chaos like a conductor leads an orchestra. I know because I volunteered to help out for a school year.

During college in Spokane, Elsa worked at KinderCare and the YMCA in what she calls the "Crawler Room," with the babies. "I loved diaper changing," she says. "I'm serious. That is the most magical time, because they're completely focused on you. I fell in love with those kids, but I never thought *I want one.*"

She also never thought she'd get married. "When Eric and I got together we formed this great partnership," she says. "He didn't want kids either. That solidified the deal. Kids traumatize him—the slobber, the tantrums. Whereas when I see a kid tantruming, I'm like, 'We all kind of want to do that. Let it go. Let it out. We're all a little envious you get to have a tantrum.' If I did that as an adult I'd be put on medicine or placed in a home of some sort." Eric and Elsa have been happily married since 2003.

The couple's practice of spending holidays with chosen family hasn't set well with everyone. "It's hard on my parents," she says, "particularly my mom. She feels like I've rejected her. I'm letting that go. It's not my job to take care of that emotional part of her."

Instead Elsa focuses on people who make her happy, inspire and challenge her. "That's not always people that have the same blood running through their veins," she says. "If I had some sort of dramatic thing happen—let's say Eric died—the people

I would call right away and say I need you here now, none of them are my blood family. They are the people I know would listen to me and know what I needed."

——————

Sometimes not having children means a woman can spend a lifetime anchoring her birth family.

"If you live long enough, you mother your mother," says Jane Dunwoodie, who has lived in her family home since she was born. "The only card game I played as a kid was Old Maid," she chuckles, "and I became one." Jane is a sunny sixty-four-year-old blonde who may be the perkiest person I've ever met.

Before mothering her mother, though, she mothered her brother. Two days after Jane's seventh birthday her eight-year-old brother, Dave, was hit by a car, resulting in a massive brain injury that left him permanently disabled. "He had a sharp mind and a great sense of humor," she remembers. "His limitations were physical. The shaking. The motor part of his brain was hurt so badly. They called it cerebral palsy back then."

Jane's mom involved her in Dave's care, because she felt it was important to her daughter's emotional survival. One of her first jobs was cleaning his urinal. "I'd dump it and clean it," she recalls. "That kind of maternal role was part of me from childhood on. You can be maternal even without the kids."

As she grew up, Jane realized she would have lifelong responsibility for her brother, especially after their parents died. "I had it mapped out," she says. "If a husband didn't fit into that plan or a boyfriend didn't accept him, that was fine. I wrote him off. I chose not to be married, and it's been very liberating. When I finally decided it's okay being single, I started switching out faucets and changing things at the house that normally I never would have thought I could do myself. It felt good. When I did my first plumbing job, I went to see the friendly guy at

Ace Hardware. He walked me through how to do it. That was liberating."

Before Jane chose not to have children, she polled all her relatives, because she knew she'd be ending her family's bloodline. "I was in high school at the time. I would go from one relative to another and ask how they would feel about it if I didn't have kids."

Her dad and grandfather were supportive. Her grandmother didn't understand. Her mom was frank. "If I had had the opportunities that you have now," Jane remembers her saying, "I might not even have gotten married, much less had kids." When Jane asked her mom where she'd be then, she recalls her mom said, "Your little spirit would have found another mom." That answer sat well with Jane.

Twenty-two years ago Jane's brother was getting ready to go fishing with their dad, when he had a sudden heart attack and died. Dave was forty-four, Jane forty-three. The following year her father was diagnosed with cancer and passed away, leaving Jane and her mom on their own. Together they cared for Jane's grandmother, managing her money and her personal care once dementia set in.

After her grandmother's death, Jane's mother began manifesting signs of dementia, too, so she's taken on her mother's finances and personal care. She also holds down a full-time job working as assistant to the dean of the local university's library.

Today Jane's mother is 101 and has lived in a nearby memory-care center for the past five years. Her dementia took a turn for the worse at age ninety-six, when she was hospitalized for atrial fibrillation and ended up dehydrated. Jane discovered she'd gone an entire day without food or water. Her mother stayed in the hospital another week, and upon discharge she had to go to assisted living for rehab. Jane hoped to get her back home, but five years later she's still confined to a memory-care home.

"It's scary, isn't it? Without children," Jane wonders, "who do you have to advocate for you?" She sees positives and negatives with her mom's memory-care facility. "You can make these places work if you're there every day. Watching, challenging, advocating. If you don't, I don't think any of them work properly. Probably people who just dump their parents there don't want to hear that."

She celebrates holidays with her mother, but since they're a different sort of family of two, Jane has made some changes to tradition. "We find the single friend who doesn't have children and include them," she says. "There's always an extra one. I anticipate that's what I'll do when Mom's gone. We'll find ways to celebrate. They're the ones who've become my chosen family. Sometimes that's better, because in some families when they're thrown together all they do is fight over the holidays. There's a reason that drinking goes up, that violence goes up then. There's a plus for us."

Jane visits her mom at least two hours each day. People sometimes ask why she does it. "The family is down to just Mom and me," she says. "If I'm not here, that's a day without family for each one of us. That just doesn't feel right."

Her mom's death will dramatically change her, Jane knows. "I've told friends 'I'm so into caregiving, it's been my whole life. When I finally lose Mom, if you see me starting to date some really needy guy, please tell me to run the other way and learn to take care of myself,'" she laughs. "In a way I'm kind of excited, though I'm hoping I won't be totally alone. I picture some friend moving in, and we'll muddle through it together."

———————

Someone, I imagine, will urge Jane to get a dog or a cat. Pets, some say, are our children. Sometimes it's us non-moms who label them as such; sometimes they seem offered up by parents we know as a sort of consolation prize—*But you have pets!* I assure you, we know the difference. And it appears we're pretty good at rearing the four-legged variety.

Shelly Volsche refers to herself as a "childfree mom." Her kids, you may have guessed, are her dogs. Two of them, with big brown eyes. One's a towhead, the other brunette. Shelly is a doctoral student of anthropology at the University of Nevada, Las Vegas and has professional experience as a canine behavior consultant.

She's studied how people raise their animals and found a demographic in her research that caught her attention—women without children. Of women who used an "authoritative parenting" style to raise well-behaved, socialized animals, says Volsche, "nearly 80 percent did not have children, and 65 percent considered themselves their dog's parent or guardian." These women's pets are being raised using "a balance of warmth and discipline, with most discipline being verbal or restraining in nature. These 'dog moms' appear to use minimal punishment only when necessary for the safety or long-term well-being of those involved," Volsche writes.

————————

When asked if she considers her pets to be family, former special ed teacher Elsa Stavney says, "Oh, God yeah. Not in a weird way, though. We don't throw our dogs birthday parties. They're not our babies. We don't say, 'You're going to stay at Grandma and Grandpa's house.' I consider them family because no other thing in the entire world is as excited to see me when I come home. They're better than family sometimes." She's always had dogs—four to be exact, starting when she was age two. She may try living without one when Sienna, her fourteen-year-old Jack Russell terrier, dies.

Marching across the rear window of massage therapist Annie Eastap's SUV are white decals of a woman, a man, three dogs, a cat, a bunny, and two chickens. "I get comments about my sticker family all the time," she says. Annie has fostered many animals, mostly dogs, for years. She's cared for creatures with special needs, she pet sits, and there's always a menagerie at home. She says she mothers her dogs and her garden. "We all need something to mother," she adds. "I just never felt it needed to be my own flesh and blood."

Beverly Williams looks at how she parents her pets and wonders what that suggests about the kind of mother she might have been. She and her husband recently lost one of their dogs. "I think we get one really great dog in our life, and she was that really great dog. Now we have two average dogs. See what a bad parent I would be?" she laughs. "I feel sad for them, because I have expectations they're not going to rise to. 'We're housebroken,'" she imagines them saying, "'we generally come when you call us. What more do you want?'"

Her real motherhood story, Beverly tells me, involves giving birth to her novel. "I just won't give up on it. I guess that's why I see it as a birth story. When mothers tell theirs, what they're really saying is, 'I had no choice but to get this kid out of me one way or another.' That's how I feel about my book. I have no choice but to get it out of me. Thank God children don't take eight years to deliver."

But not all writers feel the same. While participating in a memoir-writing workshop, Suzanne Sigafoos was asked to write about what she wants for her children. "I can't write for my children," she told them, "because I don't have any children. One woman said, 'But your poems are your babies.' 'That's not the same,' I told her. I can't quite relax about that, that my poems are my children. That just doesn't seem right."

––––––––––

Suzanne focuses on her family of origin when speaking about family, particularly the importance of the role of aunt. Now in her late sixties, she is a middle child, with a brother four years older and sister seven years younger. They grew up in Ohio. "We were aspiring to middle class," she recalls, "but we weren't there yet. I didn't have educated women forebears. I'm the first college graduate."

During summers when she was a preteen, Suzanne would go up to the big city of Cleveland to visit her aunt, her father's younger sister, who worked as a long-distance telephone operator for U.S. Steel. "She worked downtown and wore wonderful outfits, with shoes and purses that matched," she says. "I thought she was really stylish. I loved going to visit her. We really had an exclusive closeness, she and I."

Suzanne's aunt regularly took her on special outings, just the two of them. The summer she was ten, they went to a music festival to see Erroll Garner, the renowned American pianist and composer of the jazz standard "Misty." "There was a tent set up," she remembers, "Erroll Garner and a guy on bass and a drummer. They did not have music stands. We had a program, and there was the word 'improvisation.' 'What does that mean?' I asked. My aunt's white-gloved hand pointed to it, and she said, 'I think that means they just listen to each other and play.' She opened some doors for me. She would take me to the Cleveland Art Museum. If it was Fleet Week, we would go tour a ship. We would have adventures.

"My own folks, they wouldn't take just me out," she adds. "It would be the whole family. But I was my aunt's little star, and I liked being that. My aunt died so young of cancer. I was twenty-five, so she would have been about forty-four. It was stomach-related—really nasty and fast."

Someday Suzanne hoped to mimic the nurturing she received from her aunt, but her birth family scattered. Both her brother and sister have children, and she expected to become the quintessential aunt. But the brother moved to Ireland, and her sister now lives in Eastern Canada. "We're all pretty far-flung and not that close. Getting together is expensive and rare. I haven't been the really close aunt that I wanted to be."

Her sister's family used to live only a few hours away. But

that family split up and then reformed. Now sixteen, her niece shuttles between families in Tennessee and Ontario. Suzanne misses her. "My young niece is surfing all this with grace, absolute grace," she says. "She's at my sister's now for her summer break visit. There's only one guest room, and my sister's made it clear that they're so busy, it's not a good time for me to go. I feel a little bit dealt out on that one, too. I know it wasn't done intentionally, but I'm not getting my 'I'm the close aunt thing,' which is what one can be if one doesn't have one's own children. Now I have almost no contact with family."

————————

When I think about family these days, I think about changing faces and ambiguity.

My place in my family of origin straddled the generations in our household. Bigger and taller by far and four years older than the next of my three younger sisters, I lacked parental authority yet was held accountable for enforcing my folks' edicts. A no-win situation, but I tried.

Our mom was overbearing and scary, our dad a bipolar alcoholic. He did his best to keep his distance from the flock of females at home. After telling my sisters all about menstruation and sex, trying to run interference the best I could when mom or dad exploded, I moved out the day after high school graduation. Home became a series of rentals and roommates, family a place visited under duress.

One of my sisters married at nineteen, another the day after she turned twenty-one. My first niece arrived when I was still unmarried at twenty-seven. I enjoyed aunthood but never quite fathomed the scope of my role. I always felt superfluous.

Then at noon one sunny May day, when I was thirty, my dad walked me down the aisle. He clutched my hand so tightly his knuckles show white in the photographs.

Exiting the chapel on the arm of my handsome new husband, I thought, *This is what I've waited for.* I wanted to create the vision of family I'd held in my heart since adolescence. After three years of dating, the best man I knew was now my husband. I reveled in my cozy new family of two.

Soon my sisters were all families of four. They each worked tirelessly to break the family pattern of dysfunction, and in my eyes they've all succeeded. We vacationed sometimes with one family, spent holidays with the in-laws, or joined a sibling's celebration. Our family of two bounced between loved ones, hitchhiking on their rituals. We really had none of our own.

Looking back, I now see my marriage in distinct phases, a morphing marital mosaic.

The first phase was dreamy. We fell in love, then got domestic. We grew our careers, stashing away parts of our salaries for tomorrows. Maybe someday we'd add to our two-person pod.

The second phase brought the tumult many couples endure in earlier years—infertility, job and financial insecurity, the deaths of our fathers. Moving to the country might help us recover, we thought.

The third phase was one of hard physical labor as we cleared our land, kept our sheep, and built our house. Our wounds scabbed over but never quite healed.

In its last phase, the marriage floundered and fractured. Our temperaments have always differed. While I want to address conflict, he aims to avoid it, so marriage counseling never gained much traction. There was no middle ground to be found. I was sixty-three when we finally separated, Dan seventy-one, two-thirds of our lives now behind us.

Today, as our decades-old alliance fades to a ghostly shadow, our old home swells with reshuffled family. Fresh from her own failed marriage, Dan's sister moved in, creating a convenient new "we" for them both. Her daughter and offspring, son and his wife relocated nearby and now surround the family dinner table. Dan's new family is the old family I'm no longer part of.

On my side of the bloodline, geographically far-flung sisters maintain contact and invite me for holidays. Phone calls and visits from nieces and nephews remind me I'm part of the clan. This spring our mother died suddenly from a blocked liver, sparing herself and the rest of us the full experience of dementia. My branch on the family tree has been pruned and reshaped. Arborists say that generates health and new growth.

Who, I wonder, is my family now?

———————

It behooves us all to consider how we define family, whether we're talking blood, choice, or pets. I picture family as contained within a membrane. Members bind together, sure. But an important characteristic of each family is also the permeability of the membrane that defines its borders. Are outsiders welcome? Or is family more like the concrete wall that once divided East and West Berlin into them and us? What about those inside? Can they flow beyond the membrane comfortably, or is it a violation, a sign of abandonment? When we join families, is it a collision of incompatible substances or an integration of disparate parts?

Immunology tells us that the more tolerant a body is to the introduction of microbes from outside, the stronger and more resilient it is. As humans who form alliances and societies, we can choose how porous and healthy are the borders of our family membrane, just like we can decide whom to welcome into our homes.

CHAPTER 6

----------------

# WHERE WE LIVE

*I stayed in the inner city to present an image to the young people in my community that there are choices.*

*My neighbor and I pick up things at the store for each other. We're helpful without being invasive.*

*When we get older we should all move in together. We're not going to depend on anybody.*

I'm walking down the street. "Move to Honduras," says a lanky fellow right behind me into his phone. *Why I could,* I think. Then it sinks in—I can live anywhere.

Transitioning from coupledom to singleton, I realized I'd bought into the magical thinking that being married meant I would never be alone. My husband and I would share space, decisions, many friendships for the rest of our lives. I hadn't realized how much I'd taken for granted being part of a family

97

of two, even as we steadily grew further apart. I now see that for most couples, whether it's by the slow unraveling of a lifetime commitment, the gnawing degradation of terminal illness, or the instantaneous smack of a drunken driver, one day the experience of coupledom will dissolve.

Without the influence of or obligation to progeny, however, women without children—single and coupled—can choose how, where, and with whom we live. Everyone wants a home and living arrangements that support our needs, interests, and values. In this regard, women who don't have children are not that different from those who do, except we non-moms have more license to choose arrangements that suit us—living alone, with partners or roommates, or in intentional communities formed around common interests or identities. We can even uproot to try different options if we like, without worry about switching school districts or ditching the kids' friends. Our housing decisions are our own.

———————

Before getting carried away with Honduras, though, I decide to focus a little closer to home.

One late-October morning I attend a forum on housing and community alternatives at a local community college. The building is packed with a smatter of Gen Xers scattered among a bevy of boomers. Organizers, many in costume, hand out candy corn at the door and politely turn away folks who didn't preregister. Grabbing a coffee and one of the bakery-donated scones, I sit in the back row of the auditorium and rifle through the schedule. The half-day forum is organized around small-group breakout sessions on topics such as cohousing, intentional communities, shared housing, and opportunities for aging in place.

I choose a session on cohousing, because I'm not sure what that is. I learn most cohousing communities are multigenerational living designs, which include features such as a compressed neighborhood layout, resident management and participation, common-use facilities (such as gathering rooms, commercial kitchens, and laundry rooms), and non-hierarchical decision-making. The presenter shows slides of the first such community, which was founded in Denmark in 1967. It serves as a model for many cohousing communities today. In the United States, the first community opened twenty-five years ago in Davis, California. Today there are more than 160 cohousing communities in operation in twenty-five states nationwide, with an additional 120 communities under development as of April 2016.

Cohousing is one kind of intentional community, though not all intentional communities are formed using cohousing design criteria. At this event residents from several such communities share what it's like living where they do. I find the idea of living cooperatively with people of all ages appealing and perhaps an ideal option for women without children.

We forum participants are invited to visit a local cohousing community the following weekend. So I sign up, curious to see how the model works in practice.

———————

Set on nearly four acres in what was once an urban hydroponic farm within Portland city limits, Columbia Ecovillage was founded in 2009. Its surroundings have morphed over the years into mixed-use industrial, residential, and small businesses. What looks to be a machine shop is located next door.

The property's original 1912 farmhouse sits toward the rear of the property, surrounded by free-ranging chickens, stacked beehives, and the community's massive garden. The main floor of the house is in nearly original condition. A resident tells me the kitchen is countered in straight-grain walnut milled from trees that once grew on the land. The dining room retains its original lead-glassed cabinets, and the living room fireplace is edged with high-fired brick of the times. Upstairs, three small guest rooms can be rented by residents visiting family and friends for a paltry five dollars per night.

Along the busy thoroughfare at the front of the property are five two-story buildings converted from motel-like apartment buildings of the early 1970s into thirty-seven privately owned residences. They range in size from 512 square foot studios to three-bedroom units of around 1,200 square feet. Fifty adults and twelve kids—from less than a year to eighty-nine years old—comprise the village's residents. Everyone except babies works a minimum of nine hours each month to support the community. My visit happens to coincide with the quarterly Cleanup Day. Residents scurry everywhere putting the community garden to bed for winter, painting trim on the farmhouse, sorting art materials in the craft room. Other service options include cooking biweekly community meals, bookkeeping, offering classes and events, and hosting community tours like the one I'm on.

———————

I meet Martha Wagner, who invites me to see the compact studio she rents from its absentee owner. There aren't many rental units, she tells me, and she feels fortunate to have found this one. Martha is seventy-one and single. Her tiny frame makes her living area seem larger than it is.

We sit down at a compact table in her well-laid-out kitchen. She breaks small pieces of specialty chocolate onto a plate and tells me to sample them. Recently Martha took a class in chocolate tasting, and she wants to share what she's learned. Rich morsels melt on my tongue, and I try unsuccessfully to describe what I'm tasting. Martha is more eloquent than I, using terms like bitter, earthy, smoky. We agree the Cuban chocolate is more smooth and mellow than the one from Madagascar.

Martha is no stranger to community living. When she was in her midtwenties, she and her then-husband formed a commune in New Zealand. "We probably used some of the same reasoning that people talk about in cohousing today," she says, "having an easier life, sharing meals."

They leased a big house in Wellington and rented out rooms to a couple with two boys under five and a single dad with a seven-year-old. "We didn't spend much time getting to know each other before," she remembers, "like maybe none."

The eight of them later talked about moving to the country someday, leaving the city and their important jobs behind, challenging established ways of being. After a while, there was also talk of practicing free love in the household. Martha was having none of that. "It was not on my radar," she says. "My husband and I never even talked about doing this experiment as a couple or as a group." But all the men were game, as was the other woman. Seeing she was outnumbered, Martha moved out, leaving behind her husband and roommates. "It was the most stressful time in my life," she remembers.

The household arrangement in New Zealand broke up a year or so later, and by age thirty Martha was divorced and living back home with her parents in Chicago. She soon moved west and over the years has lived alone or with a series of roommates in various housing arrangements.

Martha never planned to have kids, though several of her roommates had some. "But it wasn't my job in any way to care for them," she recalls. "I never thought about having a child on my own or adopting, because I never had a lot of money." But she still wanted to live well in community.

"A long time ago I had a dream," she says. "I can still see the images: a group of attached houses that shared a conservatory running across the back, everyone sharing the space. That made sense to me."

One day at a church meeting in Portland Martha discovered

the term for her vision—cohousing. She got involved in helping plan a community already under construction. She put down a deposit on one of the condos and made an extra investment in the project from a bit of money her mother had left her.

"I soon realized I had made a lot of assumptions about project finances that were ridiculous," she says. "I never asked how much money the developers, who were also members of the community, were going to make. When I found out, I remember my jaw dropping. I began to lose my trust, and that was the climax." Then she was laid off her job and had to give up the condo. She lost her deposit and never got any money back from her investment.

Martha knew at the time that across town Columbia Ecovillage was rehabbing some old apartment buildings into another cohousing community. "I would come over here to have meals in summertime," she recalls. "Everyone would be outside. It was so appealing. When I learned I could rent here, I moved in November 2009."

Life in cohousing was idyllic for Martha the first few years. She attended many community meals, even managed the community kitchen for a while.

"My honeymoon here started dissipating once there began to be disagreements," she says. "People started moving out, frustrated at how long it took to make decisions." One of the thorniest community issues of late is whether or not it's okay to grow marijuana on the property. Even though cultivation and possession of a small amount for personal use is legal in Oregon (as long as you're twenty-one or older), some are concerned that community youth would have too-easy access. Others think it's a personal decision. There are also issues with communication, facilities, and governance.

The community hired a consultant who tried to bring everyone together, even lived at the Ecovillage for a while to see how things worked from the inside. Instead of coming to agreement, factions dug in, and some residents moved out. That's pretty much how things sit today, according to Martha. Now the community has hired another consultant to lead a session on conflict resolution. Martha has signed up to attend. "There are several threads of conflict active here," she says. "I'm not very hopeful that we're going to get our issues resolved. But if we did, I'd feel good here."

Another option she's considering is to become less involved than she's been in the past. "I can live here as independently as I want," she says. "Working my nine hours a month isn't difficult, and I can maintain a number of relationships without being active in our governance system. Thinking about leaving here brings into view what I would be giving up.

"I like the convenience. I remember living on my own, trying to coordinate getting together with people was difficult. Here it's so much easier. You say, 'I'm going to a show. Meet me at my car.' And it happens. I love the land. I love being close to food that's grown here and eating that food."

As Martha weighs her options, there's one thing she knows for sure, "I really want and need to live in some kind of community."

———·———

Who does well living in such a place? In her book *Finding Community: How to Join an Ecovillage or Intentional Community*, Diana Leafe Christian describes what makes for successful communitarians: a healthy self-awareness, emotional maturity, readiness to share their thoughts, and remaining open to others' points of view. They genuinely care about the well-being of others and support group agreements, while balancing community goals with their own personal needs. They work hard to resolve the inevitable conflicts involved in building a healthy community and commit to building strong communication and decision-making skills to create a more cooperative lifestyle with others.

As for who would find community living unsatisfying,

Christian says, "Marine drill sergeants, maharajah, and pouting princesses need not apply."

She should know. Over the past twenty years, Christian has visited over 120 intentional communities worldwide, interviewing founders and longtime residents with a goal of understanding what makes for success. Christian was the editor of *Communities* magazine for fourteen years. She now writes a free online newsletter, *Ecovillages*, and has a thriving worldwide consulting and teaching practice.

Christian and her mom built a small house in Earthaven, an ecovillage in the mountains of North Carolina, where they've lived since 2003. "I want to live in a world filled with wildly successful intentional communities," she writes, "ecovillages, cohousing communities, housing co-ops, shared group households, and every other kind of community."

---

Let's Share Housing! hawks a sidewalk sandwich board in front of the neighborhood library. Sixteen people gather on a dreary February afternoon for a Meetup group in the branch's small meeting room. I'm here not because I'm looking for roommates yet, but because I imagine the scheme might be especially well-suited to single women without kids. Living alone, I'm finding, gets lonely sometimes. Let's just say I'm curious.

After leading Let's Share Housing Meetups off and on since 2009, host Michele Fiasca is a pro at creating an open environment for people to share their housing needs. She tells us her goal is twofold: create community among residents and new arrivals and facilitate affordable housing matches.

Michele looks to be about my age, and I later learn we were born six days apart. She's wearing a fabulous tan-colored jacket embroidered with bucking broncos, cacti, and sequins that pick up the reddish hues of her curly hair.

Participants ranging in age from their twenties to midsixties sit down around a U-shaped table. We each wear nametags marked either with a pair of eyes (for those who are looking for a home) or a house icon (for those with space to rent). Michele distributes a handout with specific questions each person answers round-robin style, different ones for home seekers than for homeowners. Homeowners tell where in town their place is located, describe the space, monthly rent and what it includes, and pet and smoking policies. Home seekers say what they can afford to pay, if they're willing to share a bathroom, whether they have pets or a car.

One woman has the basement of her home available after a family of five and their big dog moved out recently. That was her first foray into shared housing after her divorce, and she liked having people around. "Kitchen and laundry are shared," she says, "otherwise the rest of the basement is yours." Two young couples, both new in town, are looking for space that will accommodate them and their pets. All four have jobs and transportation. An older single woman with two bedrooms for rent in her townhouse wants only one roommate; she's more concerned about getting along with her renter than she is about getting top dollar. A single man who owns a fourplex says he expects to have a vacancy soon. He's curious how house-sharing works. Two middle-aged women know they need to make a change, one because she's splitting from her boyfriend, the other because her place is for sale. Michele asks follow-up questions that tease out everyone's specifics. The meeting moves at a quick clip.

After introductions, Michele gets us on our feet, and we shove tables and chairs aside. Then she calls out a series of statements, one at a time. For example, "I really enjoy watching television" and "I'm a night owl." For each statement we array ourselves physically between two signs on opposite walls— Strongly Agree and Strongly Disagree. After about eight or ten statements, it's easy to see who's compatible and who might clash as roommates. I end up repeatedly standing next to Nancy, the woman who's splitting from her boyfriend.

At the end of the ninety-minute meeting, most of us walk together to happy hour at a nearby bar, where Michele has reserved a big table. There's an easy interchange as we get to know one another, much more relaxed than typical first meetings. I overhear several people swap contact information for follow up on potential rooming matches. The system seems to work in booming Portland, where vacancy rates are notoriously low and rents are going vertical. Before I leave, Nancy asks me to contact her if I ever want to look for a place to rent together. Who knows, someday I might. Making a match is that easy.

———————

Michele and I talk by phone a few days later.

She's the youngest of three girls, she tells me, and an Oregon native. She refers to herself as "sixty-four going on seven. I'll always think of myself as a child. That's why I never wanted kids. I didn't want the responsibility.

"My decision was a good one," she continues. "I can count on one hand the number of times I've ever regretted not having a kid. The thought's gone in about fifteen seconds. I enjoy my nieces and nephews, and now they're starting to have their own kids. I've never felt like children have been missing in my life."

Michele started Let's Share Housing in 2009 as an offshoot of what's been her primary business for nineteen years—the Adult Placement Network, through which she finds appropriate care settings primarily for clients' aging parents. That business pays the bills and provides investment resources for Let's Share Housing.

"I began to see there was a niche of people who weren't being served," she says, "because they couldn't afford the types of communities out there. They were independent, and they were falling through the cracks. Then there's the huge population of boomers who are aging. I saw a need for more affordable, innovative housing ideas."

Today, in addition to eldercare, Michele promotes shared housing in the Portland metropolitan area. Skyrocketing rents and the recession spawned an expansion of her vision to include intergenerational living. Her new Let's Share Housing website will complement the monthly Meetups when it launches. "People can match themselves in any kind of configuration they want," she says. "They can live with their peers. They can live intergenerationally. They can live as a group of people with similar interests or diverse interests—maybe folks who enjoy organic gardening or a household of artists or musicians." Keeping it local and community-based is important to Michele.

Shared housing is ideal for women who don't have children, Michele thinks, especially those who are single. "You can create networks of people you can rely on," she says, "like historically people have with their children. Somebody you share a home with probably isn't going to take care of you, per se, but you are going to watch out for each other. The social factor is important, because you don't have that regular family bond where you have meals or get together on Sundays. Shared housing offers that level of social interaction—having somebody there to find out how your day went or leave the light on for you.

"But shared housing is not the American Dream of having my own house and my own car. Today we tend to isolate and create our own little nuclear family situation with maybe a few friends. We don't live with a sense of community. I think shared housing offers that. People can live at a fraction of the cost and live better together. That's our tag line: Live better together."

Michele is not one of the newly converted. For years she's had roommates, first in Hawaii where rents were prohibitively expensive, then in Costa Rica. During the ten years since her marriage ended, she's rented out rooms to her nephews, a couple of guys twenty years younger than she, and several boomer women.

Sometimes it works well, sometimes not so much. After her divorce, her first roommate moved in but couldn't pay her rent. "Turned out she was a hoarder," Michele remembers, "and her rent money was going to pay for storage units."

Instead of evicting her, she concocted a novel solution. Michele had a limited wardrobe at the time and her roommate a good eye for fashion. "She was also an addicted shopper who did a lot of resale," she says. "So for a year she went out and bought me a wardrobe. I still get a lot of compliments on the things she brought home to me." Including that cute tan jacket with the bucking broncos.

"With the right combination of people," Michele continues, "single women can age together into their golden years, even beyond. If someday you need to hire a caregiver, for example, sharing one is a way to make aging more affordable. Having roommates also helps with the isolation and depression that's so common as we age. If you don't create social bonds, getting old can be very isolating."

Working from home, Michele is anything but isolated. She has several employees who work on both her Adult Placement Network and Let's Share Housing—systems designers, a bookkeeper, and her niece, who often brings along her five-month-old son. I can hear him crying in the background. "My house is a three-ring circus," Michele laughs. "I've got people coming in and out all the time."

Her housemate Enid volunteers for Let's Share Housing and comes to meetings sometimes. In fact, Enid and Michele met at one of the Meetups. "She's a doll, not that we don't have our moments," says Michele. "She's an artist and has made my house a lot more aesthetically pleasing. She brings beauty into my life. We're one of those magic matches."

*The Housemate Matchmaker*—that's what one of Michele's clients nicknamed her. "Do you remember the Asian gal who had a basement for rent in Northeast Portland?" she asks. "Well, she ended up interviewing those two young couples, and I think the one from Nevada is going to move in with her.

"When I'm able to match someone to a living situation it completes something for me," she says. "It lights me up."

————————

Happenstance can topple the towers of a well-planned life. Canadian Leslie Hill married at age thirty-nine, and six months later she was a widow. Paul's cancer had come back, "scattered like pepper all through his abdominal area," her husband's doctor told Leslie. They had been a couple for eight and a half years and had no children.

Back when he was nine, Paul was left sterile from radiation and surgery to treat kidney cancer. "My husband would have been a wonderful father," says Leslie, now sixty-seven. "He was great with kids. I married the best man I ever ran into, and he couldn't have children."

Leslie and Paul were both high school teachers, though they taught at different schools. Their romance started when they were counselors together at an intercultural outdoor camp. Leslie always figured if she got married, she would probably have children. "But I couldn't have dealt with kids at school all day and then come home to my own," she says. "I needed some peace and quiet. I felt I had a pleasant amount of children on good days, and on bad days I felt surfeited with them."

After college Leslie lived alone until she was thirty-one, then with Paul, then alone again after his death. The latter alone years were punctuated with searing, abiding grief. Life in Toronto became unbearable, so she took a leave of absence from teaching. Through a cousin Leslie knew about the Findhorn Foundation, a

New Age spiritual and learning community in northern Scotland. She signed on for three months. She stayed five years.

The Findhorn Foundation was founded in 1972 and is a world-renowned holistic learning center, community, and ecovillage. Several hundred people live and work together at various Findhorn properties located not far from one another, supporting thousands who enroll each year in courses, workshops, and conferences. "The ratio of men to women was always shifting," Leslie remembers. "It wouldn't have been more than one-third male and two-thirds female, often far fewer males. Most of the women weren't mothers. You got a place to live in exchange for work, so they definitely didn't encourage people to come with children.

"It was extremely challenging living in community," Leslie recalls, "though totally accepting, which I hadn't encountered before, other than in my marriage. I was living cheek-by-jowl with people that I would never have chosen to live with. A philosophy of the community is that everybody in your life teaches you something. It's annoying being right in the middle of righteous anger and somebody says, 'So what should you be learning from this situation?' My answer was almost always, 'Could you please just fuck off so I can be angry?' I was coerced into being more open. I learned a lot about myself and about other people. It was really tiring, but it was good."

After her first year at Findhorn, Leslie briefly returned to Toronto to quit her teaching job and sell her house, then she went back to the community. When she couldn't renew her visa four years later, she moved back to Canada, relocating to British Columbia this time.

"I would have stayed longer," she says. "I didn't want to leave at all. On the one hand, I carry the Findhorn Foundation within me. It's part of my memories, and I hold it as a philosophy. It's easy to distance myself from that philosophy when I get irritable and cranky, but basically the Foundation is very much a part of me. I learned to enjoy living in community, and now I enjoy living alone."

Today Leslie lives in a two-bedroom condo in Vancouver with her ragged-eared, bobbed-tailed, twelve-year-old rescue cat, Maggie Mae. She likes shutting the door to her place knowing it will be the same when she returns and the easy simplicity of quality time with her cat. She reads a lot, sings in her church choir, and plays bridge twice a week with her eighty-eight-year-old aunt.

This summer she's also graduating from an intense master's level writing program. "As I near the end of my thesis, I realize my deep involvement with others in our school community is winding down," she says. "I don't have that in Vancouver, and I'm beginning to feel more isolated." It doesn't help that neighbors she enjoys are selling their places, taking their profits, and moving out of the city to live near their kids. Leslie wants to stay in the city.

"So I'll live comfortably as I am now," she says, "until I feel like I need someone checking on me all the time and/or until I really do not want to cook. I'm in neither of those places yet. When that happens I'll move into some kind of assisted living, I suppose. But as long as I don't have to, I will cheerfully live on my own."

Leslie had a late menopause; she was nearly sixty. "Since that time I have occasionally wondered what it would have been like to have a child," she says, "but then I think about what I would have given up. I wouldn't change anything. I'd live my life exactly the same and make all the same decisions. I wouldn't have changed Paul for anyone else."

--------

In his book, *Going Solo: The Extraordinary Rise and Surprising Appeal of Living Alone*, Eric Klinenberg researched the booming demographic of people he calls singletons—adults like Leslie

Hill, who live by themselves. Singletons are single adults (i.e., unmarried, divorced, or widowed) who do not share their living space with anyone else. Today singletons represent 28 percent of all US households, which, according to Klinenberg, "means they are now tied with childless couples as the most prominent residential type—more common than the nuclear family, the multigenerational family, and the roommate or group home." (His definition of "childless couples" includes empty nesters.)

That's over thirty-one million singletons, and seventeen million of them are women. Most live in urban areas and are between thirty-five and sixty-four years old. A large proportion have no children.

Klinenberg is a sociology professor at New York University. Over a seven-year period, with the assistance of a team of graduate students, he interviewed more than three hundred singletons, all of whom live in major metropolitan areas—greater New York City, Los Angeles, Austin, Chicago, and the San Francisco Bay Area. These singletons ranged in age from young professionals in their twenties to the elderly. For comparison he also interviewed and analyzed data from other countries with high percentages of singles.

Living solo is not an American phenomenon, nor can the US boast the highest proportion of singletons. Each of the Scandinavian nations, Japan, Germany, France, the United Kingdom, Australia, and Canada have higher rates of one-person households than does the United States.

Young people are marrying later—American men at age twenty-eight and women at twenty-six, on average. Despite claims that marriage is at risk of becoming passé, Klinenberg reports that almost all never-married singletons believe marriage is in their futures. In fact, 12 percent of women and 16 percent of men age forty and above have never married.

"Most people who live alone are financially secure, not poor," Klinenberg writes, "and those who purposely use their domestic space as an oasis from their busy, stressful work lives report that it is a regenerative, not an isolating experience."

——————-

Singleton Laura Johnson, an unmarried, forty-seven-year-old English professor, has lived alone since graduating from college over twenty years ago. Her folks live out West, far from the medium-sized Midwestern town she now calls home. Laura's sister, her husband, and kids are back East. She rents an apartment, one of eleven in her building, partially because she worries a house would be too much upkeep, but also for safety reasons.

"As a single woman," she says, "I feel safer with neighbors living in the same building. This may be an illusion of safety, but it's comforting. I suppose I will live alone until I can no longer manage and then move into some sort of facility. When I can't do my own grocery shopping or cook or take care of myself in other ways, it will be time to seek help."

Most of Laura's free time is spent alone. Work keeps her busy many weeknights, though she does take time out for ballroom dance classes from time to time. Weekends are filled with grocery shopping, running errands, and preparing food for the week ahead. Probably every other weekend she goes out with friends, though she says she's still building her network of singletons.

Living alone suits her. "It helps to be an introvert," she says. "A certain degree of independence and a good landlord also help. And I love my apartment."

Because she's relocated so frequently, Laura has found it challenging to feel a strong sense of community. But after nine years in the same town—the longest she's ever lived anywhere— she says she's putting down roots for the first time. "Many of the checkout clerks at my grocery store recognize me," she says, "and there is one whose lane I always try to get in so that we can have a chat while she rings me up. My hairstylist knows me well enough to tell me that she will *not* give me pink highlights, even though that's what I think I want. I always buy scones from my neighbor's shop when I bring treats to class.

"Is this what it means to put down roots? I'm not sure, but that's what it feels like to me."

————-—

"I'm a full-time RVer, " says sixty-eight-year-old Julie Aegerter, who grew up in New York. "Now when people ask where I live, I say I'm a nomad."

For nearly five years Julie has been traveling the United States in her seventeen-foot trailer. That seventeen feet is an exterior measure, she points out, including the tow bar, and it's only as wide as her diesel truck. Lacking any bump outs or cab-over, the living space is slightly over one hundred square feet. Packed inside Julie's got a full bath, compact kitchen, two-seat dinette, and a bed that doubles as a couch. Lots of big windows open to let in the breeze and sounds of her environment. "If I get to spend the day outside," she says, "I'm very happy. That's why I do it."

When she lost her mate fourteen years ago, Julie was minister of a Unitarian Universalist congregation in southern Indiana. Even as a young woman, she thought she wouldn't have made a good mother, so she devoted her life energies to career pursuits. "I saw only two options," she remembers. "I had an aunt, who was unmarried and ran a business, and my mother, who was married and didn't work outside the house. If I'd had kids, I couldn't have done this work. I really gave everything to it, and it was hard on my partner."

At sixty-two, widowed, retired, and exhausted, Julie committed to a fifteen-month stint at a Zen Buddhist retreat center in New Mexico. As the months flowed toward completion, instead of re-upping Julie decided what she really wanted was to live outside. So she placed an order for a brand new trailer, finished her time at the Zen center, then headed to Texas to pick up her new rig. "Over the course of my lifetime," says Julie, "I've moved from backpacking to tent camping to a pop-up to a little-bitty travel trailer." So a bigger, residential trailer was her next logical step. On April Fools' Day 2013 Julie left housebound living behind and took to the road.

The first two years she followed the sun from her sister's place in Connecticut, down the East Coast to Florida to see her father, then traversed the bottom of the country to winter in Arizona. The following spring she returned to Connecticut to do it all over again. Julie had never known anyone who lived like this, so she had lots to learn. Along the way she gathered nomadic friends, who shared tips and tricks of the road. They now rendezvous periodically around the country. For the past several years her itinerary has been anchored with Buddhist retreats and visits with RVing buddies and old college friends, with new environs and travelers layered in between.

She did join one of the organizations that cater to RV living— RVing Women. It's been around for over twenty-five years and offers women of all ages a community of support for life on wheels, whether full time or seasonal. With eighteen regional chapters throughout the United States and Canada, traveling women have access to a like-minded community. When she was still working, Julie went to some of their weekend rallies in the Ohio Valley.

Another organization, the Escapees' RV Club, has been managed by three generations of the same RVing family since 1979. Boasting over 10,000 members, among the services it offers are mail forwarding, a job-matching center, educational boot camps, online discussions, and far-flung RV park locations.

Julie has shed possessions along the way, and today everything she has is stowed in her trailer. "Last March I got rid of even more when my truck was stolen," she laughs. "All those belongings are gone. I did get the truck back, minus the topper, so I downsized a bit more radically."

As a nomad, the one thing Julie sometimes misses is having a sense of community, where she could volunteer regularly and stay a while. "But I'm not lonely," she says. "I have lots of friends from all different walks of my life, and I keep in touch with them by email, on Facebook, and in phone conversations. I spend a lot of time by myself, even when I'm with people."

She also hikes and kayaks, sometimes with RVers she meets on the road. "Mostly we talk about camping," she says, "where we've been, where's a good place to go, or what we're doing at that moment. I'm occupying the present a little more strongly, I guess."

Most RVers she comes across have kids, even the full-timers. During school breaks, grandchildren scurry around the campground, but she encounters not only grandparents. "More and more young people are taking it up, too," says Julie, "even raising families and working on the road. There's a national group that started up particularly for younger people, providing services and ways of connecting."

Living on the road is pretty economical, she tells me, even considering the high cost of diesel fuel. Her truck gets about twenty miles per gallon while towing the trailer, twenty-five or more without. Since becoming a full-timer, Julie figures she's logged a total of about 100,000 miles, including two cross-country round trips. That's not much more than other people typically drive during the same time span. So her fixed expenses (not counting gas) total less than $1,500 a month, including Medicare and supplemental insurance, payments on her trailer and truck loans, and, because she belongs to an RV organization, an average ten dollars per night for a campsite with water and electrical hookups.

"Lots of people are in awe of what I do," she's noticed. "I don't think it's so special, but I'm always surprised that other people do."

Julie can picture a day when she'll need to adjust her nomadic lifestyle to one less rambling. "When I think I'm not a safe driver," she says, "and dementia is my biggest fear." She hopes someone will clue her in about any decline in her driving skills. After caring for her mother, who had Alzheimer's, Julie thinks she'll notice any abnormal behavior or memory loss. She makes sure to see her doctor and dentist in New Mexico every year.

This November she'll spend the month at a co-op RV campground in California, where she can buy or lease a campsite and stay put. "Just to see what it's like," says Julie. After that she says she might check out some continuing care facilities.

————————

I visit Jane Zembaty, eighty-four, in her immaculate one-bedroom apartment located in an assisted living community just outside Dayton, Ohio. Her former neighborhood in the city, where she lived by herself for decades, was one of satisfying connection. Her friend Marilyn, a fellow philosophy professor, lived two blocks away, and they frequently walked their neighborhood together. Nowadays Marilyn is a weekly visitor. "We have intellectual interests in common," says Jane, "and we're both fairly reserved when it comes to opening up to other people. Our time together goes way back. We have a lovely friendship."

Years ago another couple of professors bought the house diagonally across the street from Jane. They all shared an interest in film and over the years watched movies together nearly every weekend. "I thought that would stop when I moved here," she says, "but it hasn't. I've watched their daughter grow up. When they found out they were pregnant, it was late at night. They had to tell somebody, so they came over. Having this interaction with them and their daughter over all these years is lovely."

She moved from her house in the city to the retirement community two years ago. I ask how she knew it was time.

"I have a really bad back," she says, "and it kept getting

worse. My washer and dryer were located in the basement, and I knew it was dangerous taking my laundry down and back up the stairs. I also knew I wasn't going to physically get any stronger. It was time to do it when I was still mentally and physically in control. Just as you know when it's time to retire, you just know.

"Normally I hate apartment living, but I didn't want my friends to have to make decisions for me. Nobody should have to do that for anybody. I knew once I moved here, it's all automatic. You wear this thing around your neck, and you have a button in the bedroom you press twice a day. If they don't hear from you, they wait twenty-four hours, then come check. If you don't come down for dinner and you don't call, they check up on you.

"Because things happened in life the way they did, I can afford living in a very pleasant place. I have a secure future. That's another ramification of not having children."

—————

As a fledgling singleton, home for me is now a tiny third-floor walk-up condominium in one of two adjacent six-unit buildings built in 1925. Quite a contrast to the artsy 2,500 square foot house I left behind. My place is comfortable, except when the temperature spikes above eighty or sinks below forty, which it does about six months of the year.

The last time I lived alone was thirty-five years ago, and I didn't like it much then. Today I find it more agreeable, because I'm more secure in who I am and not itchy to find a mate. I like eating the same thing every day, so grocery shopping is mindless, and food is easy to find in the fridge. With no one to blame for messing up the place, I am becoming more self-accepting.

I chose my place because it's in a safe part of town, and most everything I need or want is within walking distance. Most of my neighbors are renters, all of them thirty-something urban-professional singles and couples. Five of the twelve units are owner-occupied, three by divorced women over age sixty. We wave greetings to each other.

————————

One rainy Saturday I miss a step going down my back stairs and end up in a ball of pain on the aptly named landing. My left foot swells up immediately and waves of pain zing up my leg. Somehow I make it back upstairs to my place, driven by some primal need to ice and elevate. Cold-packed and perched on pillows, the real pain kicks in. Tears flow. *I'm hurt, and I'm alone. What do I do now?*

I know I need help, and it won't come until I ask.

In a panic I call my sister in Seattle, a three-hour drive away. She's not home. The baker who lives downstairs is at work. I once met the couple across the hall, but I think I heard them go out earlier. The building is empty, except for me. Alone. Sobbing and scared.

I consider bumping down the stairs on my bum and crab-crawling down the street to the nearby hospital. I'm aware this is silly, but it's the only way I can think of to take care of myself. Then I remember that two nurses live in the building next door. Their contact information is even in my phone, though I barely know them and don't remember how I got their numbers. I start playing mental ping-pong:

*Call them, you baby. They both seem nice.*
*No, I don't want to bother them.*
*But wouldn't you help if roles were reversed?*
*Of course, but this is me asking. Can't do it.*
*Yeah, and your foot is swelling up and exploding in hot pain. Suck it up and call.*

119

Nurse Sally, one of the sixtyish divorcées, answers my sheepish call. Soon she sweeps in with proper icepacks, ace bandages, and authority. She wraps me up, then walks me down the stairs like a toddler, supported by my hiking sticks and her sure countenance. She drives me three blocks to the hospital. While I wait with my foot in an unladylike pose on the dashboard, she fetches a wheelchair and rolls me into the ER.

Sally pooh-poohs my repeated apologies for disturbing her weekend. "You'd do it for me," she says. She's right. I would. We chat while waiting for the doc, and I appreciate her companionship.

I'm lucky. No broken bones, just a bad sprain. Two hours later we return home, and Sally props me up on cushions, ankle nicely wrapped and splinted. She inspects my fridge and goes out for eggs, cottage cheese, comfort food. Nine months later, we're good friends.

Asking for help is integral to living alone. I have a lot to learn.

———————

According to AARP, only one in three people that divorces between ages forty and sixty-nine remarries. Of Americans aged sixty-five and above, a third live alone.

Residencewise, I doubt I'll be a singleton long. Truth is, I enjoy living with others, though I'm certainly not yet ready for a serious relationship or coffee date even. After my tumble, sometimes I fret about lying here disabled for days before somebody finds me. Like a good Girl Scout pledge, I commit to becoming more adept at asking for help and accepting the inevitability of adversity. Odds are, we'll all need help someday.

## CHAPTER 7

# USE IT OR LOSE IT

*This is not going to be the most important thing that ever happened to me.*

*I've always got the fear in the back of my mind: I could have cancer in another part of my body.*

*When other people are just encountering their own limitations and vulnerabilities, I'll have already dealt with that.*

The fear began with my breasts. I was a teenager then, and my grandmother lay flat in a chilled room at my aunt's house in Illinois. The same room I slept in five summers earlier, when I filled jars with fireflies in hopes I could read by their light. A metallic scent hovered over Grandma and flared my nostrils when I leaned in to kiss her cheek. After surgery for advanced breast cancer, her once-cozy chest was now concave and swathed in yellow-stained gauze from elbow to elbow. I had no idea what to say. That was the last time I saw my grandmother. She died soon after my dad and I flew back home.

In my thirties I read comedienne Gilda Radner's memoir, *It's Always Something*, and learned that women who've borne no babies risk an even more ominous disease: ovarian cancer. Years later I am aghast that some day the very organs I once tried so hard to put to use might go haywire, maybe even kill me. Today I'm afraid of my ovaries, too.

——————

The medical community has long known about the link between reproductive system cancers and childlessness. In 1969 researchers examined the mortality of a particular population of childless women—Catholic nuns.

Nuns don't have babies. But they do get a disproportionate share of "women's cancers." In fact, breast cancer was once referred to as the "nuns' disease." Analyzing data for over thirty thousand Catholic sisters, researchers found a much higher likelihood of nuns dying not only from breast cancer, but also from ovarian and uterine cancers, than women who had given birth. Numerous controlled studies of childless women have subsequently confirmed a non-mom's risk of these cancers is two- to threefold higher than a mother's. But why?

Since nuns don't get pregnant or breastfeed, one theory is that they have more ovulatory menstrual cycles over their lifetimes than mothers do. It may be that ovaries that continually rupture to release their monthly eggs, without taking breaks for pregnancy, have more time to develop the abnormal cell division that can become cancer.

How do you know if you're at increased risk for breast, ovarian, or uterine cancer? One factor is genetic. Mutations on BRCA1 or BRCA2 (genes named for breast cancer with mutations that are also present in ovarian cancer) can be inherited from both mother and father. The National Cancer Institute says these mutations account for about 15 percent of all ovarian and 5 to 10 percent of all breast cancers. But a woman who has the harmful mutation is at much higher risk of both ovarian and breast cancer. That doesn't seem fair.

Fortunately, testing a woman's DNA can confirm presence of the mutation. If family history includes members with gynecological cancers, breast cancer diagnosed at an early age, or lineage from certain ethnic groups (*i.e.*, Ashkenazi Jewish), genetic testing may be recommended. If the mutation is present, a woman faces a 45 to 65 percent chance of a future breast cancer diagnosis by age seventy. She is also at increased risk of developing cancer in her fallopian tubes, peritoneum, and pancreas.

Additional factors that may increase a woman's risk of cancer are a history of ovarian cysts, prior use of an intrauterine device, dense breast tissue, smoking, low levels of physical activity, obesity, and diabetes. One study from Scandinavia suggests the taller a woman is, the greater her risk of ovarian cancer.

In an especially disturbing twist of fate, women who have undergone infertility treatment, particularly those who never become pregnant, are at even higher risk than other women with no children. With endometriosis, one of the most common causes of infertility, comes the greatest risk of all. After what may have been years of trying to have a baby, invasive medical procedures, and a barrage of ever-more-potent drugs, that seems a cruel irony.

———————

During her lifetime one in eight women will hear she has the most common form of female reproductive system cancers—cancer of the breast. In 2016, approximately 250,000 women and 2,500 men were diagnosed with breast cancer.

One Friday my friend Jenny Bates got the news while shopping at Goodwill. She was there with her partner, hoping to take her mind off the biopsy of her left breast the day before. Expect results Monday, the doctor had told her. Her cell phone rang.

"I'm really sorry," she recalls the doctor saying, "but we found cancer cells. We've made an appointment for you with an oncologist and a surgeon, and I've talked with your general practitioner."

That was the moment the medical system took control of Jenny's schedule and her life.

Jenny is thirty-seven, with no history of breast cancer on either side of her family. Some months earlier, she thought she felt a lump. "I have really dense breasts, so I thought it's just a cyst or something."

She and her partner of nine years have no children. One of their best friends works at a reproductive clinic. While she and Jenny were talking about her diagnosis, a doctor overheard them and spoke up. "He offered to get me in Monday—this was Friday—to have my eggs frozen," says Jenny. "If I wanted to, with the help of a surrogate, I could have my genetic material mixed with somebody else's material someday and make a baby out of it." Jenny politely declined his kind offer.

Though raised in a conservative Southern Baptist household, where bringing up a brood is standard operating procedure, Jenny has no desire for children. "I've never had the 'I want a baby' feeling. I don't care if a part of me continues on," she says. "Knowing how genetics play a role, I really don't think there's anything about my genetic line that needs to continue. We'll nip this one in the bud with me."

A few weeks later I drive Jenny to a nearby hospital and visit with her in the chemotherapy room. She sits in a pea-green Barcalounger, one of many identical chairs lined up with military precision, most filled with other bald women. At thirty-seven she is the youngest in the room by at least a decade. During the four hours it takes for a toxic chemical cocktail to drip into her veins, friends rotate through the half circle of chairs facing her bearing nutritious snacks, cheery cards, and rub-on tattoos of menacing bears. She is sick and tired of chemicals making her sick and tired every other week. Once she finally recovers from what feels like the worst flu she's ever had, she masochistically subjects herself to another round in the recliner. And another. This has been going on for months, and her good cheer is paper-thin.

"They threw the kitchen sink at me, which means they were going to do all the treatments they could, because I'm young and my body can take it," she recalls a year later. "I got a port put in, started chemo, then had surgery, then radiation, and now it's antibody treatments." Today she suffers from post-mastectomy pain syndrome, which is a common side effect of mastectomy in younger women and those who have lymph nodes removed, and may be caused by nerve damage during surgery. Symptoms include burning, stinging, or stabbing pain in the upper chest or underarm that continues for more than three months after surgery.

"I spent two months on a lot of heavy pain medication," she says, "trying to muddle my way through before they put me on radiation. As soon as I think I feel better, I get thrown back to feeling awful for one reason or another, because they have some other treatment they want to introduce."

The barrage of chemotherapy drugs and post-op injections intentionally shut down her ovaries, and her body has gone into an early menopause. The bud is now nipped.

————————

Jenny could feel her tumor; many women can't. Often breast cancer is detected only through mammography, and women at high risk may also be screened by ultrasound and MRI. Breast cancer is confirmed most typically after analyzing a biopsy of suspicious tissue.

Risk factors, according to the American Cancer Society, include a family history of breast cancer, BRCA gene mutations, high breast tissue density, beginning menstruation early (before age twelve) and ending late (after age fifty-five), obesity, smoking, alcohol, and having the first child after age thirty or never having one at all.

Treatment typically involves surgical removal of the tumor and surrounding tissue. When the cancer is detected early, much of the breast may be preserved. Other women will have the entirety of one or both breasts removed, with the option of reconstructive surgery. Depending on the type and severity of breast cancer, chemotherapy and/or radiation may be administered.

Great strides have been made in the treatment of breast cancer since the 1960s. According to a study at M. D. Anderson Medical Center in Houston, in the past fifty years overall ten-year survival rates have more than doubled from 35 percent to over 77 percent.

Survival rates aside, women who haven't given birth are at 40 percent increased risk of the most common type of breast cancer—called estrogen-receptor-positive breast cancer—than women who have delivered. Researchers believe pregnancy causes changes in breast tissue that makes it less susceptible to hormone-fed malignancies. However, mothers are at significantly higher risk for what's called triple-negative breast cancer, a less common, but more aggressive form of the disease, which accounts for 15 to 20 percent of all breast cancers.

"The bottom line is that oncologists now have methods of upping the odds of surviving breast cancer," Elizabeth Whelan, SCcD, MS, MPH, and president of the American Council on Science and Health told the *New York Post*, "and in the large majority of cases, they are actually able to cure the disease."

—————·—–—

Judy Teufel didn't have breast cancer, but she had a double mastectomy anyway. She's a tall woman in her seventies, with a friendly face and big red-rimmed glasses. She looks hip in a disheveled sort of way and speaks nonlinearly like the artist she is.

In 2005 one of her brother's two daughters was diagnosed with invasive breast cancer. Both young women tested positive for the same BRCA1 gene mutation. "We all assumed they'd gotten it from their mother, since she died of breast cancer at age fifty," Judy remembers. "Then another niece, my older brother's daughter, was very worried, because she had daughters of her own and wanted to be tested, too." Judy went with that niece to get tested, but Kaiser refused to test her until someone from Judy's generation was tested. "I never suspected they would want to test me. I was just being a good aunt. So they tested me first and found the exact same mutation. It came through my father's side of the family, not from my other nieces' mother. When my older brother got tested, he didn't have the gene, so my niece didn't have to worry about inheriting the gene or passing it on to her daughters."

But Judy had plenty to worry about. With her genetic mutation, the likelihood of her having breast cancer someday was very high. Because of what happened to her several years earlier, she decided to undergo a preventive double mastectomy, which reduced her chances of breast cancer by 50 percent. She chose not have breast reconstruction, worried it might mask detection of any breast tissue that could someday become cancerous.

Judy tells me about Thanksgiving 1997, when she was marooned in Dutch Harbor, the largest town in the Aleutian Island chain. She'd been invited to come for several weeks to help inaugurate a new community center and excite locals about doing art. Then a megablizzard residents later called the "Storm of the Century" struck.

"There was no leaving for days. I was stuck in my room, with food and all that," she recalls. "I noticed my pants seemed to fit more tightly around the waist than usual. Like I'd gained weight, but when I stepped on the scale, I hadn't. I was just swelling up, and I had a backache. I had to go to the bathroom during the night, which was unusual for me. It's that vague. If I hadn't been snowed in, I think I would have ignored it."

Once home, she procrastinated going to the doctor. "Even though I knew something was wrong," she says, "my work was keeping me busy. I delayed getting help until after Christmas." January 6th her doctor ordered a series of tests. "You get the feeling that squishy women's parts are a kind of unknown territory to male medical people," she says. "Makes their eyes kind of roll up. After they found the mass, this [male] gynecologist looked at me and said, 'It's a really nice day, you have ovarian cancer, maybe you should go outside and enjoy it.' Like this was the last really nice day I might have."

Three days later she met with a female gynecological oncologist. "Had they not referred me to her, I think I'd be dead," Judy says, "because your chances of surviving are twice as good if you see a specialist." Two days after their meeting she was on the operating table. Judy's diagnosis was Stage IIIC ovarian cancer. Stage IIIC means cancer is present in one or both ovaries and/or fallopian tubes and has spread to surrounding abdominal tissue, lymph nodes, and the surface of the liver or spleen. Stage IV, where cancer cells are found inside the body's organs, is considered terminal.

Judy's ovaries and tubes were removed in surgery, along with cancerous tissue in her abdominal cavity. She tells me her post-surgery chemotherapy was administered by medical personnel in hazmat suits during three days' hospitalization each session.

She's one of the lucky ones, with no recurrence in over seventeen years.

––––·–––·–—

"The Silent Killer," as ovarian cancer has long been called, is the fifth-leading cause of cancer deaths in women, with over 140,000 dying worldwide each year. In the United States, the American Cancer Society projects over 22,000 new cases a year, half of which will be in women under age sixty-two. Only 44 percent of them will still be alive in five years. Understanding ovarian cancer's causes still has medical researchers flummoxed. That has me scared.

I'm not fearful by nature, except when it comes to health. I hadn't mustered the courage to stare this one down. Until now.

––––·–––·–—

The east wind blows knuckle-numbing cold the day I meet Kate Leonard, PhD and visit the support group for women with gynecologic cancers she's led since 1992. The hospital's meeting room is overheated, helpful for those with no hair, a nuisance for others in sudden postsurgical menopause. Both, she tells me, are normal outcomes of ovarian cancer treatment.

Dr. Leonard never knows how many women will attend. Could be one or more than twenty. Before they arrive, Dr. Leonard tells me most of the women who join this group come with a diagnosis of ovarian cancer stage IIIC. "Because," she says, "the symptoms of ovarian cancer whisper.

"The common symptom of bloating or abdominal pain could be attributed to gastrointestinal disorders or whiny middle-aged women's complaints. With cervical and uterine cancer there's liable to be bleeding, funny colors, things you can see, whereas with the ovaries, they're way inside, so the cancer can develop pretty far before you know something's wrong."

Soon a group of women ranging in age from their mid-forties to midseventies arrives and circles the conference table.

Dr. Leonard asks me to introduce myself and briefly describe my project. Turns out not one of these women has kids, including Dr. Leonard herself.

She's energetic, with a wide, ready smile and calm manner—one of those women you want to lean on. A seasoned therapist, she goes right to the heart of the matter. "We'll go around the table. What's your diagnosis," she asks, "and how are you doing today?"

"I was diagnosed Stage IIIC last September, and I finished chemo last month. I'm doing well."

"I had cervical and endometrial cancer, Stage III. Treatment ended three years ago. Now I've got no evidence of disease."

"Ovarian cancer. Two years ago. No evidence of disease."

"In 2010 I was diagnosed with adult granulosa ovarian cancer. A month ago I had robot-assisted surgery for a recurrence. No signs or symptoms. A scan found it." The group marvels at how healthy and strong she looks after only a month.

"I've got endometrial cancer Stage I and ovarian Stage II. My ovary was as big as two fists. Just finished chemo two months ago." She doffs the hat covering her hairless head. "This is my first time here. I'm doing okay. Tired, though."

Dr. Leonard knows talking with other reproductive cancer survivors reduces feelings of vulnerability and uncertainty, especially in women who are newly diagnosed and going through treatment. She poses a simple question to the group's newest member, "What kind of help do you need?"

For the rest of the ninety-minute meeting survivors respond to the newcomer's questions and concerns—how to get more time off work, deal with insurance companies, find sources of decent wigs. The woman's demeanor visibly shifts from shy to lively.

"You guys are so good for me," she says. "I didn't know anybody with ovarian cancer. Now I feel like I'll make it through whatever comes next."

The group's response rings out, clear and unanimous, "You will."

————————

So if ovarian cancer is "The Silent Killer," how can you catch it before it has its way with you? There are no definitive symptoms. Be on the lookout for bloating, pelvic or abdominal pain, difficulty eating or feeling full quickly, and urinary urgency or frequency. So says the National Ovarian Cancer Alliance, the American Cancer Society, and the National Cancer Institute. Sure, these things are common to many physical conditions, but if you experience any of these symptoms more than a dozen times in one month, and they're unusual for you, see your doctor, preferably your gynecologist. Try to rule out ovarian cancer.

"If women were more proactive at recognizing these symptoms, we'd be better at making the diagnosis at an earlier stage," Dr. Thomas J. Herzog, Columbia University's director of gynecologic oncology, told *The New York Times*. "These are nonspecific symptoms that many people have," he added, "but when the symptoms persist or worsen, you need to see a specialist."

The toughest challenge may be getting your doctor's attention.

————————

Call me neurotic, but as I learn more about ovarian cancer, my attention naturally drifts to my own belly. Darned if I don't notice three of the four major symptoms.

Two years ago my inner voice called me out for canceling my annual dermatology screening. Fortunately I listened and rescheduled the appointment. Turned out I had the beginnings of a melanoma, which was carved out of the surface of my upper arm two days later. No chemo. No radiation. I now pay very close attention to that wise inner whisperer.

My internist taps on her keyboard as I voice my concerns. She soon declares I have no increased risk of ovarian cancer.

"But what about my infertility, all those drugs? You know I never had kids."

No increased risk, she repeats, then refers me to a physical therapist skilled at treating urge incontinence.

I leave her office cowed, not convinced. White coat syndrome, maybe.

My symptoms don't abate, and the PT thinks consultation with a gynecologist is wise.

Six weeks later, armed with my facts and some fortitude, I perch in my crispy paper vest with matching paper drape on another exam table.

We two don't start strong. I always tape record meetings that are important, especially those concerning my own health or a loved one's. Most docs are fine; many even respect the practice. But this woman is adamant—no recordings. Instead, she'll print out my chart notes after our meeting, she declares.

Had I recorded our session, you'd hear me share my concerns and her dismiss them. I even tell her how devastated I'll be if my reproductive system turns on me, that my nether-regions have been through enough.

I don't recall our exact interchange, but I do remember feeling brushed off, minimized, like I'm one of those whiny middle-aged women Dr. Leonard talks about. While I focus on my lack of childbearing, she keeps asking if my mom or younger sisters have had breast or ovarian cancer. She seems not to care about my grandmother's terminal breast cancer. I know she's calculating the odds of a BRCA mutation, and I'm coming up short. As I leave the office, the nurse gives me the summary of my visit. "With your family history your breast and ovarian cancer risk is essentially at baseline," it reads. "You should have annual mammograms and pelvic exams."

Later it occurs to me perhaps I know more than that doctor does about nulliparous women's ovarian cancer risks. I kick myself for minimizing my concerns. Then I take them to another doctor in a private clinic.

The third doctor takes me seriously, probably because I don't play timid this time. I flaunt my knowledge and crow my concerns. I state plainly that I want a monitoring program. I want to discuss the option of having my ovaries and fallopian tubes removed. I want my next mammogram to be 3D tomography since my breasts are so dense. Based on my symptoms, she says she'll authorize an ultrasound. She doesn't sound convinced, and I don't care. We set an appointment for the following week.

I climb onto the table, cloaked this time in a soft cloth gown, and notice the ultrasound machine with its condom-clad wand at my right elbow. Waiting for the doctor, I am flooded with memories of infertility procedures and my prior trysts with what my sister and I once called the Italian Stallion. I'm glad to see he's shrunk some since we last were intimate.

The doctor comes in and gets right down to business. I exhale as she inserts the wand and focuses the monitor. She describes what she's seeing—a uterus tipped to the left and forward. Right ovary the size of an almond. She tells me it used to be like an apricot. Looks good. Same with the left. The tipped uterus could be causing pressure on the bladder, particularly when it's full. Might explain the sudden urgency I feel, she says. No sign of any growth or thickening. I exhale again.

I know many women don't have the time or tenacity to go through three doctor appointments. I also know how fortunate I am to have the means to pay for these visits and a $300 ultrasound. That worries me. If clinicians are brushing off symptoms that The National Ovarian Cancer Alliance, the American Cancer Society, and the National Cancer Institute agree should be investigated, that makes me livid. About my own well-being and that of all women. Doctors are in the delicate, untenable position of having to weigh risks and do cost-benefit analyses of a woman's symptomology. Women, especially those who haven't had kids, bear the consequences.

———-——-

While ultrasound is one of a doctor's few diagnostic tools (along with a pelvic exam and CA-125 blood test that detects a protein released by only some forms of ovarian tumors), the only way to confirm a diagnosis and determine the stage of any cancer present is by surgical biopsy.

Often the biopsy occurs during exploratory abdominal surgery with the understanding that if cancer is found, the tumor will be removed while you're still under anesthesia. In what's called debulking, the ovaries, fallopian tubes, and uterus will likely be taken. Tissue near the cancer site is also tested and, if affected, removed. So you go under not knowing for sure if you have cancer, then find out in recovery if you do, how bad it is, and what parts are now gone. Follow-up treatment usually includes chemotherapy. Sometimes radiation. Sometimes after you've recovered a bit. Sometimes immediately.

———-——-

I meet nanny Susan Gianotti at one of Dr. Leonard's group meetings, and we get together afterward. In her midforties, she's on the young side for this cancer. Petite and pretty, she has short curly hair that used to be long and straight, a common side effect of chemotherapy. "During the summer I was losing weight and felt fatigued," she says. "At first my primary care doctor thought I had a flare-up in my gallbladder. Nothing serious. The pain got worse and worse. I ended up in the emergency room, and they found the mass. They gave me two doctors' names, and I sat in the parking lot crying, looking at their pictures. Forty-eight hours later I was in surgery. It was overwhelming.

"I got through recovery and started chemo six weeks later," Susan recalls. "When I lost my hair it meant I really was a cancer patient. People look at you differently.

"I'm single and in my forties, past the prime years to conceive," she says. "But I thought there was still a chance I could have a baby. When I heard I had cancer, I wanted to get it out of me, so they took both ovaries, even though only one was cancerous. Now the option is gone. Emotionally this has been the most difficult part. 'But you've survived cancer,' say friends and family. Yes, but I've also lost something. I always wanted children."

———————

Other than getting pregnant, there's not much a woman can do to prevent ovarian cancer. But there are ways to reduce the odds. Amp up the veggies, particularly broccoli, cauliflower, and leafy greens like kale. Dairy? Not good. Same for alcohol and fat. A low-dose aspirin everyday may be beneficial. Perhaps the most encouraging discovery is that taking oral contraceptives for ten years or more can reduce a woman's risk by half. Drs. Kara Britt and Roger Short proposed in the British medical journal *The Lancet* that nuns take oral contraceptives as a preventative measure. So far the Vatican has failed to bless the plan.

———————

Marjorie Greenfield, MD is chief of General Obstetrics and Gynecology at University Hospitals Cleveland Medical Center and professor at Case Western Reserve University School of Medicine. She's leading a workshop at the NotMom Summit in Cleveland called "Nullipara: Childlessness & Your Health."

I go to the meeting room early and introduce myself to the middle-aged doctor with wavy brown hair and a friendly demeanor.

When I tell her how challenging it's been finding material specific to non-moms and our health, Dr. Greenfield tells me she spent hours combing medical literature preparing for this session. It's no wonder finding studies is so difficult, she says, because most medical research on nulliparity is about women who haven't had kids *yet*, for whom the term nulliparous also applies. My research skills vindicated, I'm curious to hear what she's found.

The room fills with women, and Dr. Greenfield shares slides showing cancer statistics. One by one she confirms our increased risk of ovarian, breast, and uterine cancers, then offers some preventive suggestions.

She talks about things I didn't know about uterine cancer, also referred to as endometrial cancer or cancer of the womb. The lifetime chance of receiving such a diagnosis is one in thirty-six for women in general, one in eighteen for non-moms. Infertility is definitely a risk factor, especially if the cause of infertility is unknown and treatment unsuccessful. So are obesity, polycystic ovary syndrome, postmenopausal estrogen-only hormone replacement therapy, and a family history of reproductive system cancer. Just like for ovarian and breast cancer, taking birth control pills can lower a woman's lifetime risk.

Abnormal bleeding is a sign something may be amiss, often presenting with a change in the amount or pattern of bleeding. Postmenopausal women are at the highest risk of uterine cancer, with 75 percent of cases diagnosed after age fifty-five. "Any irregular bleeding after menopause always needs evaluation," stresses Dr. Greenfield.

Uterine cancer is typically more easily detected than either breast or ovarian cancer and, at 82 percent, has one of the highest five-year cancer survival rates. Treatment options include surgery to remove the tumor, often including the uterus, cervix, and part of the vagina, as well as chemotherapy and/or radiation. To be on the safe side, if she is postmenopausal a woman's ovaries and fallopian tubes may also be removed.

By way of prevention for all reproductive cancers, Dr. Greenfield tells us every woman needs a Pap smear from age thirty to sixty-five, an annual mammogram after age forty, and an annual breast exam by a physician. Especially women without kids.

———————

After portions of a woman's reproductive system are removed does she feel less womanly than one who still has all her parts?

Jenny Bates doesn't. "I identify strongly as a woman," she says, "but I present as agendered, because I don't dress in a feminine way. I don't think that has anything to do with whether I'm a woman. I did not wake up from anesthesia as something completely different just because I didn't have breasts any longer. In fact, I feel more comfortable in my body without breasts, physically and in general, because I wasn't using them for anything. They were just superheavy and gave me horrible posture.

"Within the gay, lesbian, bisexual, trans community," she continues, "there is more conversation about what makes a man and a woman, because you have this community of people who are not one way or the other. We're the gray in-between."

Judy Teufel, after having both her ovaries and her breasts removed, thinks her personal conception of being female has changed. "I feel like the surgery removed my libido," she says. "That's as hard to lose as all the physical parts. Desire is gone, and it changes your relationship to your body in general." She refused when a friend suggested she wear her breast prostheses when they took a trip to Paris. "I don't see why it matters if I do. They're heavy and very painful. Anyway, I'm the same person here in Portland as I am in Paris."

———————

I'm haunted by the fact that those of us who haven't borne children get proportionately more breast, ovarian, and uterine cancer than moms do. I can't shake a disturbing image of a panel of judges, each rendering his verdict that we non-moms are guilty of some crime we never committed, and cancer is a fitting consequence for failing to reproduce ourselves.

Unspayed cats and dogs get breast, uterine, and ovarian cancers. That's really sad and another important reason for spaying them. But chimpanzees and other primates don't get these cancers, even though we share more than 98 percent of our genetic makeup. Researchers are examining that 2 percent difference and hopefully will someday find the source and cure for these cancers. If the reason we get more women's cancers turns out to be genetic, those of us without kids will be guilty of the same crime as those of us with hazel or blue eyes.

If it turns out the explanation boils down to the fact that we haven't taken time out to use our lady parts (in the case of breast and uterine cancer) or give them some time off (in the case of ovarian cancer), then the route to reduce our risk is more physiologic. Already we can suppress ovulation. Why not find a way to replicate the benefits of pregnancy and nursing without the baby?

I find it appalling that more research dollars are not invested specifically to reduce nulliparous women's vulnerability to cancer. Childfree women will never choose to have a baby simply to diminish the threat. And many of the childless already tried unsuccessfully to have one. Through our gynecologists, we are an easily identified, sizable segment of the female population, and I suspect many of us would gladly participate in research studies aimed at bringing down our overall risk. Surely we make up a sufficiently large part of the female population to warrant more medical research targeted at our health, mortality, and well-being. We owe it to ourselves, and we owe it to the nuns.

## CHAPTER 8

----------------

# SPIRIT MOVES

*I'm trying to feed my soul somehow. Children would feed your soul, and I don't have them.*

*There are so many rules in my church, but I don't really pay attention to them. I look for the spirituality and the goodness in people.*

*I think that spirituality and religion inform one another. I'm not sure you can have one without the other.*

Look at the stars on a moonless night. Survive a serious accident. Lose someone dear. These experiences offer direct access to our lives of spirit and help define our humanity. They can also shake belief systems founded in established religions and personal spiritual practices.

Growing a religion, any religion, depends on its progeny keeping the faith. None of the world's major religions gives much ink to a non-mom's purpose in life, except as relates to her barrenness and potential for reaping the gift of children, regardless of age or circumstance. So finding a place in church when you don't have any can be challenging. It falls to us, then, to explore structure and define meaning within the realm of spirit and organized religion.

But what's the difference between religion and spirituality? Gerontologist Jon C. Stuckey clarifies the contrast.

> **Religion:** *A particular doctrinal framework that guides sacred beliefs and practices about a higher power, or God, and structures how people worship.*

> **Spirituality:** *Beliefs and practices that connect people with sacred and meaningful entities beyond themselves that give meaning and purpose to life.*

Belief systems and practices originate with our families of origin and through cultural values we absorb. They evolve as we try to make sense of things along life's continuum. Not having kids impacts that evolution.

———————

Growing up as part of the only Jewish family in small-town North Carolina, Beth Rosenberg didn't use her last name much. Especially after three boys in her sixth grade class said they wanted to start another Holocaust and kill her family first.

Independent since age eighteen, Beth supported herself bartending and waiting tables, partying most every night after work. When she was twenty-six, her folks bought her a plane ticket to Israel. "That's when I had this revelation about getting my crap together and going to college," she says. "For the first time, I wanted to be out as a Jew, live life as a Jew, which is very different than just going to services and seeing Jews once a week."

She enrolled in the Jewish studies program at University of Florida and received her undergraduate degree the year she turned thirty. Her original intent was to continue on to graduate school in Jewish studies, but she found she was ill-suited to all the writing that would involve.

She did like teaching, though, and was hired to teach Hebrew and Judaism to elementary schoolers at a synagogue in Charlotte, North Carolina. "Our core curriculum was about the prophets," she says, "and our core lesson was *tikkun olam*—heal the world. I felt like I was giving kids tools to be better people. My Jewish faith tells us what to do and how to be, leaving the world a better place when we're gone."

Even during her party phase, Beth, now forty-eight, always thought she'd marry and have children. But she never did. Once she started school, her maternal urge abated. "I don't know if it was because I had so much to do—I was working full time and going to school—but from then on, I've had zero doubt. Besides," she says, "until I got my graduate degree, I didn't have the maturity to take on the responsibility of raising a child."

In Orthodox Judaism, Beth explains, having children is the purpose of marriage. "I was never Orthodox," she says. "I'm what I call a 'Buddha Jew' or 'Jubu.' I'm Jewish and belong to the Reformed Temple. I'm also a very spiritual person. In Buddhism so much of the environment and nature is God. Everything that gives me life is of the Earth. Part of why I don't have kids is because we're ruining the Earth.

"The tenets of faith I believe in," she continues, "say in order to care for others you have to care for yourself. You start with your core, how you're living. You're also there to help the elders. I always had very high regard for my grandparents and my parents, and knew at a young age I would be the one to take care of them when they got sick and old, which has happened. I wanted my life to be about them and not about a child. It's not wrong in my faith to not have one."

Beth's beloved grandfather died shortly before she finished her undergraduate studies. After graduation she worked for a while at a nursing home and found she loved serving older people. So she went back to school for a master of social work degree in geriatrics.

Since 2003 she's worked full-time as a hospice and palliative care social worker in Charlotte. Until a couple years ago, she also continued teaching at her temple's school. She figures she put in about fifteen hours a week during the school year, while working full-time at a hospital. Today she still substitutes at the temple school.

"In my community and my temple, I know more kids than I do adults," she says. "I think a lot of parents assume I have kids. The kids could care less if I had them or not."

Around *Yom HaShoah* (Holocaust Remembrance Day) Beth likes to remember gathering her third graders with her friend Tammy's fourth graders and joining the seventh grade bar mitzvah class for *tefillah*—or prayer. The room hummed with the voices of over 150 kids. "We would sit back and say, "Look at all these kids in front of us singing and praying. Hitler didn't win.""

————————

While Beth dedicated hundreds of hours to the next generation's religious education, practitioners of the Jewish faith have grown by only .02 percent in recent years. Our nation was founded on the concept of religious freedom, and religion has always been an important component of American culture. These days, how are other faiths faring?

In its 2014 Religious Landscape Study, the Pew Research Center found about three-quarters of Americans describe themselves as affiliated with a particular religion (46 percent Protestant, 21 percent Catholic, 3 percent other Christian, 6 percent non-Christian). But compared to Pew's 2007 companion study, numbers are down nearly 8 percent for Christians. This national decline in Christian religiosity is not limited to any particular geographic region or demographic subset. "The same trends are seen among whites, blacks, and Latinos," Pew reports, "among both college graduates and adults with only a high school education; and among women as well as men.

Non-Christian faiths (*e.g.*, Jewish, Muslim, Buddhist, Hindu) gained a bit since 2007. But the most significant gain—almost 7 percent—was for those who identified as unaffiliated with any religion or who said they didn't know (nearly 23 percent of all study participants).

Americans are leaving the churches of their youth, particularly young Americans. "By a wide margin," Pew says, "religious 'nones' have experienced larger gains through religious switching than any other group. Nearly one-in-five US adults (18 percent) were raised in a religious faith and now identify with no religion."

Pew's researchers conducted phone interviews with 35,071 American adults about their religious identity, beliefs, and practices. Data was collected from each of the fifty states proportional to its total population. One of the demographic slices analyzed was based on parental status, though parents were defined as those with children under age eighteen living in the home. Even so, there are some interesting facts related to parenthood. And since the US Census does not capture information on religion, the Pew study offers rare insights into the nation's religious practices and beliefs of young families compared to those with no kids at home.

Adults living without children experience feelings of wonder to a greater extent than do parents. We're about equal when it comes to meditating, attending services, and finding a sense of spiritual peace. Though the margins aren't huge, more parents of children under age eighteen believe in God, heaven, and hell, consider religion very important, pray daily, and study religious texts one or more times a month than do those with no children at home.

———·——-

Brenda Niblock has read the Bible dozens of times.

"There's no mistake about it," says Brenda, a born-again Christian, "in the beginning God told man and woman to be fruitful and multiply." Brenda and her husband follow a different life course.

Early in their marriage the couple considered having kids. They even built a big house on five acres with plenty of space for them to run around. First, though, they wanted to get on their feet financially.

"We were both working and enjoying our careers," Brenda recalls. She worked in adult health education; her husband Tom was an engineer. "We weren't opposed to having children, but it was never the right time," she says. "It sounds selfish, but I really didn't want to give up my career, because I knew if we had children, I would stop working, at least until they went to school. I know so many women who complained about how having children interfered with their careers. I thought, *then why did you bother?*"

Brenda was born again at age eighteen. "I'd started binge drinking in high school and was totally going the wrong way," she says. "It finally dawned on me—there's this void in my life. At Young Life I heard a teenage boy talk about how he'd been trying to meet all his needs with drinking, sex, and partying, and he said it didn't fill the void. I thought *he's my age, and he's speaking to me. I'm going to give this a try.* So that weekend I committed my life to Jesus Christ."

She and her also-born-again husband, now respectively sixty-six and sixty-eight, have always been active in both church and community. Since retiring early, they provide respite care for anyone who needs time off and can't afford a babysitter. "We've done it for weekends, evenings, part of a day," she says. Brenda is quick to admit, though, that she feels awkward around children. "I don't know what they like to do or what they like to talk about. I feel kind of handicapped in some way, but I bluff my way through."

Apparently young families don't see Brenda's awkwardness. "Two or three times couples with children asked if they could appoint us as guardians to raise their kids if something happened to them both," she says. "It was quite an honor they'd be willing to let a childless couple raise their own kids. We declined though, saying we had no children for a reason. It would be an injustice to them and to us to say we'd do it."

Helping out families is not confined to members of their congregation. Two years ago the Niblocks were buying a new car. The salesperson was a Muslim man from Syria, on political asylum in the States. The three hit it off, and they invited him and his young family over for dinner. Now they eat supper together every other month—the Niblocks, the Syrian couple, and their two children, ages two and four. In fact, Brenda and her husband were the children's first babysitters.

"They're so far removed from family in Syria that they don't really have anybody to dote on their kids and support them as parents," she says. "It's unusual for us, too. They came for Thanksgiving dinner last fall and said they thought of us as grandparents for their kids. It was honoring.

"We don't separate ourselves from people because they're not Christian. I do wish they would see the value of becoming Christians, but we don't preach at them at all. When we go to their house or when they come to ours, they always ask us to say grace. It doesn't intimidate them that we're Christian, and it doesn't intimidate us that they're Muslim."

The Niblocks attend the Christ- and Bible-centered Church of God in Southwest Washington. "The church is the fellowship you enjoy with other Christians," she says. "The activities that go with it aren't the important thing. We don't keep our noses buried in the Bible all day long, of course. We actually live in the real world."

When it comes to real-world advice, if a young Christian woman sought guidance about whether or not to become a mother, Brenda says she'd tell her to pray, look at God's word, and talk both to women who didn't have children and women who did. "I think any woman who has children, unless she's really dysfunctional, was blessed because she had them," she says. "I would be too had I had children. It would be up to her. I would pray about it, and she would pray about it."

Brenda reflects on what she's learned from her choice and how her life has unfolded. "Not having children taught me that they are not the answer to anyone's needs," she says. "I'm happy to be married. Tom is my best friend, but he doesn't meet my every need. I don't think children should, either. My needs are not met by the things or the people I have in my life. My needs are met in Jesus Christ.

"I don't feel like I'm missing a lot because I didn't have children," she continues. "I have some regrets. Sometimes I wish I had a child to teach and mentor. But because I have many children in the faith, I actually do have children in a way. They're people I've mentored, prayed with, cried with, laughed with. It doesn't stop at your household door."

———-——

Both Beth and Brenda found fulfilling roles within their religious communities. Neither expresses much concern about not having kids, which may help explain why they feel so accepted in the kinds of religious environments where families predominate.

Julia McQuillan, PhD, of the University of Nebraska led a team of researchers examining connections between the reason for women's childlessness and the importance they assign motherhood. Using data from the National Survey of Fertility Barriers, women without children between ages twenty-five and forty-five were divided into one of four categories based on the level of choice they wielded over their parental status: the voluntarily childfree, those with biomedical barriers, those with situational barriers, and those with no barriers but who were not mothers yet. Responses to a number of attitudinal questions measured participants' levels of concern over not having children and the importance with which they held motherhood. Based on analysis of the data, researchers found, "Voluntarily childfree women reported lower childlessness concerns because they reported a lower importance of motherhood."

Interestingly, though they also received the greatest amount of social messaging about the importance of having children, the voluntarily childfree were less concerned about it, because they were satisfied with their choice. The childless, on the other hand, wanted what they couldn't have and reported the most distress about their childlessness. "Just as reproductive options have increased, both for limiting fertility and overcoming fertility barriers," McQuillan said, "we are learning what is devastating for some women is a relief for other women."

Because motherhood is considered personally less important by the voluntarily childfree, they may not fret as much about their religions' focus on procreation. Others, however, have a more complicated relationship with the faiths of their youth.

————————

When her family shattered, Marianne Allison fell away from the church. Then last year, at age fifty-nine, she graduated from seminary and became an ordained Episcopal priest. The day we meet, the only mark of faith I see is a tiny cross hanging around

147

her neck from a short, fine chain. No bigger than a pinky nail, it looks to me more like a plus sign than a cross.

Marianne grew up in Ann Arbor, Michigan, the middle child of five born in quick succession over fewer than seven years. Her dad was an English professor at the University of Michigan; mom stayed home with the kids. Not long after Christmas 1972, when Marianne was fourteen, the family drove to Atlanta to visit relatives. On the way home, their car blew a tire in northern Kentucky. They were smacked by a semitruck.

Her father was killed on impact. Her mom and youngest brother died a few hours later in the hospital. Marianne and her younger sister escaped with minor injuries. Their older brother and sister didn't fare so well.

"My brother had a concussion and a fractured skull," she remembers. "My older sister had a major head injury and was in a coma for several weeks. Three of us don't really have any residual effects, but my sister Nell has long-term brain damage."

Marianne is part of a lineage of ministry—her grandparents were missionaries in China; her brother became a rabbi. Before the accident, the family was Episcopalian. "My parents were respectable and involved," she recalls, "but not using the church for any kind of spiritual nurture. That says something about the kind of community they had built within the church."

When the new orphans returned home after the accident, they were cared for by a cousin. Not a soul from the church came to see them, and their parish did nothing for her or her siblings. Since no one made her, Marianne quit going to church.

"Where was the church when my parents died?" she asks. Maybe her cousin told them not to come, she suggests, looking puzzled. "It wasn't like I was mad at God or anything. I think I was rational enough to know God doesn't do things like this."

As she grieved, Marianne developed her own coping mechanisms. "Relying on myself was my strategy," she recalls. "I went into this journey of hyperindependence and hyper–self-sufficiency that carried me through many years. Decades, really.

"If I had to lose my parents, I thought I was the perfect age—as if there's a perfect age. I was already pretty much raised, and I hadn't yet rebelled against them. I was ready to go out into the world and finish the job myself. I was invested in a story of not needing parents. That story was very important for me to hold everything together."

After high school Marianne attended Oberlin College in Ohio. She met her future husband at freshman orientation. He, too, was a loner—estranged from his family for years—but more introverted and prone to depression than was Marianne.

"He was self-reliant, a perfect complement for me," she says. "We had this orphan thing together, like the Boxcar Children were for each other. We finished growing up together."

Neither she nor her husband ever felt ready to start a family, though they talked about it periodically over the years. "I think the collateral effect of the accident was I did not feel safe enough or vulnerable enough to have children," she says. "I think there was part of me that knew my coping story was at risk if I had children."

After graduation, Marianne's professional life blossomed as her husband's floundered. "We couldn't hold it together," she recalls. "We didn't have enough skills to work it through." After almost twenty years together, she filed for a divorce she didn't really want. "He was supposed to be on the path with me," she says. "That was our agreement: we were not going to be alone. I went into crisis and realized this myth of self-sufficiency was crumbling. That is when I say I joined the human race."

She also noticed her values had changed. Working in a high-powered public relations job, Marianne found herself caring more about the people she was working with than the work itself—what she characterizes as a crisis of integrity. "I was running out of gas in my job, and there was no longer any work I wanted to do there." After twenty-three years, she and her employer came to terms. Marianne left the company and started therapy.

As a condition of treatment, her therapist required that she have some sort of spiritual practice. "The only thing I knew to do," she says, "was go back to church. That began my journey back. I became more able to feel my emotions. I have a lot more compassion. Especially in doing service work, I found my humanity."

Over the years she took classes and attended programs about spirituality, ministry, and faith. While at a conference on social justice, Marianne learned about an intercultural studies graduate program run by a consortium of four seminaries. She enrolled in a few of their courses and found her spiritual peer group. "A year into it I started thinking I might be called to holy orders," she recalls. "I went and told my priest, 'now I understand—I'm supposed to do this.'" At age fifty-five she entered divinity school.

After four years studying subjects like indigenous religion, the history of the church, and theology, Marianne received her master of divinity degree and became an Episcopal priest. Today she splits her time between ministering to a suburban parish and acting as chaplain of a church-run social services organization that serves vulnerable populations.

"It's a weird thing to say, but I'm attracted to people who are in the midst of loss," she says. "The thing about loss is it's dynamic. Your relationship to it changes over time. Sometimes it feels more like loss, and sometimes it feels more like redemption—in my case, making good out of the loss.

"If I were the person I am now when I was in my twenties, I probably would have had kids. Not having children was one of the necessary losses that came with my situation. It's wistful and sad, but not like I blew it. But I do think of it as an experience that I missed.

"The idea of limitlessness is a great illusion," she continues. "I think women who don't have children have accepted a boundary and are working with what God gave them in this life in the best way they can. That is the same as women who do have children. It's just a different choice. One of the definitions of love I really like is 'holding space for the other's greatness.' In that way we should love women who don't have children; we should hold space for them."

This spring, on the Saturday before Mother's Day, Marianne will hold a special evening service to acknowledge the losses and pain that can surround motherhood, like infertility, sterilization, miscarriage, abortion, unwanted pregnancy, death of a child, and stillbirth. "We will search for hope and meaning," she says, "and we will comfort in music and prayer together."

————————

Such openhearted outreach might help reverse a decades-long trend—women without kids are taking up less and less space in church.

While they were still living with their families of origin, those who would ultimately never have children attended church at rates similar to those who would later become mothers. Researchers Joyce C. Abma and Gladys M. Martinez came to this conclusion after analyzing data from three cycles of the National Survey of Families and Households. During the more-than-twenty-year time span they studied, the childfree by choice showed a steady increase in not identifying with any religion, while the involuntarily childless remained about the same over time. However, as adults 30 percent of both subsets never attended religious services, compared to 18 percent of mothers.

Abma and Martinez's study was cited to in an article titled, "Childless and Godless," published in *The Family in America: A Journal of Public Policy*. Authors Bryce J. Christiansen and Robert

W. Patterson summed up the study's findings by saying, "This study highlights—among other things—the sterilizing consequences of irreligion."

It's ridiculous to suggest that those without children would have procreated if only they'd remained regular churchgoers. There are way too many variables for that to be so. And with nearly one-third of non-mothers never attending services, might those "sterilizing consequences" originate in exclusionary religious dogma or behaviors?

Christiansen and Patterson also link the study's findings about religion with the higher earning levels of the childless. "Voluntarily childless women do seem to be finding their way to the bank," they write, "but not many of them are finding their way to church."

We know the way, though some of us have found the church less than welcoming. Castigating women for not bearing children, as if having them is a simple and obvious option for all, portends ever-dwindling congregations and runs counter to the forbearance of most world religions.

———————

Fortunately, many diverse paths lead to the divine.

"I was in a period of deep longing for something meaningful in my life," says Jen Hofmann, forty-four. "I was going through the motions of running a business, being married, and paying bills. There was this itchy dissatisfaction." She scratched that itch by walking a 500-mile path. Twice.

"My biggest question was, 'What am I here for?'" she says. "Because I don't have kids, it's not spelled out for me in a beating heart and cute shining eyes. I can't look down at my progeny and say, 'This is why I'm here.'"

The Camino de Santiago (the Road of Saint James) wends its way through the Pyrenees, beginning in France and ending at the

Cathedral of Santiago de Compostela in northwest Spain, not far from the Atlantic Ocean. More a network of paths than a single route, spiritual pilgrims since the Middle Ages have trekked its hundreds of miles. In 2013 and again in 2016 Jen walked The Camino's entire length (except, she says, for a snippet she covered by bus after an ear infection left her too dehydrated and weak to walk).

Jen was raised Catholic and graduated from a tiny Northeastern college where she led the choir, played guitar at mass, and was active in campus ministry. Her work-study advisor, who was also a nun, tried to recruit Jen to "consecrated life." "It didn't take hold," Jen recalls.

Her relationship with the church became strained during her junior year, after she came out as a lesbian to her friends. "I didn't feel welcome in the church," she says. "I felt like my sexuality needed to be kept secret because it would never be accepted or tolerated." Looks like her hunch was accurate, because the year after Jen graduated, her former advisor fired a friend of hers for being gay.

Walking The Camino each time took Jen seven weeks. She put work on hold. Contact with family and friends was limited to periodic calls and emails with her wife and a few in her inner circle. "I gave myself permission to leave behind every role I had," she says, "to find out who I really was when I didn't have any of those hats to wear. It was really unnerving, because I like knowing what my responsibilities are. I've also always been very other-oriented, wanting to know what people expect of me so I can be whatever it is they expect."

Why did she feel compelled to walk The Camino twice? "Ancient pilgrims got to Santiago," she explains, "and they were only halfway done. I wanted the experience of completing it by returning to the beginning. I didn't think I could bring back home the person I'd discovered when I was in Spain the first time, so I left her there. I tried to live like I was okay, like I hadn't awoken, but I had.

"I got the opportunity to do two things. One was to pay attention to what the divine's voice sounds like and be able to hear it, because there were so few distractions and so little noise. There were moments of profound clarity. I heard voices. I had visions. I trusted them, and they came throughout the walk. Secondly, there were people I met along the way who had messages for me. Pilgrims call them 'Camino angels.'"

It was on her second trek, when she started at Santiago and walked back through the Pyrenees to France, that she met the priest. She was lost in a little town, trying to find her way back to The Camino. She rounded a corner and found the doors to the Church of Santa Maria wide open. She went in.

"It was all dark. There was music playing, and it was really beautiful. I scooted in, kneeled on a pew, and said a prayer. When I stood up to leave, there was a priest in the doorway. A young, beautiful guy with vibrant energy." She told him this was her second time walking the Camino; he was curious to know more.

"He asked if I was married. I said yes—I didn't get into the details about who or what gender. He asked if I had any children. I said no.

"Then he said, 'I feel called to say a blessing on you. Is that okay?'

"Who turns down a blessing? 'Sure,' I said. So he put his hand on my forehead, and I bowed my head. 'Blessings on this pilgrim. Blessings on her soul. May God bless you with many, many children.' He paused, then added, 'If God doesn't bring you children, may God bless you with many spiritual children.'

"All the hairs on my body stood up. I felt acknowledged as who I actually am, rather than who I'm supposed to be in the eyes of the church. It was so powerful. He gave me a hug and sent me on my way.

"It was one of those Camino-angel moments, offering me the opportunity to stay on the lookout for things to which to give my whole life. That's what you do when you have a child—give your whole life, your whole soul to that person so they can flourish. I took it to mean that my next task was to find the thing I was going to create in the world, and there was room for me to define that for myself."

Today Jen blogs regularly about spirituality, and she's writing a book. "It's Camino-inspired," she says, "but mostly about spiritual transformation beyond the church walls. What I now know is that my role as a writer is to report from the front lines of spiritual growth so other people can step into their own. My purpose is about helping people find their voice.

"The time since the second Camino has really been about me stepping into my own power and using it for the benefit of others. We all have power we don't claim. One of the things I realized is I was not serving the world by staying small."

As if receiving another Camino-angel message, her insight was soon confirmed. After the 2016 presidential election, every week Jen developed a checklist of recommended action items and began emailing it to a few friends. They passed it on to other friends. Her "Weekly Action Checklist for Americans of Conscience" went viral and currently boasts over 70,000 subscribers.

"I was thinking of my book as my spiritual child," she says, "and my cousin's kids, my brother's kids, and my friends' kids. Those subscribers are my spiritual children, too, because they're finding their voices. That's what they're telling me. Just having one person willing to share their truth and giving them a little glimpse of what direction they might go to feel less lost—that's everything."

———–——-

Pope Francis might frown on Jen's conception of spiritual children, as he surely would the sanctity of her same-sex marriage. But he's clear that children are important for the married.

At a morning mass celebrating long-wed couples in 2014, he shared his views on marriages that do not create offspring. Fidelity, perseverance, and fruitfulness, he said, make for a successful marriage.

The Pope made a distinction between the childless and the childfree. He suggested that couples who are unsuccessful having children "look to Jesus and draw on the fertility that Christ has with His Church."

However, he didn't mince words when it came to the childfree. "These couples who do not want children, in which the spouses want to remain without fertility . . . in the end this marriage comes to old age in solitude, with the bitterness of loneliness. It is not fruitful, it does not do what Jesus does with His Church: He makes His Church fruitful."

———————

"I like the first part," says Barbara Hanna, a practicing Catholic for over seven decades. "That's a pretty theological way of saying there can be many ways to give birth." But she doesn't agree with the part about the destiny of couples who choose against having children. "For some people," she says, "that decision can be made out of selfishness, but for others it's made out of an understanding of who they are and how that would not work with children. The church has a long way to go.

"Religion can and should be a helpful community in which to be enriched in your spirituality," she continues. "Your spirituality is the way you relate to God, the way you relate to others, yourself, your prayer. Religion should encourage growth.

"What happens with most religions," she continues, "is that more and more structures, more and more rules keep getting added. You lose the basic reason why it was created in the first place. The rules become more important than the heart."

Barbara's vantage point is pretty unusual. From the time

she was a teenager until her early forties, she was a sister. As in Sisters of the Humility of Mary, a Catholic religious order.

Technically there's a difference between being a nun and being a sister, Barbara explains, though even she mixes terms sometimes herself. Nuns are cloistered. That is, they typically live a contemplative and inner-focused life in a monastery. Sisters, on the other hand, actively engage in ministering to a broader community. Barbara entered the sisterhood at age eighteen. She's now seventy and has been married for twenty-five years.

Adult life before marriage was dedicated to God and educating children. As a schoolgirl Barbara had hints of her destiny. "I can remember in fifth grade we had to draw a picture of what we wanted to be," she says, "and I drew a picture of a nun. Then in high school, my guidance counselor, who was a nun herself, met with each of us. I told her I wanted to be a nun."

So she joined a busload of fellow high school students for a daylong visit to the nearby Sisters of Humility of Mary's Villa, just a few miles from the Pennsylvania-Ohio border. Not long after, Barbara became one of thirty first-year "postulants," moved into the Villa, and began her training and education. Three years later she took her vows.

"I was in a good, caring community," she says. "I naturally have a sense of giving and outreach, but the reason I think I entered was security. I was always very insecure and fearful. I loved the structure of teaching. I also liked being in charge. You closed the door, and the classroom was yours."

Weekends posed a challenge, however. "I would get so depressed on Sundays," she says. "Now that I look back, I think that's because Sunday was family day, and I wanted a family. But I wasn't able to articulate that then."

By the time she was in her late thirties, Barbara had become so depressed she sought help from a counselor, who also was a sister. "We worked through a lot of family issues, a lot of my fears," she says. "She asked why I entered the community. I would never answer her, because I was afraid I would find out I had to leave. That would mean I'd have to go out and fish on my own." Barbara had also made a permanent commitment and didn't want to break her vows. She continued counseling.

But her counselor could tell she was stuck and suggested Barbara take leave and not come back until she'd done three things she'd never done before. In Barbara's community, when a sister goes on leave, she's typically given up to three years to decide whether to stay out or return to the religious community.

"So I left, got myself an apartment, got myself a job," she says. Within a year she decided to stay out. "There was an inner knowing by then that this was right for me. I had a wonderful sense of freedom." Barbara was forty-one and on her own for the first time in her life.

"I still wanted to have a family," she says. So she joined her parish's group for separated and divorced people. "I thought, *I don't exactly fit, but what else am I going to do?* I went to a meeting and explained that my situation was not so different, it was still a big change. They accepted me."

Once Barbara started dating, she was forthright about what she was looking for. "I felt my timeline was running out," she recalls, "so I just told people. If you date somebody three months and it doesn't get deeper, it's not going to. So I would break it up."

Before long a new teacher at Barbara's school introduced her to an acquaintance. Their first meeting was at his family's pharmacy, where they sat at the soda fountain and ate hot-fudge sundaes.

"We had things we both liked to do," she says. "He's such a gentle guy. Shy, in a nice way." Barbara liked him right away.

"He was over forty and had dated a little bit," she says. "He told me he said to God, 'You've got to send me somebody, because this dating world isn't for me.' I guess his prayer was answered."

Within five months they were engaged. Five months after that they married. She was forty-four, he forty-three. "I still really wanted children," she says. "I wanted nine boys." She soon conceived but then miscarried.

The day we talk by phone, she tells me it's the Feast of Mary Elizabeth, also the anniversary of her miscarriage. "I thought it was very symbolic that we were having this conversation today," she says. Twenty-two years ago, Barbara found out the hard way she would have had a baby girl. "We call her 'Mary Elizabeth,'" she says, "because we believe life is life. Wherever she is or isn't, we still refer to her as that. She would be in college now, I'd be broke, and I wouldn't be talking to you."

After the miscarriage the couple consulted with their doctor, then tried to adopt. Once they'd filled out all the paperwork, they were told they were too old. It took time to accept the loss.

"When you go to church on Sunday and hear about the old ladies in the Bible who get pregnant, like Hannah," she says, "you think well, maybe. Then I got to a certain age, and there were no more maybes. It wasn't going to happen. It wasn't a sudden moment, but I just gradually let it go. Eventually I was at peace with not having kids."

Today Barbara still attends mass regularly. But her most profound spiritual connection is with a tight-knit community of four women—two former Sisters of Humility and two who are still in the order.

The four meet monthly, and currently they're discussing Eckhart Tolle's book *A New Earth: Awakening to Your Life's Purpose* and the ramifications of living in the present moment. "It's very challenging," she says. "That's the type of thing that could be happening with parishes, but it's not. We were just saying at the last meeting we wish we'd known this stuff when we were younger."

Barbara is the baby of the group. "I'm seventy," she says, "and this year they're all turning seventy-seven. It's exciting to see they haven't given up on growth at their age. Their minds are still going, and they want to learn more."

Her community isn't mainstream or conservative, Barbara says. Instead it's about "living with awareness and consciousness. It just dawned on me that what's nice about this group is that none of us has children, so that doesn't distract from our purpose."

She's silent for a moment, then tells me a photo of her parents just caught her attention. "They were older then," she says, "but they still loved our family reunions. They'd sit and watch their children and grandchildren and beam with satisfaction."

"Not having kids, *our* beaming is not as easy to gather around us. But we have to make sure we don't miss it. We have to create our own ways of gathering."

———————-

Forty-seven-year-old Meg Woodard knew as a preteen she wasn't having children. She's had decades to develop a fulfilling spiritual life without them.

At age ten Meg learned she had Type 1 diabetes. She's since been giving herself insulin shots every day for thirty-seven years. Within a year or two of being diagnosed, she realized there was no way she'd risk bearing offspring for fear they'd be diabetic, too. Because of her medical condition, she decided against having children.

Meg was married for fifteen years, amicably divorced now for five. Her ex agreed with her decision not to have kids, and no one in either family expressed any concerns. "I feel like the decision was completely within my control," she says. "I can appreciate that for some women it's not. What is in their control is the attitude they choose to have about it. I would imagine you have very different inner peace depending on that perspective alone."

The youngest of three siblings, Meg grew up in a rural Oregon town, population 610. She was raised Bahá'í and was recently elected Chair of her local assembly. Bahá'ís believe there is one God, and all religions come from that one God.

Mohammed, Zoroaster, Jesus Christ, Abraham, and the Buddha are all God's messengers, sent in response to the needs of their time. They also believe all mankind is part of the same race and that men and women are equal.

The tenet of faith Meg finds most personally meaningful is the independent investigation of truth. "That is my own journey in understanding my spiritual nature," she says, "in identifying who I am and not who somebody else has told me I'm supposed to be. So it's a journey both on a spiritual and human level— being genuine and true to who we are and what is right in our own lives."

Meg took that tenant to heart and left Bahá'í when she was in her early twenties. "I didn't know if this was really my truth," she remembers. "So I wrote to the national spiritual assembly and said until I can see that this is right in my heart, I'm not a Bahá'í." After twenty years away, Meg came back and joined some study circles to see how the faith fit. "Now I can't ignore it," she said. "Bahá'í is true for me."

Community building is an important part of Meg's spiritual practice. Every Wednesday she and a ninety-three-year-old friend reach out to other Bahá'ís. "I think doing home visits is a replacement for not having kids," says Meg. "Helping Persian friends practice speaking English, giving them the opportunity to talk instead of just reading doesn't feel like a make-do. It feels like that's exactly what I should do."

––––––––––

An accident of geography—that's how Susan Hammer, sixty-eight, sees religion. "If I had been born in Jakarta, I'd be a Muslim," she says. "If I was born in Tibet, I'd be a Buddhist. If I was born in India, I'd be a Hindu probably, depending on where I was born. This idea that you had to be a Christian, and you had to accept Jesus as your personal savior or you would not go to Heaven, what kind of a god would leave out all these people who have never heard of Jesus, who are living in all these other parts of the world?"

Susan was raised Presbyterian and went to Sunday school, sang in the choir, and became a member of the church when she was fifteen. But she questioned the structure of the church and its beliefs. "I wondered why women were left out of church leadership. The sexism inherent in even a rather benign Protestant situation seemed weird to me."

Susan is the second of four siblings, the only daughter. She doesn't remember her parents pressuring her to have children. "I'm sure they would have wanted me to have kids," she says, "but they were always suspicious of the men in my life. I think they would agree, there was never really an appropriate partner out there."

Susan went to a psychic once, when she was in her twenties. "I don't know if it was entertaining or informative," she recalls, "but I certainly remember what she said. She told me I was in my ninth lifetime. I'd been a woman four times and a man four times. I'd had many, many children. She said, 'You probably don't need to do that again. You do different things in each lifetime depending on what it takes for your soul to evolve.'"

During her fertile years Susan was ambivalent about whether or not to have children, because her life was already full with a busy law career, outdoor adventures, community, friends, and family. Though open to the possibility of having kids, she ultimately chose to remain childfree and is happy with her decision. Susan enjoys many close relationships with nieces, nephews, and other young people and doesn't feel she needs children of her own.

Susan has traveled the world—China, Africa, South America, Southeast Asia. In her thirties she met her partner, Lee, when he was her trek leader in Nepal. They've since led many trekking groups to the Himalayas. "The people there seem so happy with so little," she says. "That fascinates me. People with such big hearts and so few material goods. My connection is much closer to Buddhism than any other form of religion. I definitely feel the presence of the spirit in life."

Last year Susan severely injured her shoulder and spent most of the past twelve months housebound, except for a series of medical procedures and physical therapy appointments.

"My year of healing is what I call it," she says, "to stay put for a year and watch the sky change and the seasons change and know where the moon was all the time. To be in one place and study the world. I thought maybe this is training for being old.

"I see that souls are born and are probably reincarnated in various ways," she says. "It doesn't have anything to do with family lines. It has to do with when people are ready to come into the world and in what form. So I don't really believe in the biology of owning children.

"We can't know what the road not taken would have been like. Parents I'm close to have experienced both great joy and terrible pain over the lives of their children. They say that choosing to have children is choosing the unknown. Some, in quiet moments, say they regret their choice." Susan pauses. "Young women considering children need to know this. I'm very happy with the road taken."

———————

Awareness of roads traveled over a long lifetime can offer a retrospective itinerary of our spiritual development. Anne Wennhold has followed many routes over her eighty-plus years.

As a kid, she went to Catholic school, though the family was Protestant. As she matured, Anne grew increasingly weary of being told she was a sinner, with no hope in her life without Jesus. Loud preaching from the pulpit antagonized her.

First she was drawn to the Quakers, because they were

quiet. Later, she meditated, quieter yet, and studied Buddhism. Then the Great Spirits of Native American cultures drew her in. Today in her local community in New Jersey Anne leads shamanic drum circles and helps individuals access inner guidance and creativity as they discover their paths to elderhood.

When Anne was seven her mom and maternal grandmother decided to take in foster kids to assure the family had enough to eat, because her dad was often unemployed. As many as fourteen children packed their second-floor walkup near Chicago, Anne's only sibling, a three-year-old brother, among them. She learned quickly how to diaper, burp, and comfort babies. "I never wanted children," she says, "because they represented time and energy taken away from myself. I don't look back and wish I'd had some."

After college Anne married a classmate and moved to California. Three months after the wedding, her diabetic husband had a massive heart attack. Doctors gave him three to five years to live. The next year he went blind. "He needed a seeing-eye dog," she says, "and that's who I became. His secretary and nurse, too, because he insisted on teaching until the day he died. My marriage was like the caretaking I did as a child, except he was bigger."

Her husband made it eight years. At thirty-three, Anne was a widow. She'd been taking care of other people every day for twenty-six years.

Anne believes that periods of personal challenge and change often nudge a person toward the spiritual realm. She believes chaos disrupts lifelong systems, offering us the opportunity to put the pieces back together in a new way and transform our lives into something different. "But few are willing to invest the time and weather the discomfort to work through the chaos," she says. "It's much easier to brush inner stirrings aside." For those who heed the call of spirit, Anne is clear on her role. "My purpose here is to help others," she says, "whoever asks for help getting in touch with their inner selves."

When she was in her early seventies, Anne attended two retreats organized by the Center for Conscious Eldering. She knew she'd found her life's work: supporting others as they explore the difference between growing old and becoming an elder. She now co-leads intensive weeklong retreats in remote places of natural beauty in New Mexico, British Columbia, and New York.

"Some workshop participants have noticed I get up in the morning to drum up the sun," she says. "For me that's my way of honoring Nature, and if they're touched by seeing me do that, that's my legacy. My legacy is what we give each other through our interactions."

Anne feels more strongly connected spiritually with the children she has by choice—younger people she's taught, mentored, or befriended over the years—than she thinks she might through genetic lines. "My belief system includes the possibility of multiple past lives," she says. "People who are close to us in our current lives may have had a genetic relationship with us over a larger dimension, over more than one lifetime.

"As I look back on my life, everything I've done, absolutely every crooked pathway that I've taken off the main path, has contributed to where I am now. I look back and I say it all fits. It all makes sense."

————

If chaos and personal challenge can beget spiritual growth, infertility offers an arduous path to transformation. A team of researchers at Harvard Medical School studied the spiritual and psychological well-being of women with the greatest distress over their childlessness—the infertile. Nearly two hundred women undergoing in vitro fertilization treatments completed a series of questionnaires covering depression, fertility problems, spiritual well-being, and personal demographics. Alice D.

Domar, PhD and her colleagues at Beth Israel Deaconess Medical Center, one of Harvard's teaching hospitals, analyzed their responses.

Over 90 percent of these women identified with a religious denomination. Seventy-five percent were Christian (51 percent of whom were Catholic). The rest identified as Jewish, other, or none. Two-thirds regularly attended religious services at least once a month, and almost one-quarter of the women had become more active in their faith after starting infertility treatment.

"The results of our study suggest that infertile women with higher levels of spiritual well-being report fewer depressive symptoms and less overall distress from their infertility experience," concludes Dr. Domar. But the researchers stop short of suggesting spiritual practice for everyone. "Depending on the patient and the circumstances," she continues, "religious issues can be either healing or disruptive."

This hedging may be because of the different ways infertility can affect a woman's belief systems and relationship with her faith. How one differentiates between religion and spirituality may also play a role.

In their review of academic literature on religion, spirituality, and fertility, a team from the European Institute of Health & Medical Sciences at the University of Surrey cited a study which identified five themes of religion's influence on infertility: "as a punishment for wrongdoing; as a destiny in preparation for a higher mission in life; as an opportunity for growth and positive change; as something beyond human power; and as a biological error that is not attributed to God."

Another study mentioned in their review captured the dilemma. "Women with fertility problems on the one hand struggle with the body and earthly issues," says University of North Carolina's Margarete Sandelowski, PhD, "and on the other hand have continuing confrontation with God, faith, and other sacred concerns."

————-—-

When I was in the midst of infertility treatments, my concerns involved trying to reconcile physical and emotional experiences with matters more existential.

On one of my many neighborhood wanderings one day, I discovered a little church nearby and needled Dan into going to services with me one Sunday. I hoped returning to the faith of my youth might add spiritual heft to our efforts to get pregnant.

My sisters and I grew up in the Episcopal Church, forced to attend at the risk of losing our meager allowances. As a teen, the parish youth group became my social clique and source of budding political consciousness. After high school graduation I left home and lost interest in going to church anymore.

As a grown woman in my thirties, husband by my side, it felt good to be back. Parishioners and clergy were nice. I relaxed into the familiar cadence of prayers memorized in grammar school, hymns sung while in kids' choir.

Monday through Friday no one at work cared if I was a mom. At church, though, I felt markedly different from other women. The language of the liturgy and parish chatter was full of family, not to mention the makeup of the congregation. Except for those of newlyweds and widowed old ladies, ours was the most sparsely populated photograph in the church roster.

I stopped going to church again not long after my dad committed suicide.

He'd recently retired from the aerospace company where he worked for thirty-four years. After the family home sold, he and my mom moved to a remote town in Washington state. The bottle became his closest friend. Late-night phone calls to my sisters and me devolved into incoherent, sloshy nuisances. The last time, I told Dan to hang up. A few weeks later Dad parked his car on a windy bluff and fired the gun none of us knew he owned.

Afterwards, I tried going back to church again, but I felt even more like an outsider, raw, disoriented, and introspective. Reading about suicide and near-death experiences, spending time in nature, and sessions with the infertility therapist all offered more comfort than did going to church. My soul was deeply seeped in the dark night.

Someone gave me a book about rituals for living and dying. In hopes of finding private space to try to heal, I called the retreat center where I'd attended a youth conference in high school. I was offered a self-contained room below the chapel. Dark, simple, utterly private.

I fasted most of the time I was there, walked vaguely familiar paths, kicked fallen leaves. I journaled, lit candles, and crafted a death mask, grieving both my father and the child I would never have. There, below the sanctuary floor joists, I found respite and released the religion that seemed to have left me already. Except for sporadic Easters and Christmases, I've never gone back.

But I've never abandoned my sense there's energy greater and more profound than humanity's simple existence. My spiritual life continues to evolve as life experiences offer new potential for growth and integration. I taste various spiritual practices as if courses at a nutritious buffet.

Today I find nourishment on my yoga mat, meditation seat, and in the wonder of nature and community. Though my life takes some meaning from what's missing, what's present now matters more. The sharp pain of infertility doesn't sting anymore, it's simply part of who I am.

Another finding of Dr. McQuillan's research on childlessness jibes with my personal experience. "Each additional year of age," she found, "was associated with decreased importance of motherhood."

---

Interpersonal neurobiologists, narrative gerontologists, and other brain researchers tell us that our well-being is dependent, at least in part, on the stories we tell ourselves and others. Much of the sense we make of our lives can be derived from our spiritual and religious beliefs and practices. Yet some of those beliefs are challenging to reconcile with organized religion and societal judgment.

Family-centric themes of what is normal, right, and good offer little relevance as far as sense-making is concerned for those who don't have children. Yet many of us are called to the sacred and spend lifetimes constructing fulfilling spiritual identities. I'd like to think there's sufficient space in the realm of the divine to embrace all those identities, especially for the marginalized.

Life is sure to be messy at times for everyone, when we search for the meaning and purpose of our very existence. We all deserve sources of comfort as we navigate challenging times, acceptance as we abide the mundane, and peace as we contemplate our mortality.

---

## CHAPTER 9

# ELDER ORPHANS

*I know nobody's going to take care of me. I have to make sure that I've got things in place.*

*Who will speak for me when I can't speak for myself? One sister has her own grief. The other I simply do not trust.*

*I've thought about bribing my nieces and nephews, who are in my will.*

Let's not kid ourselves. Making plans that assure our elder years are managed to our liking and fit within our budget is more crucial for those without children. We know we can't count on offspring to oversee our dotage. There's even a name for what we may someday become—elder orphans.

"Aging seniors face all sorts of uncertainties," writes Susan B. Garland in Kiplinger's *Retirement Report.* "But older childless singles and couples are missing the fallback that many other seniors take for granted: adult children who can monitor an aging parent and help navigate a complex system of health care, housing, transportation, and social services."

Perhaps we can push planning aside for a while, but then our care may fall to an inattentive relative, acquaintance, or potentially nefarious do-gooder to make decisions for us when we can't make them ourselves. If we're really in a jam, some judge will appoint someone to manage our affairs. No one wants to face the fact, but none of us is getting out of here alive.

Some steer clear of making plans, procrastinate, or remain in denial that their day will come. Even partial planning risks chaotic consequences.

————————

Fiasco. Phone calls ricochet between a small island in northwest Washington, Austin, San Francisco, and Portland.

Ninety-one-year-old Imogene "Tex" Gieling passed out sometime before dawn, fell down, and lay unconscious in her otherwise empty home on one of the San Juan Islands for who knows how long. When she came to, she couldn't move and was in severe pain. She'd been stuck on her side for hours before inching her way across the floor to the phone, where she called for help.

A bunch of EMTs showed up, many of whom she knows. "One of them I'm very fond of. I didn't want to be on the floor in this condition and have somebody come and see me—I was a real mess in the morning. When they all came in, I looked up. 'Goodness, I didn't know you were going to be here,' I said. 'I would have fixed my hair.'"

Her medic buddies, she says, "cleaned me up, washed me down. Then they put on some decent clothes and took me to the hospital."

Tex is an art jeweler, and many days still find her at her bench producing new work. She and her mapmaker husband, John, moved from Texas to San Francisco in 1952 and bought a big, derelict house just north of Market Street in the Castro district. Over the years they restored the house to its former glory and focused on art and their work. Having children wasn't part of their plan.

Artist friends invited them to visit one of the San Juan Islands, and the Gielings were smitten with its rolling hills and bucolic seaside living. They came back to the island several times searching for land and finally purchased a number of acres in 1958. "Our first construction project was a platform under a tree at the high point of the land," she recalls. "We got mattresses and sleeping bags and slept on that little platform. Then we extended it to make an outdoor kitchen. I was happy as I could be out there."

In 1980 John was diagnosed with multiple myeloma. "His whole body, his bones were completely hollow," she says. "It's a terrible, terrible disease." He was fifty-six when he passed away in 1982.

After John's death, Tex spent summers on the island. In the '90s she decided that she wanted to come up in the wintertime, too. "I built this funky shed," she remembers. "It had an outdoor shower and its own water heater and a little propane stove. It was a tiny little thing, but there was room in it to put a bed, stay warm, and get a bath." A few years ago she built a proper house with an eclectic, open floor plan. The remodeled little shed serves as its guesthouse. Now Tex travels north several times every year, frequently filling her home with colorful locals and visiting friends from the mainland. She's become something of an island legend.

Tex broke her collarbone this time. She's lucky she came to. Last year she broke her hip; the year before it was something else. She calls these her Annual Spring Breaks. She also has glaucoma and can barely see. "My eyes are so bad. I kept looking at that roll of toilet paper over there thinking it was a pint of ice cream," she laughs. "I do have creative thoughts sometimes."

After this fall she needs round-the-clock care. Her neighbor called Tex's nephew in Texas, who called Tex's housemate in San Francisco. The neighbor can't stay; she needs to go to work. Who can come on such short notice? Who has her medical power of attorney? No one knows.

I happen to call her housemate just as he finds himself in the midst of the tizzy. "I can go," I offer. I'm several rings outside Tex's inner circle, but the situation strikes me as a pay-it-forward type of crisis. I call her nephew in Texas, who says I'm a godsend. She needs help, I say, and I can work from anywhere, giving the nephew, housemate, and neighbor a cushion of time to make longer-term plans. The next morning I head north from Portland. It takes me all day and a ferry ride to get to her house.

Road weary, I knock and quietly open the door, hoping not to wake her from what's sure to be a drug-induced sleep. Instead I find Tex propped at the dining room table, arm in a sling, with two middle-aged friends from Seattle serving her seconds of supper. "Why are you here?" everyone wants to know.

Why, indeed? The visitors' arrival was planned long ago, they say. Their timing, pure coincidence. Tex was expecting them, or perhaps she forgot. Nobody knows for sure. I learn Tex's distant loved ones never spoke directly to her after she'd fallen. Information flowed via the next-door neighbor. They couldn't imagine Tex was in any state to communicate, and being left out of the loop peeved her some. Sitting at the table, we sputtered and stewed through the confusion. The Texas nephew was embarrassed; the neighbor wanted me to stay. Pshaw, Tex and her friends said nicely. I left the next afternoon amid talk of calendars and phone trees and profuse apologies.

———————

A responsible woman without children ensures she has a support system of friends, family, and neighbors who take note of her well-being. She puts plans in place and completes documentation to manage her legal and financial affairs, assembles a team of pals, relatives, and/or professionals who knows what matters to her and can ensure her wishes are implemented, even when she can't. She chooses housing options that keep her safe and anticipates changes in the level of care she might need someday. She reviews her plans regularly and makes changes as her circumstances dictate. It's a tall order, but nobody else is going to do it for her.

What's needed documentwise varies from state to state, but the basics are:

> 1) Instructions about how you want to be treated in case you're in critical or life-threatening condition and who can act on your behalf when you can't speak for yourself (often called a health care power of attorney, health care advance directive, or living will);

> 2) Designation of who you want to manage your assets and financial affairs when you can't handle them yourself, including paying your bills if you're incapacitated (durable power of attorney); and

> 3) How and by whom you want your possessions and financial resources to be distributed once you die (a will naming your executor or a trust, which names your successor trustee).

It's not enough to identify a gaggle of loved ones and enlist sharp service providers. We also need to be clear with our close friends and relatives about whom to contact when we're in trouble. Which can be a bit of a challenge for us independent types.

———————

There's a crucial way station between independence and dependence, says Keren Brown Wilson, PhD, widely credited as the architect of assisted living. That way station is inter-dependence—a mutual reliance on one another. She doesn't equivocate when she talks about the importance of leaning on others. "People think, *I'm a professional woman. I've done all these things, and I can take care of myself.* I think that nobody can take care of themselves. Gender has nothing to do with it. Age doesn't have anything to do with it. It's recognizing that there's a need to be interdependent."

Pragmatic and plainspoken, with only a trace of her West Virginia roots apparent when she speaks, Wilson knows what she's talking about. Not only was she awarded her doctorate in social policy in her thirties, she and her husband have dedicated themselves to improving life for elders, particularly those of limited means.

Wilson didn't have children, though she wanted them. "In the absence of adult blood relatives," she says, "we have to figure out what to do. To deny it is kind of silly. There are lots of ways to form relationships that go beyond blood. What is it I can do to connect with others and stay connected?"

Wilson is a strong believer in building relationships with people of all ages, not just with contemporaries. "Lots of young people need older people," she says. "It's okay to reach out. It's incumbent on all of us to figure out how to do that. It's good to be interdependent."

———————

In his bestselling book *Being Mortal*, author and physician Atul Gawande traces our culture's bias towards independence.

"Modernization did not demote the elderly," he writes. "It demoted the family. The veneration of elders may be gone, but not because it has been replaced by veneration of youth. It's been replaced by veneration of the independent self."

I squirm as I say this, but aren't those of us without children the pinnacle of "veneration of the independent self?" When I ask non-moms about the positives of not having children, *freedom and independence* are always their first responses. How does this bode for our future? Unless we're in a position of caring for others due to injury, infirmity, or disability, we choose when and how we accept others as our dependents. How we become dependent on others is murkier.

Mortality is guaranteed. "Sooner or later," says Gawande, "independence will become impossible. Serious illness or infirmity will strike. It is as inevitable as sunset."

So we make plans and learn to ask for help. Without taking action to plan for our life's probable degradation and inevitable ending, we run a high risk of blindsiding ourselves and creating havoc for those who care about us. Making connections and finding sources of reliable support will become more and more important as we age, particularly as our contemporaries die off.

I'm coming to believe that independence and aging are not good bedfellows. I think those of us without kids will find learning how to incorporate the dependency side of day-to-day living a greater challenge than many parents will.

————

Fortunately, there has never been a broader range of options for living a connected retirement, from aging in place to affinity group homes to corporate housing developments with multiple levels of personal care, all of them conducive to providing support to women without children (others, too, of course). There's also a lot of jargon.

Naturally Occurring Retirement Communities (NORCs) are neighborhoods, sometimes apartment buildings, with a lot of older people living in them, whether by chance or because folks bought adjacent properties on purpose. Some have services funded by community grants or local governments. One not-for-profit community service system, The Village to Village network, supports elders who live independently within a specific locale. For an annual fee, participants have access to a team of peers, community volunteers, and vetted professional services for non-medical assistance, including transportation, home maintenance, and social activities.

Beacon Hill Village in the Boston area, established in 1999, was the first such community. Today there are over 190 Villages in operation across the nation, and another 150 are now in the process of being set up. The model is gaining popularity so quickly it's starting to be referred to as The Village Movement.

Niche retirement communities are organized around a common identity, such as religious faith, labor union membership, or sexual orientation. Living space may be purchased, rented, or provided by a not-for-profit organization. An example is a retirement facility for aging nuns or former union members. Care services for the aging may or may not be available.

Congregate care community living offers individual dwellings, either apartments or cottages, which are either owned or rented by residents. Professionally managed, services can include dining facilities, social activities, housekeeping, and often some assistance with activities of daily personal care. The most comprehensive option is the continuing care retirement community (CCRC), which offers a full range of options, from independent living units to skilled nursing, sometimes memory care. An ownership interest, which may include a hefty buy-in and monthly service fees, guarantees lifelong residence. Such guarantees come at the cost of some of that sense of independence common to many non-moms. Even with your very own kitchen in your unit, for example, you typically have to pay to eat at least some meals in the community dining room.

————————

Keren Brown Wilson is a proponent of congregate care living, because she played a major role in its inception.

When Wilson was a nineteen-year-old college student, her mom had a debilitating stroke that left her fully dependent on others physically, while her mental capacity remained intact. She lived in nursing homes for more than ten years until she died, because her care needs were beyond what her children could provide. Yet she wasn't happy about it. When Wilson entered her doctoral program, her mother begged her to find a better way to live. That plea inspired Wilson's work in gerontology and assisted living.

In 1983 she and her husband built a simple residential facility in Canby, Oregon, with private rooms, doors that locked, and individual kitchens. Like home. "This was an experiment many people thought could not work," she recalls, "because it was in a smaller community. It was not fancy. For me it will always be my firstborn, the model of assisted living that I think represents what assisted living can and should be." She and her husband went on to build and manage over two hundred assisted living facilities for elders.

Now nearing seventy, Wilson is making plans for her own future. "If I'm left alone," she says, "I'm moving myself to a setting with people around to help take care of me, because I don't have anybody else. A retirement community of some kind. There are so many options it would be foolish not to consider one, and I'm fortunate enough I can do that."

She's already identified two or three communities that could work for her, using a basic system of evaluation. "I'm a big believer in doing your own sensory testing," she says. "You go and you look, you listen, you smell. Mostly you look at the people. You know yourself well enough to know what kind of place is a good fit for you."

She also freely shares her way of validating her options. "Develop relationships before you need to go in," she suggests, "maybe as a volunteer. If you were going to apply for a job, I don't know too many people who wouldn't investigate the place."

———————

However, the thought of living in what some stubbornly refer to as an "old folks' home" can be tantamount to an admission of weakness. If we want to grow old in our own homes, we had better make sure our houses are aging-friendly or get work done before the time comes for ramps or grab bars or doorways wide enough for a wheelchair. We'll also need to build a good network of reliable friends and neighbors nearby and be connected to a variety of supportive services and resources we can call immediately if we need help. Aging in place offers the best bet of maintaining aspects of independence. But someday we might need to arrange live-in assistance or move to a care facility anyway.

———————

Or build a community of our own from the ground up.

After over sixty years living in her childhood home, Jane Dunwoodie is finally moving out. She's building a 3,000 square foot house on a half-acre lot about three miles from what she's called home for her entire life. Complete with an elevator big enough to fit both wheelchair and caregiver, basement art studio, and two Toto Washlet toilets. "They wash you, they dry you," she says. "Because of the frequency of urinary tract infections in the elderly, that's good. With a serious UTI, it makes it seem like you got dementia overnight."

One of the reasons Jane can pull this off is she's been a lifelong saver. She also lives in Dayton, Ohio, where construction costs are reasonable. She's rushing her contractor in hopes of moving her 101-year-old mother in before her next birthday. "My mom's over one hundred," she says, "and my grandmother was ninety-four when she died, so I have parents who live long enough that I can see what aging does."

Practicality plays into Jane's scheme. "I wanted a place to stay out of assisted living as long as I could," she says. "I built it with three bedrooms so a couple friends, or one friend and a caregiver if need be, could live there. We could age together. I jokingly said to my friend, 'If we age like our parents, I'll probably lose my mind and not know how to do anything. You're going to lose your body, but as long as your mind can tell my body what to do, we'll be okay.'"

Economics figure in, too. "I see what Mom's spending every year," she says. "It's atrocious, and our generation will probably be twice the cost. With just a few years in the nursing home, my house is paid for."

I think she's bound to have a waitlist for her spare space and wonder how she'll know which friend to move in. Jane's not worried. "In my circle of friends, I love them all so dearly, any of them would be wonderful companions to age with," she says. "Recently one of my married friends told me her husband said, 'If I die before you, maybe Jane would take you in.'"

As you can imagine, Jane also has all her documentation ready. "I've made sure, both in my mom's case and in mine, we have three different people lined up to be power of attorney, and three different people for health care decisions," she says. "I have one dear friend who I thought would be so good with the business part, but she would not be able to pull the plug if she had to, so I didn't want to make her my power of attorney for health care, too. It would be too hard for her.

"The person who can pull the plug on me has the health care decisions. You let them know how you feel: 'In this case

I want you to let me hold on for a while.' You have this frank discussion so that they know.

"It wasn't hard asking friends to do it. I'm fortunate to have a lot of friends who didn't have kids. We know we have to rely on each other. Ultimately it all comes down to having an individual you totally trust."

Jane is also thinking about who might watch over her down the road. Given the longevity of the women in her family, eventually she anticipates involving younger people in her plans. "I've had such wonderful friends who have shared their children with me. 'I have my eye on your children,' I tell them. 'This young lady is turning out pretty good. Hm, maybe,'" she laughs. "I just come out and ask my friends' kids, 'Are you going to take care of me?' We are very close, and their parents say, 'Of course they will.'"

Jane does worry about a few aspects of her plan. Before breaking ground she went to see her attorney, concerned a live-in friend might get kicked out should Jane die first. The attorney eased her mind. She could add a provision to her will that after her death, the house will still go to charity, but not until her occupant is gone. As a lifelong single woman, Jane also thinks about shifting governmental definitions of what counts as family. "I worry about city ordinances in the future that you can have only so many people who are not blood related live with you. What harm could a bunch of old ladies living in community come to?"

The wild card in anyone's plan for tomorrow is dementia. "When you make the decision or find you can't have children," says Jane, "right from that day you start looking at taking responsibility for yourself. I think the dementia card scares me the most, because as much as you plan, that can really throw you for a loop. Because now you don't have control."

———————

According to the Alzheimer's Association, in 2016 over five million Americans were living with dementia. Two-thirds of them were women. There is no prevention or cure for what is now the sixth-leading cause of death in America, claiming more lives each year than breast and prostate cancers combined. While other major causes of death are declining, those from dementia have increased more than 70 percent in the last decade and, unless there's some medical breakthrough, will skyrocket in the future. A future with dementia for those without children can be downright bleak, because every article and book on the subject tells family members what to do and how to take care of their loved ones. When you have dementia, someday you won't be able take care of yourself. You will become dependent. Who will manage your care?

———·——·——

A woman who calls herself Naomi Gregory knows she needs help figuring out her future care needs, so she shared her situation on a website ironically called *A Place for Mom*. "I'm a seventy-one-year-old single woman with no family, no relatives," she posted, "and I need to make some financial decisions. Who do I talk to? When should I move? How do I figure out how much money I will need?" No one replied. She didn't even mention that her mom died of Alzheimer's.

Naomi is clad in swirling bright colors, complete with head-scarf and arty earrings. She's an only child, and she never liked kids much. Only once did her mother give her any flak, though what she really wanted was grandchildren. "It didn't occur," Naomi says. "Mother knew that both of my marriages weren't ideal."

One of Naomi's aunts was a former college dean and childless widow living alone in Greenville, South Carolina. When she got a nasty dual diagnosis—breast cancer and ALS/Lou Gehrig's Disease—Naomi went to take care of her. She wasn't there long. Her aunt died in the hospital soon after her cancerous breast was removed. "I knew it was going to be ridiculous for her muscles not to work and her mind still strong," she says. "She was on morphine and just went to sleep."

Naomi was fifty-five then. After the funeral she moved to Los Angeles to be near her mother, who had been acting strangely of late. Her mom was soon diagnosed with Alzheimer's. The doctor said she couldn't live on her own anymore. The polarity of her mother's and her aunt's life sentences was a cruel juxtaposition.

"I have a two-bedroom condo and moved her in with me," Naomi says. "She stayed downstairs in the master bedroom and just watched TV. I was lucky. She did not roam, she did not start fires, she did not drive."

At the time Naomi had a part-time job she enjoyed—teaching ESL (English as a Second Language) classes. She arranged for a family friend who was a professional caregiver to come stay with her mother while she was at work. With the cost of care about the same as her paycheck, Naomi soon decided to take care of her mother full-time herself.

"I was trying to do it all myself," Naomi recalls, "and it is 24/7 with Alzheimer's. You have to watch them. You have to put a baby monitor in the room to make sure she wasn't doing something that was detrimental to her health."

This went on for three years. Naomi got help from Meals on Wheels and took caregiver classes. "I was getting to the point where I knew I needed help," she recalls. "One of the hospice nurses knew a young woman who was in nursing school." Naomi hired her on a Thursday, and her mother died that Saturday.

"Taking care of my mom is the best thing I ever did in my life," she says, "because I had done so many other things that were all about me. This was my way of paying back. I did what needed to be done at the time, and I'm very proud of that."

Today Naomi is trying to figure out what to do about her own aging, "so I can check out without causing a whole lot of problems for me or anybody else."

Because of her mom's Alzheimer's, Naomi had a baseline cognitive study done. Then she joined a behavioral therapy group at UCLA, where she meets twice a month with other participants over age sixty. A therapist facilitates discussion of topics like how to build new support systems, mortality, isolation, and long-term care decisions. Being in the group helped Naomi appreciate that everyone has stressful issues. "Life is a soap opera," she says. "There's still crap that comes up every day—your internet provider gets on your last nerve, and you have to figure out if you go with them next year or not. Every day life is happening, and you have these issues that have to be decided."

Naomi loves where she lives, and she tries to keep active. "I'm across the street from the ocean," she says. "It's very safe. Community is quite important as you age, and I went walking with friends this morning. Then I went to lunch on my own. I make myself go out. Now I'm back home. The rest of the evening, it's like I'm waiting to go to bed.

"What I want is a community where there's transportation, and somebody's looking at me to say, 'She's acting crazy now, we'd better put her in assisted living.' How do you know when it's time to go?"

———·———

An aging life care manager might be just what Naomi is seeking. Formerly known as geriatric care managers, these professionals work with elders, their families, and friends to oversee our aging care. They go through a formal education and certification process, much like accountants and financial planners do, only they're focused on the process of aging.

Mary Jo Saavedra, author of *Eldercare 101: A Practical Guide to Later Life Planning, Care, and Wellbeing*, is an aging life care manager. She designs plans for clients and their families that focus on what is important to them as they age and experience various life transitions.

Her assessment is holistic and examines what she calls the Six Pillars of Aging Wellbeing™: medical, legal, financial, social, living environment, and spiritual. By talking with clients, she identifies what's in place in each of the pillars, as well as what's missing, then develops action plans to fill in the gaps. Sometimes that involves referrals to experts like attorneys, medical professionals, and financial advisors. Sometimes the focus is on assessing the home environment or identifying care communities that are a good match. Activating the plan, she supports her clients and, when need be, advocates for the elder with doctors, attorneys, family, and financial institutions. She oversees implementation of her clients' hopes and needs.

The initial assessment takes about two hours. "We create safety for deep conversations about issues that clients often are not comfortable having with other people," she says. "I'm a partner who wants to know what makes them tick, their meaning and purpose. That's always the foundation of every plan." After the assessment, Saavedra prepares a comprehensive written report tailored to the individual's circumstances and needs, including resource identification and action plans. Like many professionals, Saavedra charges by the hour. The costs for a care manager are not often covered by Medicare or private medical coverage. Depending on the policy, long-term care insurance may cover some care management expenses.

"My number-one message is don't let someone else make your important life decisions for you," Saavedra says. "That's what the planning phase is all about—putting together a team of people who will oversee your well-being as you age and make sure they know what you want. Like an elder attorney to make sure your will and/or trust are in good shape, also powers of attorney and end-of-life instructions. Or a financial advisor who knows where you have your accounts and how you want your savings managed.

"When we're in the planning stage," Saavedra says, "we're building a relationship for the future when you may need me for care management. Because we discuss sensitive topics, our relationship gets intimate pretty quickly."

Ideally clients would establish a relationship with their aging life care manager before they have acute needs. Unfortunately, most people Saavedra sees are in crisis.

"Either the doctor will call me, the Alzheimer's Association will refer to me, or they may be referred by a lawyer or CPA or friend," she says. "Typically people are unaware of my role until they actually need it."

Even in crisis, Saavedra considers her job one of education. "It's a matter of walking through the options in a gentle but very clear and concise way," she says. "Once clients understand the options and threats, they're more likely to make the right decision for themselves and avoid others making decisions for them they may not like."

Saavedra represents the rights and needs of the elder under care management, even if someone else, like a friend or family member, is paying the bill. "The elder's opinions and rights always come first," she says. "We keep in the forefront what the elder would best be served by, but also what the elder wants. Their quality of life, the way they perceive it, is the most important aspect of their ability to thrive."

Aging life care managers are also aware of details, laws, and regulations most of us have no reason to know about until we need them. That's why it's best if the care manager works in the same state where her clients live. "The aging life care manager can do spot-checks," says Saavedra, "to make sure care management is sound, and plans are consistently adapted to a client's needs."

The care manager's role can also extend into the spiritual and psychological realm. Saavedra defines the spiritual pillar as "your meaning and purpose in the world, what gives you joy, what gives you fulfillment, what gives you purpose at the end of the day.

"Let's say for some reason you're confined to bed or a wheelchair, or you have cognitive decline like dementia. Our goal is to understand and integrate into daily life what brings you joy and purpose at a time when your body or mind is diminishing. This can bring comfort and familiarity."

One way Saavedra can influence a client's quality of life is to zero in on an appropriate living environment. If a client loved gardening, and going out in nature is where she finds peace and meaning, Saavedra wouldn't be looking at a city environment, unless there was some sort of horticultural program. If the client is not interested in being around lots of people and social activity, she can focus on small care homes with four or five residents. She goes over the pros and cons of each situation with clients.

"We're not meant to do this alone," Saavedra says. "We all need help. There comes a point in life where we do have to depend on others, whether they're in our family, our community, social nets, or part of a professional service. We are companions on this diverse and complicated life path. With seventy-eight million boomers entering their retirement years at the rate of 10,000 per day, how do we provide for everybody, and how do we keep it personal? Everybody is individual in this process. There is no normal."

———————

Planning for our potential future care can be daunting, both emotionally and financially. According to the *Wall Street Journal*, the median cost of a nursing home or memory care facility in 2015 was $91,250 a year. Twenty-four/seven home care can exceed $170,000 a year. Once diagnosed with dementia, a person typically lives four to eight more years, though some may live as many as twenty.

Paying for care without going broke can be challenging, especially for Americans aged sixty-five-plus, whose median net worth is $171,135. The major component of this figure is home equity, so to cover even a year's care, the house would probably have to be sold.

Long-term care insurance is an option, but the premiums are expensive and become more so the older you are when you first buy it. Figuring out what kind of coverage to purchase is a quagmire of detail—daily rate benefit, inflation protection, coverage for home health care—and frequently the person explaining your options stands to gain from whatever you decide. Rates increase with age, and consumers may be offered the option to save on premiums by reducing their benefits, just as they reach the age when they might need them.

Then there's the challenge of managing a complex insurance policy as one gets older, especially if dementia is becoming apparent. My mom bought a long-term care policy when she was in her midsixties and paid her monthly premiums religiously for nearly twenty years. After she had heart surgery a couple years ago, her dementia worsened as her heart healed. Her ninety-one-year-old husband apparently overlooked her monthly long-term care bill. He doesn't recall receiving any communications from the insurance company, but her policy was cancelled. Once my generation got involved in her finances, the matter was referred to the State Insurance Commissioner to force reinstatement. The insurance company said no way, and it lost. What if she had no children to advocate on her behalf?

————————

When Susan Ross was in her midforties, she was offered long-term care insurance through her government employer. She popped for the "Cadillac" plan, with the highest daily benefits and an adjustment for inflation, all for a monthly premium of around forty-five dollars. "The fact that I do not have kids motivated me to enroll and continue my coverage all these years," she says. "It gives me a certain peace of mind."

Susan is far from wealthy. Over the years her premiums crept up, and Susan paid them. Then last year, when she was sixty-six, they escalated a whopping 85 percent to $250 a month. This year she understands they'll increase again to between $350 and $375 per month. At her age, were she to buy a policy today on the open market (if the type of coverage she selected is even offered anymore), the monthly premiums would be much higher. "I decided I don't care how much it costs," she says, "I'm keeping my long-term care. My decision is affirmed on a daily basis now that I am working in palliative medicine, hospice, and end of life. I have seen so many patients languish in Medicaid nursing homes or squalid conditions."

Susan became a social worker later in life. When she was nearing sixty, she returned to Cleveland to care for her beloved mother after years working for the Peace Corps in Botswana and Kenya. That was in 2007, as the Great Recession was just beginning. She knew she'd need work after her mom died, but the administrator jobs she was well suited for were nonexistent. So she enrolled in Case Western Reserve University's Master of Social Work program, specializing in aging. Her mom passed away in 2013 at age ninety-three, shortly after Susan finished her two-year program. "The commitment to school, the commitment to Mom, I don't think I've ever experienced that level of exhaustion," she says.

Susan was raised Southern, conservative, and Catholic, the eldest of three, with a sister fourteen months younger and a brother over five years her junior. Growing up in Virginia, Susan was always independent, and she never thought she'd make a good mother. The Zero Population Growth movement of the 1970s also held sway with her. "It was both a conscious and an unconscious decision," she recalls. "I didn't have a very happy childhood—dysfunction, alcoholism. My mom, who I dearly loved, was so unhappy in her marriage. I can remember on a very childlike, subconscious level thinking I'm never going to have kids."

Then Susan married a man who wanted them. "I later realized," she says, "I didn't want to have kids with him, because he was a big kid." They divorced after five years together, nearly thirty years ago.

Today she thinks a lot about her future. "I left a job to take care of my mom," she says, "but who's going to take care of me? I'm the one who's got to set all that up." She has an advance directive for health care and a will, both of which she prepared while her mother was dying. They need updating.

"I've been thinking about this chapter of life," she says, "the final third. It really is a lot about dealing with loss and unexpected catastrophic events, often on the medical side of things."

Susan is inspired by how one of her close friends, a university professor with no children, chose to die. He had AIDs and passed away in 2001. During his decline he created his own support system. "He intentionally chose people who had different skill sets," Susan says. "His business partner was to be the executor of his will. Another woman was very methodical and precise, so he worked with her to sort through all his papers and correspondence."

As his disease progressed, he held weekly meetings with all his caregivers—some did meal planning and made food, others helped with medications, filled pillboxes, or provided transportation. "There was an intimacy between these people, most of whom knew each other," says Susan, "but they became much closer. They were honored to honor him. It was a synergistic community all centered around his care, and he organized it all himself."

Susan designed her own funeral while in graduate school, in a course she took on death and dying. "I really liked what I came up with," she says. "I have friends in different places that have special meaning to me. I don't see them all coming together in one place, but I could go to them in the form of my ashes. One friend was in the Peace Corps in Botswana with me. I'd like to have some of my ashes scattered in the Chobe River, which feeds into the Zambezi, which then flows over Victoria Falls. That's a spiritual place for me and has great significance in my life. In my will I can leave the money for her to make that trip. She'd go in a heartbeat."

Hopefully, Susan will capture that beautiful vision and make it a meaningful reality for herself and for those who love her. "My whole life has revolved around making plans and taking care of things," she says. "There is this part of me that doesn't want to have to work at planning my death. Can't I just leave that for someone else to do?"

---————-

Of course she can, but we all know that really means kicking the job toward the funeral parlor and maybe the judge. Susan's ahead of most, because she has some plans in place and long-term care insurance. She has other desires she's considered putting in writing. Most people don't. We can put it off until tomorrow, but some of us won't make it that far.

Three days after doctors told Karen Steinmetz she had terminal cancer, she was at her attorney's office putting her affairs in order. "Three days, can you believe that?" her sister Kristin marvels. A year and a half later, in 2013, Karen passed away at age fifty-five. Kristin, bereft, then learned she'd been named trustee of her sister's estate.

"I had no idea," she recalls. "Before she died we talked about a lot of details, but she never told me I was in the role. I assumed it was Peter, her husband."

Neither Kristin nor her sister had children themselves, though both stepmothered their partners' youngsters. Their brother adopted a son. "I was ambitious and into animals," says Kristin. "I never wanted kids, but I accepted the role and did my best. My sister did, though, and she was her stepchildren's primary mother." Kristin's seventeen-year marriage ended in divorce nearly six years ago. She has little ongoing contact with the stepkids and hears about their lives mostly through periodic conversations with her ex.

Soon Kristin was settling not one, but three estates—her sister's, her uncle's, and her aunt's—in addition to managing her spry, eighty-three-year-old mother's affairs. Her sister and uncle both died in 2013, her aunt a year later. She's also been making adjustments to her own arrangements to incorporate what her sister bequeathed to her.

"I'm a generalist, an executive kind of manager." That's how Kristin characterizes her skills, and that's probably why her sister put her in charge. Kristin launched her first enterprise at an early age. "I've been making jewelry since I was seven," she tells me. "At nine I got these little velvet panels, pinned what I made on them, then sold them on consignment through two or three beauty parlors in Stockton, California, where I grew up." She parlayed her success into a multifaceted corporate career in business planning, sales, marketing, strategy, operations, and consulting, all the while continuing to make jewelry. "I've done everything," she says. "I'm an all-purpose person."

Despite her sister's diligence, there were a few glitches after her death. Her IRAs, for example, had to go through probate, because Karen hadn't named her trust as successor beneficiary. That was a nightmare, Kristin recalls. There was also a house in San Mateo to dispose of. Through a crackerjack real estate agent, they spiffed the place up and sold it quickly in the red-hot Bay Area market. She and her brother shared the proceeds, as their sister intended.

Kristin's skills were put to the test again when her uncle, who lived in Kristin's grandmother's family home, died within months of her sister, his wife following soon after. Everybody who had been named in their wills to settle their estate was long dead. Someone needed to sort through things. Kristin volunteered.

"I knew they'd left everything to charity, and I had mixed reactions about that," she says. "They didn't have kids, and it was their choice what they wanted to do with their money. It was access to family stuff that mattered most to me."

After the court appointed her trustee, Kristin found herself walking through paths of Grandma's stuff piled near to the ceiling. Her uncle and aunt likewise were hoarders. Everything was in disarray, but Kristin wasn't fazed. "I'm anal," she says. "I like to find clues. I opened every box."

Sorting through treasures and detritus, Kristin pieced together evidence of bank and brokerage accounts. She found 1800s era silver dollars among thousands of See's Candies boxes, most of them empty. Wedged between piles of newspapers she came upon a few nice pieces of jewelry she remembers belonged to her great aunt. Pocket watches. Twenty binders listing every letter Grandmother wrote to Grandfather during the war and originals of the letters he wrote back. And Kristin's favorite find: two human skulls.

She emptied the house and hired the same real estate agent that sold her sister's place. Because proceeds were going to charity, Grandma's former house was sold as is. Liability, said the lawyers. "My aunt and uncle hadn't updated their wills since 1998," says Kristin, "fifteen years before they died. I don't think they had any idea about San Francisco real estate values. Who knows if they'd have done anything differently, but they'll end up leaving millions to charity."

A few blocks away, her aunt's family home awaits Kristin's attention. It's next on her to-do list.

Kristin may be good at settling other peoples' estates, but she struggles about what to do with her own. "If you don't have kids," she says, "it's not obvious who you leave your stuff to." Of what might remain, Kristin wants to leave some to charities and causes she cares about. She avidly researches organizations to make sure they're well managed and the money will go where she wants it to. She's also considered leaving money to her nephew. "But he's getting the trickle down from his mom and dad and grandma," she says. "Plus he's successful in his own right and doesn't need even more money." Friends, family, and for sure Larry, her partner of the past three-and-a-half years, are on her list.

"The hardest question, if you don't have kids," she says, "is who do you ask to do all the work? Are they capable? Do they have the time? Are they skilled?" She's discarded the idea for now of choosing a bank or trust company. "If my sister were alive I would have named her, no question. I trusted her completely." A friend of thirty-five years has kids and a full-time job. "Is that fair to her?" Kristin wonders. "I decided on her as a default."

That involved asking her. "'I'm thinking of putting you down as trustee,' I said. 'Here's what's involved. You know, you can charge for your time, and you don't have to know what to do. The attorney walks you through it. And you can hire people to do a lot of the work.'" Her friend agreed.

Larry is her medical power of attorney. "He knows what I want," she says. "I may make some changes. It's probably a good idea to review everything every year or two, because things change.

"Who I need to name to do the job is me. I know how to do it."

———————

More than half of Americans age fifty-five to sixty-four don't have wills. Two-thirds of women age forty-five to fifty-four don't. Neither did Amy Winehouse nor Billie Holiday. Only 26 percent of Americans have a health care directive. We're in denial of our mortality.

"The prevailing attitude is you really don't talk about aging," says eighty-two-year-old elder Anne Wennhold. "You make fun of it and send birthday cards to each other about being over the hill. I'm not against any of that. I'm only saying that's a defense system that keeps people from aging at a deeper level."

Anne lives alone in an apartment in Tenafly, New Jersey, with a few close friends nearby who are her go-to people. No one has mentioned it, but she knows any day she could trip and fall. "I'm beginning to pay attention to wearing one of those alert systems around my neck," she says. "I don't feel as well-balanced as I have felt for most of my life, and I can't rely on my body balancing the same way as it could."

Her brother and his family live in Minnesota, and Anne has considered moving there. "I know they would do their best to make sure I was physically taken care of," she says. "Emotionally and spiritually it would be difficult. It has never meant anything to me to have people around me when I die. At the actual point of dying, I want my spirits available to me. I'll have that internal support rather than depending on external support."

She skirts the subject every time I bring up the mundanity of planning. "I have a 'do not resuscitate,'" she says. "That's what I would like to have happen. It's very hard for me to envision myself being so mentally out of it due to injury or accident or illness that I'm not aware of what's going on, and I can't make any choices. In that case I figure it's out of my hands anyway." She has a will, with her brother as point person, and she says getting a power of attorney deserves her attention. She enjoys those possessions that reflect the spiritual aspect of her life, though she has little of material value. "When I'm gone," she says, "whoever comes to clear out the house is welcome to whatever they see. I'm not wedded to it.

"I will do what planning I can within reason. I have to laugh, because whatever I plan is not what happens. It's always some other something that sneaks up behind and takes me by surprise. I figure long-term planning just doesn't work for me."

———————

As a stalwart planner, I have a financial power of attorney, a will, a trust even. However, with my marriage kaput, they all need to be changed. I did fill out a new health care power of attorney, and a couple of divorced girlfriends witnessed it for me the other night. They applauded my foresight. My sisters are now in charge of my person if I can't be. I hope they outlive me.

It's my job to tell them what I want. Fortunately, there's help. *The Conversation Project*, a not-for-profit started in 2010, guides people through talking about their wishes for end-of-life care. A survey they conducted in 2013 discovered that while 90 percent of us say that talking with our loved ones about end-of-life care is important, only 27 percent of us have actually done so. So, *The Conversation Project* designed an online starter kit that takes you through the process in a thoughtful, purposeful, easy-to-use way. It begins with a broad, fill-in-the-blanks question: "What's important to me at the end of life is..." What follows is a step-by-step exploration of specific elements that matter, like how much information you want to receive about your own life-threatening condition, whether you'd prefer to die at home or in the hospital, how much you want loved ones to know about your health. It's all there, clear and well organized.

For years I've obsessed about who would hold my hand when I die. I know I'm not the only one—it's the most frequent worry women without kids have shared with me. Perhaps because the answer often doesn't point to an obvious person. Perhaps because we're afraid to ask someone to come. Perhaps because we're scared of dying alone. Thanks to *The Conversation Project*, we can make our plans and have our conversations, then hope everything goes as desired.

I'm not worried anymore about who will hold my hand when I die. Sure, I'll still make plans, but not long ago I shifted my thinking about my last day. Instead of worrying about it,

I now am intently curious to discover who will be by my side. Maybe it will be someone I've known forever, or maybe it will be a kind face I won't even recognize. I picture feeling a loving presence nearby, opening my eyes, and seeing them clearly. "My, my," I will say, "So, it's you."

----------

## CHAPTER 10

# WHAT WE LEAVE BEHIND

*I don't want to wonder if I've really made a contribution. Most people's legacy seems to come through their children.*

*I'm the last of my family. What do I do with the family silver and china, all the old Christmas ornaments?*

*My legacy is in the here and now. I hope those I've mentored will mentor others in turn.*

As the contrail of our existence dissolves, vestiges of what we had and who we were remain. What happens to all we've amassed? And what do our lives mean, anyway, as our genetic lines go extinct?

————-—-

In 2013 *Time Magazine* ran a cover story showing a chiseled couple lying supine on a bleached sandy beach, lolling arms entwined, satisfied smiles on their beautiful visages. "The

Childfree Life," read the headline, "When having it all means not having children."

The article covered the years when we're vital, free, and unencumbered, as life without kids certainly can be, touting all the material goods and experiences we may have. But what happens when that handsome couple or, really, any of us without children face our mortality?

————————

Buried deep within myriad studies are data nuggets that help explain such things about those of us without kids. Like income and wealth, how it compares when you have them and when you don't. Every two years researchers involved with the *US Health and Retirement Study* interview more than 20,000 couples and singles over age fifty and collect data about health, income, and wealth. Using data from 1996 to 2004, Michael Hurd, Director of the RAND Center for the Study of Aging, noted that those without children had greater average income and wealth than those who do. For couples, the average income gap was about $4,000 per year, for singles over $10,000. When it came to wealth, the gap grew. Couples without children had about 15 percent more wealth than those with children, singles about 17 percent. We know that parents bequeath mostly to their children—about 90 percent of their assets go to the kids.

So who benefits from the possessions and financial resources of those who have none? Relatives? Friends? Communities? Is stuff of material value all we leave behind?

There's also the existential question about the purpose of our having lived. If our lives have made a difference, what form does that difference take when we no longer walk the Earth? How do we want to be remembered? By whom?

Memory and meaning can't be quantified, and our direct genetic line ends with our death.

———·———·—-

Kristin Steinmetz touched every item stacked in her grand-mother's house. As court-appointed trustee, it was up to her what to keep and what to let go of generations of family possessions. She sorted through big binders of letters, winnowing out a few with key family information. The rest went into the dumpster. "I had to become less sentimental," she says, "because I couldn't take it all home with me."

Even so, her basement is now heaped with boxes full of her great-grandmother's china, her mother's silver, and other treasures. Antique dealers won't take it. Kids today don't want sets, they told her. The human skulls and her uncle's glass beakers were sold in a garage sale. Useable furniture went on Craigslist, free for pickup. Her adopted nephew got her dad's military uniforms, her uncle's dog tags, and some medals.

"I'm the last Steinmetz," she says. "Someone will have to clean all this up after me."

She did keep the little box of jewelry she found wedged in a stack of newspapers. She couldn't let go of anything with initials; they felt too close and personal. She has nine or ten diamond rings, not high-quality stones, but the filigree settings are beautiful. The good thing about being a jeweler, she says, is she can repurpose these small pieces, put them into more contemporary settings perhaps.

———·———·—-

While we can fret over material possessions, it's our money that has power to change lives. We can leave some to siblings, nieces, nephews. We can also leave some to organizations that support efforts we care about.

At the intersection of age and not having kids sits the

demographic most likely to leave money to charity. According to one study, childless Americans over age fifty are "more than four times as likely [as people with children] to report having a charitable estate plan." Another study attributes the sharp spike in charitable estate planning among fifty-five to sixty-four-year-olds between 1996 and 2006 to the childless. We're prime prospects for philanthropic organizations, and our gifts can take myriad forms: donor-advised funds, scholarships, family foundations, conservation of land, construction of buildings. How it's spent can be our prerogative.

————————-

Gathered around a conference table on a rainy spring afternoon, nine non-moms meet at The Oregon Community Foundation (OCF). I had the pleasure of co-leading the meeting. These women look like your typical fifty-five to seventy-five year olds, not particularly posh in either dress or demeanor. Some are married, some single. Half of them had worked with children in various capacities in the past, and three were social workers before they retired. They've never met each other before, though they all have established relationships with OCF. You could say what they have in common is a commitment to community giving.

OCF is one of 1,700 community foundations worldwide, more than half of them in North America. Their common mission is to improve the quality of life in a given geographic area. When you contribute to a community foundation, you receive a tax deduction, and the foundation assesses a modest annual administrative fee to manage your fund.

As a donor, you explore giving options with foundation staff, who then write up an agreement that captures the specifics about where you want your money to go. To safeguard against supporting a defunct non-profit, OCF verifies the non-profit's charitable status before making any grants. Donors' contributions are pooled and invested together. With assets of over $1.6 billion, OCF ranks as the eighth-largest community fund in the United States, distributing a total of over $103 million in grants and scholarships in 2015.

Granted, these women may be better off financially than your average woman of a certain age. Most have already established what's known as a "donor-advised fund" with OCF. That means they've given at least $25,000 to start their funds, some much more than that. Contributions qualify as a charitable donation for tax purposes the year you give it. Then each year donors can recommend a percentage of their fund's balance (typically 4.5 to 5 percent) to go to not-for-profits focused on causes they care about. Donors can name their funds as they wish—some use their family name, others are more comfortable with a descriptive word or phrase.

Many donors like to visit the organizations they've targeted, both before and after making grants. Foundation staff can update a donor about an organization's effectiveness and fiscal health. Donors also direct how their funds should be used after their death. They can name others to advise on the fund's grants, or specify particular organizations or fields of interest (such as education or the environment) to support in perpetuity. OCF distributed $34 million from its donor-advised funds to non-profits throughout Oregon in 2015. A sizable chunk of that came from the childless, but they couldn't say how much because numbers aren't tracked that way.

One woman at the meeting gave a $5,000 grant to a high school program called Community 101, which teaches young people about philanthropy. After learning how to research organizations, read financial statements, and interview those running the different charities, the students decide how to distribute every dollar of the grant to local non-profits. "I attended the event they hosted to give out the checks," she says. "I loved seeing the connections these teens had made with people in need in their own backyards."

Another woman chose to remain anonymous in her giving. She says she feels a bit like an invisible angel that shares good news with people who could use some. Others at the meeting direct their funds to the arts, animal rights, environmental education, reading-readiness programs, and job training. Seeing the impact of their financial gifts while they are still alive is gratifying, they all agree, and there's pride in knowing their efforts will continue long after they're gone.

Most have also named OCF as beneficiary of at least part of their estates. They've directed how those funds will be managed after their demise. As one woman pointed out, "What I give through OCF has far greater impact than it would if I gave it to my relatives who don't really need it." Every woman around the table nodded. One added, "When I die, my loved ones will get enough of my estate to feel remembered, but not enough to change their lives. That part goes to my community."

Our individual temperaments and goals will suggest whether we give anonymously or use our names. Perhaps we establish a scholarship fund at our alma mater as a way to support young people entering a beloved profession and leave a named legacy to our school. Maybe we're the sort that shirks public recognition, preferring private acknowledgment of the fact of our giving. Bottom line: our giving makes a difference.

———————

German researcher Professor Frank Adloff, PhD, of the John F. Kennedy Institute of North American Studies, Section of Sociology at Free University Berlin, found that those who set up private charitable funds are three times more likely not to have children. Adloff explains why. "Establishing a foundation is attractive for childless people, both as a means of ensuring that one's name lives on, and as a way of organising [sic] bequests. Childless donors were significantly more likely to list 'giving to posterity' as an important motivator for establishing their private foundation."

After examining the demographics of American charitable bequests between 1992 and 2012, Russell N. James, III, PhD, professor of personal financial planning at Texas Tech concluded, "Childlessness is the single strongest demographic predictor of including a charitable bequest in one's estate plan." For married couples with no kids aged fifty-five and above, about half have named a charity as beneficiary.

Italian researchers Marco Albertini and Martin Kohli point out that increasing numbers of childless elders are "a valuable source of charitable giving. In fact, by giving to philanthropic foundations—instead of consuming their wealth or leaving inheritances—childless donors may develop into pioneers in the field of postfamilial civic engagement."

According to the New York–based Foundation Center, in 2013 there were over 87,000 foundations in the United States, with assets totaling nearly $800 billion. Annual giving that year was nearly identical to gifts received—around $55 billion. That's a lot of money, and there are many ways to make charitable contributions. Some do good while you're still here, others pay out after you're gone. I like seeing the childless referred to as "pioneers." When talking philanthropy, boy do we make a difference.

————————

Here's lifelong Dayton resident Jane Dunwoodie's advice for how women without children can amass resources that will someday make a difference: "From a very young age, start saving. You can really start building security for yourself in a way that people who want to put their kids through college might not be able to. Now I've amassed enough to know that, provided the stock market doesn't go bottoms up, I'll be all right."

She's thinking beyond her own lifetime to the possibility she may leave behind a financial legacy. That is, if she doesn't deplete what she's set aside for her own care. Some friends have suggested she travel some, live it up a little. Jane has a different strategy. With her mom already 101, she wants the security of knowing she's set aside enough to last another forty-five years, when she'll be 110.

She was at work one morning recently when her department's secretary arrived.

"I almost had a wreck on the highway when I saw you," she told Jane.

"You did not see me on the highway," Jane replied.

"Yes, I did. You're on a billboard."

Jane chuckles at the recollection, "I guess The Dayton Foundation put my mug up: You too can have your fund at The Dayton Foundation. I never saw the billboard. I purposely kept away from that highway."

She and her mom have made arrangements that whatever's left after Jane's death goes to a family foundation they set up. "I'm saving for that legacy, the monetary legacy," she says. "It's so nice to know that what I don't spend is going to go to the Dayton community, to things we care about. You don't have to pay a thing to set it up. It's fun."

The arts matter to Jane, as do her church and the university she works for. Her degree is in fine arts, and in her free time she paints, sculpts, and does photography. After her brother died, Jane began making what she calls the "Brother Boxes." "They're sculptural," she says, "plain gray on the outside, but filled with colorful pieces and projections, symbolic of people not seeing past the exterior handicap to the person inside." They range in size from a few inches square to nearly six feet high. She made hundreds of them, and they sold quickly, though not without some misgiving on her part. "It was hard to sell them," she says. "It was like selling my brother. But I don't want to be found when I'm ninety-eight with a million boxes in the house, like the lady with a dozen cats. I have only about six boxes left."

Jane hopes some of her art will outlast her. "It might not be like Antiques Roadshow," she says, then puts on her announcer voice, "That was made back in the old twenty-first century by an artist named Jane Dunwoodie." Her voice returns to normal. "It might not be like that, but somebody will have a precious little box or a painting or a piece of photography that says 'J. A. Dunwoodie' on it and wonder who that was. Maybe they'll never find out, but there's the fun of the mystery."

She likes that she's preserving the family name with her fund, too. "Arts organizations will see this money trickle in every year, and they'll say, 'Sometime there lived a Dunwoodie.' I really want to keep saving so it will be a healthy fund with enough to make a significant impact each year on some arts organizations, keep the church going, and all that.

"It's also a good feeling to know you're doing something for the next generation," says Jane. "Some people have kids to do things for posterity. I have this."

———————

Deb Fischer figured out a way to help educate the next generation of givers. After Christmas dinner a few years ago, Deb, her partner Paul, his grown children, and their spouses were sitting around the table talking. One of his daughters was in nursing school at the time, and she brought up the subject of health care directives. They ended up having a conversation about what life-sustaining interventions they each wanted. Because of how deeply everyone engaged in that conversation, Deb had an idea.

A few years earlier, she'd set up a donor-advised fund through Charles Schwab. As a certified financial planner, Deb knew her tax benefit would be greater if she set up the fund while she was still drawing a salary. She also knew she'd continue giving to non-profits once she retired and sold her business to colleagues. "I liked the endowment fund concept—having a bucket of money that could then be a source of charitable giving when my income was going to fluctuate over time," she says. "I was in the higher-income-earning years of my life, and I wanted more of that to go into charitable giving, but I wasn't yet sure how I wanted to spend those charitable dollars."

Not long after the Christmas conversation, Deb asked Paul and his kids if they would be interested in suggesting organizations to benefit from some of her annual grants. "They're great kids who really care about the world," she says. "I knew their money at this stage of life was really tight. There are also people doing all these cool things, and we could support them with some dollars. They all liked the idea and said yes, yes, yes, sign us up."

Twice a year now Deb tells the kids the total amount of funds available for grants and gives them a deadline for submitting their proposals. She outlines what they should consider: whether it's a 501(c)(3) tax-exempt non-profit organization, what the organization's work means to them, and why the rest of the family would care about it. The process was designed so it can evolve, and they have made a few changes along the way. "I fully expected that maybe we'd do it once or twice and they'd say, 'We don't have time, not interested.'"

Instead, they've all participated twice a year, every time. Deb was surprised. "Even this time Elizabeth, who has a brand-new baby, said she's really excited about her organization. It's folded into the way they look at the world," Deb says. "This thing has given them eyes to be on the lookout all the time for what might be a good organization."

One of the changes they instituted early on was the role of "family liaison," who partners with Deb to review proposals and make recommendations. Each year they rotate who fills the role. Deb researches each proposed organization, looking at their financials, mission statements, and sources of revenue. Then, using consistent guidelines, both she and the liaison compare notes and suggest grant recipients and amounts. "I'm the Grand Pooh-bah," she says, "so I get to make the final decisions."

We're not talking huge dollar amounts. The minimum grant is $250, and the most they've ever given a single organization is $1,000. Non-profits they've chosen over the years have been involved with efforts like providing legal help for refugees, supporting people getting out of prison, women and children's programs, and environmental and medical endeavors.

"There hasn't been any unhappiness so far," Deb says, "but we have run into a few delicate situations trying to balance everybody's interests. There are a number of small, local organizations that some like and benefit from more than others. Sometimes I will personally do a grant, but I tell them about it. They seem to be very interested in organizations I'm giving to and why.

"We're learning about each other beyond what the grandchildren are doing, what's happening on the job, and where to go on vacation. It seemed like something really cool to have in common, as long as we figure out how to do it so it's easy, simple, and fun."

When it comes to her own legacy, Deb downplays her personal importance. "I'm one of seven billion people," she says. "People come, people go. When I die, return me to the earth. Money is only money. My little bit in the whole scheme of things isn't really going to make a big difference."

The other day someone told her about how they'd spent a significant amount of time and money building a hiking trail in the forest. They now have a legacy many people can use. "To me legacy is leaving behind a mark," says Deb, "whether it's a child or a building or a company. I don't have a need to leave anything that has my name on it. I'm part of the fabric of the greater whole, where little bits of my time, talent, and treasure are given. A lot of people will say, 'But your name dies with you.' Who cares? There are a lot of other Fischers around.

"I don't think I will be remembered," she continues. "It's like the roses in your garden. They grow, they mature, they bloom. They're gorgeous for a while, then they die and go back to the earth. Somebody might remember that rose for a little while, but after that they won't."

———–———

Real estate plays a big role in Tex Gieling's philanthropic plans. Built in 1870 as the first house on the block, her home in San Francisco survived the 1906 earthquake and fire that destroyed over 80 percent of the city. "The house was condemned when we bought it in 1952," she remembers. "The building inspector was determined that it be torn down. He kept saying, 'it's just perpetuating a mediocrity.'"

But she and her long-deceased husband prevailed, fixing the house bit by bit, accepting contributions of beautiful objects from friends searching for a place to put them. In her home library alone there are Native American baskets and scrimshaw and a multidrawer sea captain's chest full of knotting. The whole place is furnished with Victorian pieces appropriate to the era of its construction.

"I gave the house to the Oakland Museum," says Tex, ninety-one, "because it's the only museum that has any kind of interest whatsoever in crafts. The gift of the house is to create a curatorship in craft and decorative art." Years ago, when the museum's former curator went to work for the Smithsonian, acquisition of craft items lapsed. Tex's idea is that the new curator will focus on acquiring crafts from the 1980s to the present and fill that gap.

As for the property she and her husband John purchased on one of the San Juan Islands in 1958, that too is destined to a cause greater than blood relations. When they bought the property, every bit of the land edging the secluded bay below was privately owned. Old-growth stands of Douglas fir draped over the rocky shore, nearly touching water's edge. The tiny, keyhole-shaped cove would be perfect for secreting pirates.

A change in property tax laws—charging for waterfront footage instead of total arable land—resulted in land-poor owners having to sell off some or all of their holdings. That's how Tex and John managed to buy their three parcels. "They walked us around everything they owned," Tex recalls, "and we came through the woods from the beach on this wonderful trail that had been used for over a hundred years. We got to what we later called John's Point, and both of us said, 'This is it.'" The sleeping platform and outdoor kitchen they built their first summer are still used by visitors today.

During the over fifty-five years she's owned her place, land values and tourism have soared. Locals were worried the nature of island living would be lost. So in 1990 county voters approved a real estate tax that funded a land bank to preserve special places on all the San Juan Islands. Today over five thousand acres on eight islands have been protected, including Tex's land.

The way Tex tells the story, the Seattle developer who owned a seven-acre parcel next door planned to remove more than half its trees and build a 6,500-square-foot house at the head of the bay. Tex was pivotal in what happened next. "I made a deal with the San Juan Preservation Trust," she says, "and told them if they would buy that piece of property, I would give them the next piece."

Islanders raised almost half of the $1.225 million purchase price, public agencies ponied up the rest, and the trust succeeded in buying out the developer. In the end, Tex put two parcels of her own land—over three acres—into a conservation easement that effectively completed a contiguous horseshoe of protected land around the bay.

The conservation easement assures her land will stay as it is in perpetuity. She retains title, pays reduced property taxes, and she can pass ownership to her heirs when she dies. But they'll need to honor the terms of the easement attached to the property forever. "I hope to be able to leave enough money so that the interest will cover the taxes and the upkeep," she says, "and the kids [her great nephews and nieces] can come when they want." Some of her relatives have been visiting Tex on the island since they were two years old.

Compare a 1950s picture postcard of Tex's bay to one photographed recently and the only differences you'll see are woods that are slightly narrowed and her house far off to the side, almost out of the frame. And that's how it will always be, at least in part due to Tex's largess.

———————

While Tex's giving thwarts future construction, Cheryl Katen and her husband invested in renovating space for students. Cheryl loved the library when she was an undergrad at Lowell Technological Institute, now UMass Lowell. As one of five women in her freshman class of three hundred students, Cheryl needed a place of respite, away from all that testosterone. Although an engineering student, she indulged in a unique diversion. "When I was really wrung out studying," she remembers, "I'd go to the medical section and look up skin diseases. Skin diseases were my favorites."

During her sophomore year Cheryl met her husband, Paul, in that library. He was a senior. "A library," she says coyly, "is the heart and soul of a university."

A few years back, Cheryl contacted her alma mater with an offer to purchase some journals for her beloved library, aware that subscriptions are quite expensive. Their proposal came back at far less than she'd anticipated giving. "What else do you have on your mind?" she remembers asking. "They said they'd really like to take a whole floor of the library and make it a learning center, with a commons and whiteboards."

The Katen Learning Commons was dedicated in 2011—a comfortably furnished, second-floor open area, ringed with a computer lab, group study spaces with projection screens, and private study rooms. "We paid for the whole thing," she says. "That's what I consider my legacy."

She's not worried about her genetic line ending, either. "They say all you need is eight cousins to be covered in the gene pool. Both my parents came from big families, so I have plenty of coverage."

Cheryl is not shy about challenging the prevalent practice of children inheriting their family's assets. "I look at parents who are going to leave their estate to their kids," she says, "and I wonder if there's something else in the world that could be done that would benefit a lot more people than one kid."

———————

Regardless what riches they may leave their kids, I'm sure parents hope the children remember them fondly. The most mysterious legacy of all is what we leave behind in the memories and lives of others. When we leave no skin in the game, what purpose has our life served? What is our intangible legacy?

Marie Erickson found her legacy in both business and family. Because she's well known in the yoga world and wants to protect her private life, Marie goes by a pseudonym here. She's lithe and limber, just like you'd expect of a woman who's practiced yoga for over forty years. It's impossible to believe she's a year shy of turning seventy. She recently sold her successful studio after more than twenty-five years in business.

"There's professional legacy," she says, "and there's family legacy. If my 'children' at the yoga center see that I've created this amazing business, that's my professional legacy. The yoga center is all the people who come and go. Whether I own the business anymore or not, I will always have that legacy.

"I never would have been able to put into the business what I have in terms of heart and soul had I had children. I mothered my business. I always saw it as my baby. That's why people thought it would be hard for me to let go. But it's grown up now. We want our children to blossom and evolve beyond us."

Marie says she was never really in a position to have children. Her first husband was killed in Viet Nam when she was twenty-one. Learning yoga supported her through her grief and healing process. "Out of the worst experience of my life, which was losing my husband, came my life's work," she says.

She's been with her current husband for twenty-five years and feels very close to his three daughters and their children. She feels more a friend than a stepmom to the girls, but she's recently begun introducing them as "our daughters." She considers the grandkids to be hers, because they've never known anything different. They call her, "Grammy."

"If my grandchildren see me as being a good person," she says, "that's also my legacy. I think that the only legacy anybody can ever really have is how you've lived your life. I try to feel like I live from my heart, that I am kind.

"It's not about being perfect. It's about being real, and showing the kids that we all make mistakes, and we can learn from them. Mistakes are our teachers. Was it Beckett who said, 'Fail again. Fail better'? I love that.

"We can't know how the ripple effect of our lives will touch others," she continues. "Think about the people we look up to. Do they necessarily know they've influenced our lives? I was thinking of writing to my first yoga teacher. I need to tell her how meeting her propelled me into my passionate experience with yoga. It wasn't just something I did, it was something I loved."

——————

Trying to make sense of it all, one day poet Suzanne Sigafoos shared her concerns about legacy with her brother and sister, both of whom are parents. "I finally said to them, 'I want you to know that when I think about my death, one thing that makes me really sad is that there won't be children on the earth who will talk about me, have my picture on the shelf, quote me, look like me, walk forward with part of me in them.'"

She was saddened by their response. No, they told her, their deaths will be more difficult than hers, because they will be leaving their children as they die. "I didn't want to win the conversation," says Suzanne, "I just wanted them to acknowledge that it's lonely for me in this way.

"My husband and I are both without heirs," she says, "and it feels like the end of an era. I have no map. I have to proceed to getting old without a map."

She's trying to create her own route, but it still lacks direction, at least in part because she has difficulty engaging her husband in the planning process. "I keep saying to him, 'Let's think about setting aside some money for what you consider really important, like a scholarship for an engineering student.' I get really excited, and he just collapses. I don't think he's ever going to face it. I'll have to figure it out my own."

Suzanne has lots of ideas, all of them celebrating words—giving to the library's foundation, perhaps setting up a scholarship for writers. "I certainly don't have it worked out yet," she says, "but it seems exciting to me that I could have my name on something that would benefit someone's creative life."

Still, she wonders about her afterlife. "Will there be any lore? Do I just end?" she asks. "The frightening part is I want to be thought of as a loving person. If you're not a good mother, I don't know how you get love cred."

———-——-

For eighty-four-year-old philosopher Jane Zembaty, legacy happens in this life, not after she's gone.

"I don't think in terms of legacies, not at all," she says. "As far as the general question of the meaning of life, one thing I learned in college was that it's a meaningless question.

"I'm not religious; I'm an atheist. So for me, when I think of a life, I think of whether it's well lived or not. Is it a life that gave you satisfaction? Is it a life that helped you contribute to other people? Is it a life with friends and with joy?"

———-——-

I find a semblance of love cred and legacy in the classroom. I find it in little things.

A first grader, snarled raven hair in braids, leans into my side as we look at letter combinations the teacher just covered in class. Her workbook is open to the "ph" page, and I have a stack of flashcards at the ready.

"Do you know what sound the letter 'p' and the letter 'h' make together?" I ask.

Her lips contort, trying unsuccessfully to join the airy pop of "p" with the diaphragmatic exhale of "h." She looks to me for a hint. I press my upper teeth into my lower lip and blow the "f" sound three times. Her brow furrowed, the little girl looks skeptical.

"It's one of those trick combinations," I say. "The letter 'p' plus the letter 'h' sound just like the letter 'f.' Do you know the 'f' sound?"

She looks at me like I'm loco and sounds out a perfect "f."

"That's it. Can you sound out this word?" I point to a flashcard drawing of a phone, then run my hand along chunks of the word as she puts the new sound combination together, first very slowly, then more and more quickly. Eureka.

"Yes, it's 'phone.' Nice job," I say. We high five. "What about this one?" I hide the next drawing and ask her to sound out the new word written at the bottom. It's a long one, and she keeps trying.

"You just said it," I nod. "Listen to what you're saying."

"El-e-phant. El-e-phant. Elephant!" The spark of understanding ignites, and she registers triumph as I unveil the picture. We go through a few more flashcards—dolphin, microphone, alphabet, then she runs to tell her classmates about "f" and "ph" as they line up for recess.

In no other aspect of my life do I have this much patience. From few do I derive this much gratification. In our short time together, this little girl realizes she can read many new words, and a budding reader builds confidence to try the next trick combination. She will never make a conscious connection between the brief moments I spent with her and her growing vocabulary. I will never forget.

These moments constitute my legacy, and much of whatever resources I may amass will someday benefit early-childhood literacy. If even one child I encounter derives meaning and joy from learning to read, my life will have mattered.

I now know that the time and life energy I can invest in others is a direct result of not having children of my own. My care and influence cover a scope that surely would have narrowed had I raised my own progeny. Their absence gives me capacity to touch other lives.

—————-

It's surprisingly easy to quantify at least part of that capacity, thanks to interviews and time-use study data gathered by the Pew Research Center. Conservatively estimated, a mother

217

dedicates on average 20,970 hours to caring for her kids from birth until they turn eighteen. Assuming a forty-hour average American workweek, that's the equivalent of over ten full-time work years (forty hours per week times fifty-two weeks equals 2,080 hours). Ten years.

What's not included in that calculation is time spent planning for, worrying over, and talking about one's children, as well as all those years of each child's life after they turn eighteen. It's fair to say, the average woman without children is likely to have considerably more time available to pursue other life endeavors. Yet many of us risk frittering it away without even being aware it's ours to invest.

My purpose here is not to distill childbearing into units of time, but rather to spotlight the rich potential non-moms have to impact our own lives and the lives of others. When we're not attached to children of our own, our lives are self-directed and composed of other cares, joys, and concerns. By mindfully considering our capacities, we can purposefully craft lives congruent with what we value.

Malcolm Gladwell, in his bestselling book *Outliers* examined the relationship between time and the development of expertise. Ten thousand hours. That's what it takes to master a given skill. If we direct our "extra" 20,000 plus hours towards something we care about, we can become the kind of people we hope to be. Or we can divvy up our time into smaller chunks spread over a wider scope. There is freedom, power, and creative potential inherent in living life without having children.

—————

Soon that little first grader who learned the "ph" sound will become a preteen. She and her pals will hear pretty much the same talk their aunts, mothers, and grandmothers did as they approached puberty. Each girl will try to conjure up how children might feature in her future womanhood. She'll stand at the portal of her tomorrows.

After my own girl-into-woman talk I remember taking comfort in the teacher's assurance that no matter where I was, if I unexpectedly got my period other women would be able to help me, whether I knew them or not. I imagine expectant mothers hear a variation of the same theme before they give birth and as their children mature.

My wish for my little first grader and her cohort is that they grow up with the comfort of knowing should their tomorrows follow a different path than the route to motherhood, they likewise will be supported and celebrated by women of every age and destiny.

Manifesting that vision is within our reach. When we seize opportunities to share how we're navigating life without kids, we add vista points and rest stops to the atlas of non-motherhood. Story by story, woman by woman, we flesh out options for leading satisfying lives at work, at play, in relationship, and as maturing human beings. Cross-generationally, with women older and women younger.

Who we are is not the antonym of being a mother, and our options and lifestyles do not imperil motherhood in any way. Rather, we represent a complementary dynamic of what it is to be women of a different ilk. Regardless why we don't have children, we grow up outside the mainstream of motherhood and can cultivate lives we never expected.

----------------------

# DO YOU HAVE KIDS?

*What difference does it make? I don't think there's a need to ask the question.*

*When I was going through infertility, I'd go cry in the bathroom. Fortunately, it's morphed. Now it's who I am.*

*Once I say I don't have kids, I know they're going to ask a weird follow-up question.*

**O**f all the indicators that ours is a pronatal culture, the social acceptability of this ubiquitous icebreaker question is perhaps the most emblematic. How can we better integrate the realities of childfree and childless living into the social discourse? We don't ask about religion or whether and with whom someone is having sex. But inquiring at first meeting about one's reproductive output is standard social operating procedure. By now it should be apparent—for many, answering this question is neither simple nor benign.

Inquiries about children come up at social functions when we first meet someone, in the course of our everyday encounters with acquaintances, merchants, and coworkers, and between family and friends over the entire course of the relationship. While some conversations will not unfold perfectly, taking the risk to include childless and childfree perspectives will help release stigmas and stereotypes.

When the answer to the kid question is "No," it can feel like the air is sucked out of the room. What usually follows is a pregnant pause while everyone tries to figure out what to do next. *Oops*, the mom is probably thinking, *I wonder why not? But I know I shouldn't ask her. What do I do now?* The non-mom is likely getting ready for the mom's encouragement, judgment, or pity. No one knows quite what to say.

That pregnant pause is a golden moment for non-moms to lead the conversational dance in a direction of our choosing. The question is inevitable, and we have the advantage of already knowing our answer. So why not thoughtfully honor ourselves and rescue the tongue-tied questioner by responding in a way that suits our intentions and current emotional state? With preparation and practice, we can smooth divots in the conversational dance floor.

Mothers also have an opportunity to fill that pregnant pause with curiosity, tempered by attentive awareness of how their inquiries are being received. A respectful conversationalist can ease the flow of information and open up an authentic exchange.

Non-moms talking with each other can be a potent source of exploration, support, and appreciation. By maintaining awareness of differences in our individual circumstances and responses, we can find common ground and learn from non-moms of all ages.

Trouble is, most of us don't know what to say or do with

that pregnant pause. And even if we try to fill it, we're bound to make gaffes while we develop new skills. But try we must if we want to better integrate the full spectrum of who and how we are in the world, regardless whether we have children or not.

————·——-

So how do we talk to each other? Here are some thoughts, dos, and don'ts, first for non-moms responding to inquiries about their reproductive status, then for moms who learn the woman they're talking with has no children, and lastly for non-moms who encounter other non-moms.

## FOR NON-MOMS TALKING WITH MOMS

Those of us without children can try to meld into the edges of family-centric connections, limit our community relationships to other childless or childfree women, or fabricate some mix of the two. Fabricating a mix is in everyone's best interests.

For years I've fielded the kid question with a mixture of dread and confusion. Do I tell the truth? If so, I'm exposing myself before having any idea what the other person is like. If I make light, the mom might assume I don't like children. If I bring up my pets, she may parry with stories and photos of her kids *and* their pets. Depending on my gut sense of who's asking, my mood, or some other internal barometer of what I think is expected of me, I might be glib, gloomy, or frank. That stutter-step in the space between the kid question and my answer is weird.

And almost always there is a tone to my response I don't like:

"No, *but* I really like kids."

"We tried, *but* it didn't work."

"No, *but* I have wonderful nieces and nephews. And
I dote on my animals."

All true, yes, but why all the defensive-sounding *buts*?

A wily trial lawyer I once worked for delighted in asking
outrageous personal questions, and people almost always
answered him. "Never forget," he told me, "a question asked is
not necessarily a question answered."

Maybe you're feeling tender, defensive, or vulnerable. Maybe
you're not in the mood to explain your situation. Maybe you'd rather
talk about something, anything, else. Frankly, you have every right
to evade the topic, because it's no one's business but your own.

People who know your situation, of course, won't ask if
you have kids. Instead they'll inquire either directly or furtively
about details of your status, intentions, and conclusions about
having them. When that happens, you have a choice: either
evade the topic altogether or engage in it with the person asking.

I think it's wise to be skillful at both evasion and engagement strategies, because there will be occasions to use each of
them, often in tandem. Be sure to have your options at the ready
for what surely will come. You're going to be asked about kids
over and over for the rest of your life.

Here are a few ways to evade the question:

**Bait and switch.**

It's highly likely the person asking has kids. If you're genuinely
interested, inquire about them. If not, switch to a less personal
subject.

*Some examples:*

"You're a mom, am I right? How many kids do you
have? What are they like?"

"I don't have kids. I also recently moved here. How long have you been in the area? What are some of your favorite local places to go?"

"I bet we can find something we have in common. I'm passionate about the environment/adult literacy/cooking. What about you?"

**Use humor and shift.**
If it fits both your personal style and the social occasion, humor can serve as a light-hearted way to evade.

*Some examples:*

"I haven't found a worthy baby daddy yet. Where'd you meet your partner?"

"We're still practicing. I'll let you know if anything changes. We're also working on our ping-pong skills. Do you play?"

"A long time ago my sisters and brothers made me promise not to. Do you have siblings?"

In an article he wrote for *The American Scholar* titled "Child-free in Toyland," Penn State professor Christopher Clausen shared two of his humor-based evasion strategies when the kid question comes up. "If I could be sure of getting one just like yours, I'd do it in a minute," he responds. "Most people prefer flattery to imitation," he says. "Alas, it seldom works with your own parents."

What I like about this approach is it also works when you know and honestly admire someone's child. I can think of numerous friends' kids I'd like to hear about.

Clausen goes on to describe a time his wife dealt with a nosy relative. "On one occasion my father, always an outspoken man, took my wife aside and blurted experimentally, 'Chris should have given you a child.' To which she responded: 'I would have given it right back.' My parents never raised the question again."

***Cut and run.***
There will be occasions when, for whatever reason, you'll simply want to exit the conversation as soon as you can. It's not rude; you're simply taking care of yourself.

*Some examples:*

"Please excuse me for a moment. I need to go to the restroom."

"Pardon me. I see someone who's been trying to get in touch with me."

"My drink needs refreshing. Can I get you something?"

These days I find myself taking the initiative to engage others on the topic, regardless whether or not I think the person I'm talking to has kids. I ask them first. That way I get to choose the timing and, because people almost always reciprocate and ask whether I do, it's up to me what happens next. I've bought some time, feel less defensive, and am better prepared for the rest of the exchange.

I enjoy talking about what life is like not having kids. When we're ready and willing, engaging with someone else about our experiences and identity can open doors to new understanding and connection. We can offer access to the experience of not having children and try to make it more real for them. We're also taking our rightful place as women manifesting our gender roles differently than the norm. Trying to engage is also potentially risky, so ease into it and be ready with a fallback strategy.

Here are some ways to engage others and open up the conversation:

### Talk about talking about the subject.

The least risky way to open up the subject of not having kids is to talk around the edges of the topic.

*Some examples:*

"I don't have kids, no. Do you know other people who don't?"

Give them a moment to think. Of course they do, but they've probably never been asked before.

"This can be challenging to talk about, especially between moms and non-moms. Some of us wanted kids and some didn't, but it's usually not so clear-cut. How often have you had the chance to talk frankly with someone who doesn't have kids?"

Probably rarely. A possible follow-up is, "Why do you think that is?"

### Share statistics or other impersonal factual information.

Data and hard facts are a safe way to scratch the surface of the subject in an engaging way.

*Some examples:*

"You know women earn on average eighty-one cents to a man's dollar, right? But a married mom with a child at home makes only seventy-six cents, and a woman without kids earns ninety-six cents."

"Depending on what generation they're from, up to 20 percent of women will never have kids. There are a lot of us, and I heard projections for the next generation are higher."

"Charitable organizations love people without kids, you know."

**Talk about someone else's experience.**
Especially when we're trying to get more fluent talking about life without kids, it may be easier to talk about someone else's experiences instead of our own.

*Some examples:*

"I read recently about a childfree couple who did their jobs entirely online while they traveled around the world for two years. Can you picture doing something like that?"

"My sister doesn't have kids. She never met anyone she wanted to have them with. She's a preschool teacher who's devoted her life to making sure kids start reading and know their numbers. Do any of your kids' teachers not have kids?"

"An older woman I know is starting a scholarship fund for homeless women. I hope to consider something like that too someday. What about you?"

### Disclose something about your own experience.

When you want to bring the conversation to a more personal level, someone has to take the initiative. By diving in yourself, you guide where the conversation might go.

*Some examples:*

"I don't have kids, and I imagine it's different than you think it is." If they bite, you can tell them some of the pluses and minuses you've discovered.

"I loved my school librarian, and I'm pretty sure she was a non-mom, too. Other than your own parents, when you were a kid who were important role models in your life?"

"I like to think of 'mother' as a verb. For example, I mentor a dozen young people who are starting out in my profession. Other than your own kids, who or what do you mother?"

### Turn the tables.

Shifting the focus to the other person can provide valuable information about their level of interest and willingness to engage. Staying open and curious may lead to interesting conversations.

*Some examples:*

"That can be quite a personal question. Why do you ask? Really, I'm curious."

"What will you think if, for whatever reason, one of your kids doesn't have children?

"Let's assume for a moment you didn't have kids. What might you have done differently with your life?"

I asked my mother that last question one day. She got a far-off look in her eyes and told me about how she would have gone for a PhD in English literature and taught at a university. Then she looked directly at me, horrified.

"That doesn't mean I didn't want you and your sisters."

"I know," I told her. "I like that you can picture another life for yourself. Maybe you can see my world differently now." It was the most authentic exchange I ever had with my mom.

—————

Sometimes it's helpful to study an expert's approach.

In April 2016 Hillary Frank, co-producer of the podcast "The Longest Shortest Time," scored an interview with the master interviewer herself—Terry Gross of National Public Radio's *Fresh Air.* The topic? Not having kids. During the interview Gross responds to a string of questions about whether she ever wanted to have a child (not really), what kind of mother she might have been (she'll never know), the benefits (she got independence and the life she wanted), does she like babies (she likes cute dogs and cats more), who will care for her as she ages (she hasn't made plans yet). Then, a good three-quarters of the way through the interview, Gross asks if she can pose a question of her own. Frank agrees and hears what she later refers to as "a superscary personal question."

Gross's question: "Do you ever have second thoughts about having had a child?" (Frank does.)

With that question, the traditional ask-and-answer format

shifts to more of a conversational give-and-take. How did this occur? I think it's because Gross was vulnerable and honest in her answers to Frank's questions, disclosing personal information multiple times. Only then did she pose a probing question herself, which allowed the two to find areas of both agreement and contrast. Gross took a risk, albeit the well-calculated one of a professional interviewer, and the payoff was sincere exploration of the space between two people. She brought the conversation back into balance.

Whether by providence, maneuvering, or skillful editing, Gross also ends up with the last word. She ties the entire conversation up with a bow of firm personal conviction: "It's great to be a parent when you're not forced to be," she says, "when society isn't demanding it, when they're not making it an obligation. And in order to no longer be an obligation, I think some people had to choose not to have children and rewrite the rules a little bit. And you know—hooray for all of us."

When asked about your reproductive output from people with kids,

### Do:
- Take care of your personal needs.
- Try leading the conversation.
- Eliminate the "but" after the "No."
- Respect your own boundaries.
- Acknowledge and respect differences between your life and theirs.

### Don't:
- Answer any questions you'd prefer not to.
- Justify, compensate for, or defend not having kids.
- Apologize, attack, or criticize.

## FOR MOMS TALKING WITH NON-MOMS

Mothers can benefit from better understanding women who aren't, because non-moms are everywhere, and numbers are increasing.

A proud mother is nearly always the person asking about kids. She's simply trying to make some sort of agreeable connection, and what's wrong with that? Most women eventually become mothers, so odds are she'll meet a kindred spirit. Or will she?

Asking if someone has kids isn't as innocuous as it might seem. There's a lot attached to the question, even when the woman is a mother. For instance, what if the person once had a child, and he or she died? Or relations with an adult child are strained. What if there are chronic substance-abuse issues, or the son or daughter is in prison for some heinous crime? On the other hand, you might be about to learn their kids are brighter, prettier, or more successful than yours. Potential minefields abound.

What's your intention behind asking about kids? If it's to break the ice, can you substitute another, less personal question? It's highly likely if the other person has kids and there are no extenuating circumstances, they'll soon bring them up anyway, without being asked. And if you later discover someone doesn't have kids, you can decide how to approach the subject, if at all. Your options remain open.

Building skills and exercising conversational options today may pay off tomorrow. As daughters grow up and enter their potentially fertile years, fewer may end up bearing children in the future.

The Cassandra Company has tracked emerging trends in youth for over twenty years. In its 2015 *Ages and Stages* report, it revealed that "nearly one-third [of millennials] do not want to have kids at all, either because they don't want to give up their flexibility (34 percent) or they don't want to take on the responsibility (32 percent)." If these projections become reality, today's parents and grandparents will have fewer grand- and great-grandchildren and, consequently, more opportunities to better understand their daughters and granddaughters who may not have kids.

So how can mothers approach non-moms effectively? Even if you think having kids is the best thing ever, touting your conviction will likely serve only to frustrate or hurt those who wanted them and raise the defenses of those who didn't. Nothing you say will change their reality anyway.

Deciding to accept differences is a process that happens in the privacy of one's own mind, of course. And while it's human nature to disagree with other people's situations and decisions—where they live, their religious or political bent, how they handle their money—offering value judgments can be counterproductive to building strong relationships. If you can accept that not having kids is a valid way of being female, non-moms will be more inclined to be open with you. If you can't, consider not asking about kids or gracefully change the subject when she says she doesn't.

Yet many parents seem to have a stockpile of responses ready when they encounter someone who doesn't have kids. In fact, these comments are so predictable, new usage has been coined for an old game—bingo: *A put-down or criticism of a life choice.*

> **Usage:** *A bingo. It's when a person says they don't have children, and someone tells them they'll change their mind or that it's different when they're theirs.*

You might even hear a non-mom utter the word under her breath sometime. If you're curious, you can find images of "Childfree Bingo" cards (sometimes snarkily referred to as "Breeder Bingo") online.

Here are some typical responses that may elicit a "bingo":

"You'll live to regret it."

"But you'd be such a great mom!"

"Aren't you lonely without them?"

"You think you don't want them, but you'll change your mind."

"You'll never know true love until you look into the eyes of your child."

"Children give life its meaning."

"Being a grandmother is the best role there is."

"Not having kids is selfish."

"Who's supposed to take care of you when you're old?"

"It's the most important job in the world."

"You aren't a real woman if you don't give birth."

These retorts are not reserved for the childfree. I can vouch for the fact that those who wanted kids frequently hear them, too. Try rereading the list with a woman experiencing infertility in mind.

What's tough about all these comments is the underlying assumption that one way of being, *i.e.* having kids, is both the right way and accessible to everyone. Neither is true, and what comes off as pressing one's own position on another results in a funky shift in the interpersonal dynamic, even (sometimes especially) between friends and family members.

Fortunately, most people are less confrontational and judgmental. Open minds are curious. Accepting hearts are compassionate and kind. Interested voices are soft in tone. When the topic of children comes up (even if you're not the one asking), consider trying to explore the subject with the non-mom.

Here are some ideas:

**Be considerate of the other's reactions.**
Make it a habit to pay attention to how someone expresses herself about not having kids. People often signal their feelings non-verbally. When you notice subtle cues, you'll be able to respond more thoughtfully. Take a breath before continuing, and trust your gut.

*Examples:*

"That's a personal question, isn't it? How about we talk about something other than kid stuff."

"I imagine you sometimes hear insensitive comments from parents about how important they think having kids is. Will you share some of the most offensive ones?"

**Own your experience; be open to hers.**
You don't have to drop all references to progeny. They play a huge part in most parents' lives, and we know that. See if you can find middle ground.

*Examples:*

"I love being a mom but worry about what I'll do once the kids leave home. Tell me about what captures your time and attention these days so I can see life from a different perspective."

"Raising kids has been hard but worth it for me.
What matters for you?"

"My cousin is getting a lot of pressure to have kids,
and I'd like her to know I'm a source of support.
Do you have any suggestions how I could do this
tactfully?"

**Notice your airtime.**
Talking about your own children might be natural, but with a
non-mom the conversation is sure to become one-sided. With
non-moms you already know and care about, consider whether
they know more about your life than you know of theirs. If so,
try to learn more about them.

*Examples:*

"Tell me more about yourself."

"I promise I won't show you every kid photo I
have. Here are three of my favorites that give
you a sense of who they are, then I want to hear
about you."

"Look at me—talking about all my grandkids again.
I haven't heard what's new with you yet. Please,
bring me up to date."

When learning a woman doesn't have kids,

**Do:**
- Ask if it's okay to ask her questions about not
  having them.
- Notice her reaction to your questions.

- Express your curiosity respectfully.
- Watch out for "mombarding."

***Don't:***
- Offer condolence, suggestions, or solutions, unless asked.
- Pity, pamper, or try to comfort her.
- Judge or make assumptions about her situation.

## FOR NON-MOMS TALKING TO EACH OTHER

The stigma that attaches to women without children is hard to shake.

A 2017 study by Annalucia Bays of Virginia Commonwealth University analyzed how women were perceived based on their parental status. "Mothers were the most admired group," she found, "eliciting helping behaviors; childless women elicited pity; and childfree women elicited envy, disgust, and harm behaviors [from others, for example, in the workplace]." She cites in her study considerable prior academic work on stereotypes. Some of the adjectives researchers found routinely used to describe women without children include: materialistic, immature, emotionally unstable, selfish, and less likely to live happy and satisfied lives.

The same year another study, this one out of Indiana University–Purdue University Indianapolis and provocatively entitled, "Parenthood as a Moral Imperative: Moral Outrage and the Stigmatization of Voluntarily Childfree Men and Women," concluded that the stigma remains. In fact, researcher Leslie Ashbury-Nardo found that those who go against cultural stereotypes by intentionally choosing not to have kids can be met with what researchers refer to as "moral outrage."

A powerful means of overcoming stigma is by becoming better known and understood. We do that by being seen and heard, and we might as well start with each other.

During our lifetimes we will have many opportunities to fully show up, speak our truths, and be heard. But how do we do that? By keeping quiet about our life experiences, we play a major role in perpetuating the stigma. By talking, we can help dispel it and take our proper place in the diverse world of normalcy, even when our reasons for not having kids differ vastly.

By the time she closed the first NotMom Summit in 2015, Karen Malone Wright had masterfully narrowed the gap between the child*less* and the child*free*. To spark connections, nothing on participant name badges indicated who was a non-mom by choice and who was by chance, so we had no way of knowing another woman's story without asking her. That took us all into a vulnerable place—will the woman I'm about to talk to have a story similar to mine, or is hers different? Malone Wright urged us to ask and explore each other's experiences of being other than mothers—at meals, in workshops, and during happy hour. With exploration came connection, understanding, and insight.

Malone Wright is a spunky professional communicator with a background in public relations, marketing, and social media. She launched her website TheNotMom.com in 2012. It "embraces all women without children," she says, "including their diverse life stories about 'how' and 'why.' Each woman sees herself and defines herself in her own way—I want this site to feel like family when she gets here."

She isn't interested in further polarizing or distancing women from each other. In her eyes, whoever considers herself a NotMom is one. "It's a self-defined term," she says. "I think there really is power in the concept of tribe. There is something human in finding another person that makes you see yourself and know for certain that you are not alone. Somebody else who gets you."

But what about the distance that separates stories of choice from those of chance? "There's more that you have in common than you have that's different," Malone Wright says. "I can compare it to the tension between working moms and stay-at-home moms. They're all trying to do the best they can, trying to balance time with impossible demands upon it. Yet they push each other away.

"As a black woman, I will say it's also like house slaves and field slaves. If we divide, we are apart from each other. I don't like the pettiness that divides obvious communities."

When you meet another woman who doesn't have kids, odds are about even whether she wanted them or chose not to have them. Wanting them can involve sorrow and choosing not to may elicit defensiveness. So the conversation can stall from the start. However, there's lots of common ground to explore after taking the risk of including your own reality and being open to different experiences and perspectives.

Here are some options for connecting with other non-moms:

### By choice or by chance?

A first step to connect with other non-moms is by acknowledging your own situation and opening a door of welcome to the woman you're talking to. How you start sets the stage for where you might go next.

*Some examples:*

"I don't have kids and never thought I'd have them, so it's worked out fine for me. But I know that's not the case for every woman. How has it been for you?"

"We tried, and it didn't work. That was a couple years ago, and it still hurts sometimes. But I'm also relieved we don't need to save for the kid's college. Are you childfree by choice or childless by chance?"

"I've just begun sharing my story with others. What do you tell people who ask? What has worked for you, and what didn't go so well?

**Be curious and respectful.**
In many social situations it can be a relief to meet someone who doesn't have kids. Some may express interest, but others may not want to talk.

*Some examples:*

"I don't think anyone has ever shared that with me. You've got me thinking."

"This is still a sensitive topic for me. Do you mind if we talk about something else?"

"I never thought much about how not having kids has affected my life, but it really is a different perspective. What about you?"

With the ice now broken in a new way, it's time for the juicy part—discovering how someone else has experienced life without children in all its complexity and vast range of options.

**Explore ways you've both managed circumstances you have in common.**
Most life circumstances can be impacted by not having kids—work life, how you spend the holidays, financial planning, dealing with aging parents. Possibilities are endless.

*Some examples:*

"One of my best friends just had her second child. Have you had any luck figuring out how to maintain close friendships, especially during the baby years?"

"Who in your family will take care of your parents? My siblings are counting on me, since I don't have kids and live closest, but my mom and I have never really gotten along."

"I'm trying to figure out where to live. Being single, I can go anywhere. What parts of town do you like best?"

***Share the pluses and minuses of not having kids.***
Chances are good you'll agree on several of the advantages and disadvantages, though there will be differences based on choice versus chance, women's ages, and life circumstances.

*Some examples:*

"It's great not having to buy all the things kids need. What are some of the ways you've used the time and resources others have spent raising their kids?"

"Have you figured out who would be a good advocate if something happens to you? What do you think is a good way to ask someone to do the job?"

"What experiences have you had that might have been impossible if you were a mom?"

***Compare and contrast life experiences.***
Without children, we have more autonomy about life choices, including how we spend our time and what we do with our resources.

*Some examples:*

"Since you said you wanted kids, I'm curious about your involvement with other people's children or other ways of nurturing you've found. How satisfying is that for you?"

"As time goes by, what has surprised you about not having kids? What do you think might surprise family and friends who are parents?"

"What are you thinking about retirement? A number of my friends retired early, but I'm not sure that's right for me."

When talking with other women who don't have kids:

*Do:*
• Find an approach that works for both of you.
• Maintain sensitivity and respect.
• Listen and learn.
• Be ready to change the subject.

*Don't:*
• Assume the other woman wants to talk.
• Go into detail, especially at the outset.
• Tout your experience over anyone else's.

Like embarking on a new exercise regime, talking about not having kids can be challenging to initiate. These suggestions offer some basic equipment for getting started, but we reap the best results when we customize an approach that honors our personal style and idiosyncrasies.

The potential payoff for trying is huge. As we approach each other with more openness, we learn about and appreciate the value of a broader range of adult experience. We come to know our friends, siblings, offspring, and neighbors in new ways that include more reproductive diversity and different ways of experiencing life. Younger women and men find answers to their questions and support for their decisions and circumstances. The air around us all can circulate more freely.

# NOTES

## INTRODUCTION
**2—Depending on when and where they were born:** US Census Bureau, "Fertility of Women in the United States," *Current Population Reports* (May 4, 2017): https://www.census.gov/topics/health/fertility/data/tables.html.

## CHAPTER 1. WHO WE ARE
**6—Even a nationwide network of women and gender studies professors was stumped:** Marilyn Fischer, "Any Suggestions for a Term?" Email exchange in WRAC-L forum, *Google Groups*, March 21–May 5, 2014.

**7—The United States is one of the most pronatal cultures in the world:** Kristin Park, "Stigma Management among the Voluntarily Childless," *Sociological Perspectives*, vol. 45, no. 1 (Spring 2002): 22, https://journals.sagepub.com/doi/abs/10.1525/sop.2002.45.1.21.

**7—At the start of the twenty-first century:** Sarah Hayford, "Marriage (Still) Matters: The Contribution of Demographic

Change to Trends in Childlessness in the United States," *Demography*, vol. 50, no. 5 (October 2013): 1643, https://www.ncbi.nlm.nih.gov/pubmed/23595495.

**7—In 2016 overall childlessness:** Gretchen Livingston, Julianna Horowitz, and Jessica Pumphrey, "They're Waiting Longer, but US Women Today More Likely to Have Children Than a Decade Ago," *Pew Research Center* (January 2018): 3, http://www.pewsocialtrends.org/2018/01/18/theyre-waiting-longer-but-u-s-women-today-more-likely-to-have-children-than-a-decade-ago.

**7—Demographers in the United States define childlessness:** Gretchen Livingston and D'Vera Cohn, "Childlessness Up Among All Women; Down Among Women with Advanced Degrees," *Pew Research Center, A Social & Demographic Trends Report* (June 25, 2010): 1, http://www.pewsocialtrends.org/2010/06/25/childlessness-up-among-all-women-down-among-women-with-advanced-degrees/.

**7—We still don't know how the Great Recession will affect:** Livingston, Horowitz, and Pumphrey, "They're Waiting Longer," 5.

**8—An oddsmaker might say today's women without children:** Livingston, Horowitz, and Pumphrey, "They're Waiting Longer," 6.

**8—Approximately 18 percent of all childless women:** Joyce C. Abma and Gladys M. Martinez, "Childlessness among Older Women in the United States: Trends and Profiles," *Journal of Marriage and Family*, vol. 68, no. 4 (November 2006): 1045, https://www.jstor.org/stable/4122892.

**8—Studies suggest that being childfree is not so much a single big decision:** Renske Keizer, Pearl A. Dykstra, and Miranda D. Jansen, "Pathways into Childlessness: Evidence of Gendered Life Course Dynamics," *Journal of Biosocial Science*, vol. 40, no. 6, (December 20, 2007): 864, https://www.ncbi.nlm.nih.gov/pubmed/18093349.

**9—According to one, with each academic level a woman completes:** Keizer, "Pathways into Childlessness," 872.

**9—Since 2010 women have held more than half of all managerial and professional jobs:** Kate Bolick, "All the Single Ladies." *The Atlantic Monthly*, vol. 308, no. 4, ProQuest (November 2011): 120, https://www.theatlantic.com/magazine/archive/2011/11/all-the-single-ladies/308654/.

**9—During her period of fertility:** Livingston, Horowitz, and Pumphrey, "They're Waiting Longer," 5.

**10—Karen Malone Wright, an energetic sixty-year-old:** Karen Malone Wright, "Welcome to The NotMom.com Summit," Cleveland Marriott Hotel. (October 4, 2015).

## CHAPTER 2. ON THE JOB

**18—Not having children is a boon to a woman's career:** Claire Cain Miller, "The Motherhood Penalty vs. the Fatherhood Bonus: A Child Helps Your Career, If You're a Man," *The New York Times*, September 6, 2014, https://www.nytimes.com/2014/09/07/upshot/a-child-helps-your-career-if-youre-a-man.html.

**18—Adrienne Casey walked the streets with a badge and a gun:** Adrienne Casey, in recorded personal interview with the author, June 9, 2015.

**22—Bobbi Hartwell looks much younger:** Bobbi Hartwell, in recorded personal interview with the author, May 13, 2015.

**24—A quarter of a million dollars:** US Department of Agriculture Center for Nutrition Policy and Promotion, "Parents Projected to Spend $245,340 to Raise a Child Born in 2013, According to USDA Report," Press Release 0179.14, August 18, 2014: https://www.usda.gov/media/press-releases/2014/08/18/parents-projected-spend-245340-raise-child-born-2013-according-usda.

**24—Chris Clarke was in graduate school:** Chris Clarke, in recorded telephone interview with the author, May 26, 2015.

**26—But back in 2002 Sylvia Hewitt, in partnership:** Sylvia Ann Hewlett, "Executive Women and the Myth of Having It All," *Harvard Business Review* (April 2002): https://hbr.org/2002/04/executive-women-and-the-myth-of-having-it-all.

**27—Women's earnings overall have been stalled:** Michelle J. Budig, "The Fatherhood Bonus & the Motherhood Penalty: Parenthood and the Gender Gap in Pay," *Third Way: NEXT* (September 2014): 7, content.thirdway.org/publications/853/NEXT_-_Fatherhood_Motherhood.pdf.

**27—Una Cadegan crossed the academic finish line with a PhD:** Una Cadegan, in recorded telephone interview with the author, September 10, 2015.

**28—A generation ahead of Una, Jane Zembaty worked at the same university:** Jane Zembaty, in recorded personal interview with the author, October 12, 2015.

**31—A baby girl is born with a lifetime supply of one to two million eggs:** Wendy Sachs, "The 'Big Lie' in Putting

Off Pregnancy," *CNN*, January 22, 2014, https://www.cnn.com/2014/01/22/living/pregnancy-big-lie-tanya-selvaratnam-books/index.html.

**31—Hence the employee benefit first offered to women employees:** Sarah Elizabeth Richards, "Do You Have to Be Rich to Freeze Your Eggs?" *Slate*, August 22, 2013, http://www.slate.com/articles/double_x/doublex/2013/08/the_cost_of_egg_freezing_after_years_of_prohibitive_pricing_clinics_are.html.

**32—Had she been born three decades later:** Cheryl Katen, in recorded personal interview with the author, May 2, 2015.

## CHAPTER 3. BORROWED FROM THE BEGINNING

**39—"If I had stayed in England, I'd probably be a midwife now":** Annie Eastap, in recorded telephone interview with the author, June 30, 2015.

**39—Poet Suzanne Sigafoos was twenty-five when her friend asked her:** Suzanne Sigafoos, in recorded personal interview with the author, May 27, 2015.

**39—A yoga teacher I'll call Marie Erickson didn't regret:** Marie Erickson, *pseudonym*, in recorded personal interview with the author, June 18, 2015.

**41—Canadian writer and former high school teacher Leslie Hill:** Leslie Hill, in recorded telephone interview with the author, April 27, 2015.

**41—Virginia activist Chris Clarke and one of her best friends:** Clarke, interview, May 26, 2015.

**42—World traveler Bobbi Hartwell tried to participate in a stranger's birth:** Hartwell, interview, May 13, 2015.

**44—Trying to figure out why fewer babies are being born:** Ariana Eunjung Cha, "It Turns Out Parenthood Is Worse than Divorce, Unemployment—Even the Death of a Partner," *The Washington Post*, August 11, 2015, www.washingtonpost.com/news/to-your-health/wp/2015/08/11/the-most-depressing-statistic-imaginable-about-being-a-new-parent/?utm_term=.42bcf6286df4.

**45—Developmental psychologists call this "generativity":** Kendra Cherry, "Generativity Versus Stagnation: The Seventh Stage of Psychosocial Development," *Verywell Mind*, March 12, 2018, https://www.verywellmind.com/generativity-versus-stagnation-2795734.

**45—But two PhDs at the University of Missouri examined previous studies:** Tanja Rothrauff and Teresa M. Cooney, "The Role of Generativity in Psychological Well-Being: Does It Differ for Childless Adults and Parents?" *Journal of Adult Development*, vol. 15 (October 11, 2008): 155, aging.wisc.edu/midus/findings/pdfs/727.pdf.

**46—Cheryl Katen, the Hewlett-Packard engineer also known as:** Katen, interview, May 2, 2015.

**47—Years after she tried unsuccessfully to give her eggs to a stranger:** Hartwell, interview, May 13, 2015.

**48—Nanny Susan Gianotti has cared for the two boys in her charge:** Susan Gianotti, in recorded personal interview with the author, November 12, 2014.

50—*Alloparenting* **sounds like what Susan is doing:** Daniel J. Siegel, *Brainstorm: The Power and Purpose of the Teenage Brain* (New York: Tarcher/Penguin, 2015), 143.

50—**"Human attachment can be understood as involving four S's":** Siegel, *Brainstorm*, 144.

52—**Sometimes sources of security live across the street:** Barbara Hanna, in recorded telephone interview with the author, June 14, 2017.

53—**I heard once that in the Crow Nation:** Brooke Medicine Eagle in Jane English, ed., *Childlessness Transformed: Stories of Alternative Parenting* (Mt. Shasta, CA: Earth Heart, 1989).

## CHAPTER 4. ABIDING FRIENDSHIP

56—**"The childless friend may feel like she's been knocked down":** Irene S. Levine, *Best Friends Forever* (New York: Overlook Press, 2009), 146.

57—**Poet Suzanne Sigafoos is a redhead who wants what she will never have:** Sigafoos, interview, May 27, 2015.

58—**Suzanne wrote a poem about these important relationships:** Sigafoos, *"Still and All."* Printed with permission of the author.

59—**The ongoing, decades long Nurses' Health Study:** Joan Borysenko, "Gal Pals," *Prevention Magazine*, June 2006, http://www.joanborysenko.com/dev/mind-body-balance/spirituality-inspiration/gal-pals/.

**59—True friendships, the ones that last, have consistent elements:** Levine, *Best Friends Forever*, 136.

**60—"When my closest friend told me she was pregnant, I cried":** Laura Johnson, *pseudonym*, in recorded telephone interview with the author, October 4, 2015.

**61—Beverly Williams, another forty-six-year-old, is a writer and a teacher and a knitter:** Beverly Williams, in recorded telephone interview with the author, August 24, 2015.

**64—Michelle Callahan, PhD, is a psychologist:** CBS News, "How to Make Your Friendships Last," aired on February 2, 2010, https://www.cbsnews.com/news/how-to-make-your-friendships-last/.

**64—"When you're single, you depend on your friends for your basic nourishment":** Cadegan, interview, September 10, 2015.

## CHAPTER 5. FAMILY MATTERS

**72—Indiana University's Brian Powell:** Laura Carroll, "Are Families of Two a Family? Where Americans Stand," *Lauracarroll .com*, October 14, 2013, https://www.lauracarroll.com/families-of-two-3/.

**73—According to the US Census Bureau:** US Census Bureau, "America's Families and Living Arrangements: 2012, Population Characteristics," *Current Population Reports* (August 2013), https://www.census.gov/prod/2013pubs/p20-570.pdf.

**73—Aziza Cunin (not her real name) is an artist:** Aziza Cunin, *pseudonym*, in recorded personal interview with the author, March 22, 2016.

**76—Less than 20 percent of young adult stepchildren:** Karen S. Peterson, "Divorce Need Not End in Disaster," *USA Today*, January 13, 2002, https://usatoday30.usatoday.com/news/nation/2002/01/14/usatcov-divorce.htm.

**77—On the *HuffPost Divorce* blog:** Mary T. Kelly, "Help for the Childless Stepmom." *HuffPost Divorce*, June 22, 2013, https://www.huffingtonpost.com/mary-t-kelly-ma/help-for-the-child-less-st_b_3102893.html.

**77—McMinnville, Oregon is a rural town of thirty thousand:** Jenny Berg, in recorded personal interview with the author, March 17, 2015.

**81—Deb Fischer was forty-two when her marriage ended:** Deb Fischer, in recorded personal interview with the author, April 23, 2015.

**84—Amy Blackstone knows a thing or two about the morphing definition:** Amy Blackstone, "Who Are the NotMoms?" NotMom Summit. Marriott Hotel, Cleveland, OH, Keynote Address, October 9, 2015.

**85—"When we talk about families, be it in politics":** Amy Blackstone, "Blackstone's Research Doesn't Kid Around," *UMaine News*, January 30, 2014, https://umaine.edu/news/blog/2014/01/30/blackstones-research-doesnt-kid-around/.

85—Blood family. Chosen family. That's how Elsa Stavney, forty-five, differentiates family: Elsa Stavney, in recorded personal interview with the author, March 23, 2016.

87—If you live long enough, you mother your mother: Jane Dunwoodie, in recorded telephone interview with the author, August 25, 2015.

90—Shelly Volsche refers to herself as a "childfree mom": Shelly Volsche, "Parenting Dogs: Are Childfree Dog Owners Really Childless?" *We're {Not} Having a Baby!* April 14, 2015, http://werenothavingababy.com/childfree/parenting-dogs-are-childfree-dog-owners-really-childless/.

90—When asked if she considers her pets to be family: Stavney, interview, March 23, 2016.

90—Marching across the rear window: Eastap, interview, June 30, 2015.

91—Beverly Williams looks at how she parents her dogs: Williams, interview, August 25, 2015.

91—But not all writers feel the same: Sigafoos, interview, May 27, 2015.


## CHAPTER 6. WHERE WE LIVE

99—In the United States, the first such community: The Cohousing Association of the United States, "Cohousing in the United States: An Innovative Model of Sustainable Neighborhoods," Initially published April 22, 2016, www.cohousing.org/StateofCohousing.

**99—Set on nearly four acres in what was once an urban hydroponic farm:** Columbia Ecovillage website, *"Who We Are,"* columbiaecovillage.org/who-we-are/.

**100—I meet Martha Wagner, who invites me to see the compact studio:** Martha Wagner, in recorded personal interview with the author, January 28, 2016.

**103—Who does well living in such a place:** Diana Leafe Christian, *Finding Community: How to Join an Ecovillage or Intentional Community* (Gabriola: British Columbia, New Society Publishers, 2007), 97-99.

**106—She refers to herself as "sixty-four going on seven":** Michele Fiasca, in recorded telephone interview with the author, February 16, 2016.

**109—Happenstance can topple the towers:** Hill, interview, April 27, 2015.

**112—Today singletons represent 28 percent:** Eric Klinenberg, *Going Solo: The Extraordinary Rise and Surprising Appeal of Living Alone* (New York: Penguin Press, 2012), 5.

**113—Singleton Laura Johnson, an unmarried, forty-seven-year-old:** Johnson, interview, October 4, 2015.

**114—"I'm a full-time RVer," says sixty-eight year old:** Julie Aegerter, in recorded telephone interview with the author, October 14, 2017.

**117—I visit Jane Zembaty, eighty-four, in her immaculate one-bedroom apartment:** Zembaty, interview, October 12, 2015.

**120—According to AARP, only one in three people who divorce:** Xenia P. Montenegro, "The Divorce Experience: A Study of Divorce at Midlife and Beyond," Report conducted for *AARP Magazine*, 2004, https://assets.aarp.org/rgcenter/general/divorce.pdf.


## CHAPTER 7. USE IT OR LOSE IT

**121—Epigraphs for this chapter only:** from Katherine M. Leonard, "Women's Experience of Surviving Cervical Cancer: Maintaining the Self," (PhD dissertation, University of Alberta, 1990), 82, 26, 91, doi:10.7939/R3KP7V08W.

**122—Nuns don't have babies:** Kara Britt and Roger Short, "The Plight of Nuns: Hazards of Nulliparity," Comment, *The Lancet*, vol. 739, no. 9834 (December 8, 2011): 2322, http://www.thelancet.com/journals/lancet/article/PIIS0140-6736(11)61746-7/fulltext.

**123—The National Cancer Institute says these mutations:** National Cancer Institute, "BRCA1 and BRCA2: Cancer Risk and Genetic Testing," *Fact Sheet*, January 22, 2014, https://www.cancer.gov/about-cancer/causes-prevention/genetics/brca-fact-sheet.

**123—Additional factors that may increase a woman's risk:** Norbert Gleicher, "Why Are Reproductive Cancers More Common in Nulliparous Women?" *Reproductive Biomedicine Online*, Elsevier Ltd., vol. 26, no. 5 (May 2013): 416–419, www.rbmojournal.com/article/S1472-6483(13)00015-1/fulltext.

**123—During her lifetime one in eight women will hear:** American Cancer Society, *Cancer Facts & Figures 2015*, https://www.cancer.org/research/cancer-facts-statistics/all-cancer-facts-figures/cancer-facts-figures-2015.html.

**124—One Friday my friend Jenny Bates got the news while shopping at Goodwill:** Jenny Bates, in recorded personal interview with the author, November 25, 2015.

**126—Risk factors, according to the American Cancer Society:** American Cancer Society, "What Are the Risk Factors for Breast Cancer?" *Learn About Cancer Guide*, May 4, 2016, updated version available at: https://www.cancer.org/cancer/breast-cancer/risk-and-prevention.html.

**126—Great strides have been made in the treatment of breast cancer:** MD Anderson Communications Office, "MD Anderson Study Finds Increases in Five, Ten-Year Survival at Every Stage of Breast Cancer Over Six Decades," *News Release*, September 29, 2010, https://www.mdanderson.org/newsroom/2010/09/md-anderson-study-finds-increases-in-five-10-year-survival-at-ev.html.

**126—Survival rates aside:** Fred Hutchinson Cancer Research Center, "The More Times a Woman Gives Birth, the Higher Her Risk of Rare but Aggressive 'Triple-Negative' Breast Cancer," *News Release*, February 24, 2011, https://www.fredhutch.org/en/news/releases/2011/02/triple_negative_breast_cancer.html.

**127—Judy Teufel didn't have breast cancer, but she had a double mastectomy anyway:** Judy Teufel, in recorded personal interview with the author, November 7, 2014.

**129—"The Silent Killer," as ovarian cancer has long been called:** Renee Twombly, "Cancer Killer May Be 'Silent' No More," *Journal of the National Cancer Institute*, vol. 99, no. 18 (September 19, 2007): 1359, https://academic.oup.com/jnci/article/99/18/1359/925194.

**129—The east wind blows knuckle-numbing cold the day I meet Kate Leonard, PhD:** Kate Leonard, in recorded personal interview with the author, November 12, 2014.

**129—Soon a group of women ranging in age from their midforties to midseventies:** Ovarian cancer support group meeting, Legacy Good Samaritan Hospital, Portland, Oregon, November 12, 2014.

**131—"If women were more proactive at recognizing these symptoms":** Denise Grady, "Symptoms Found for Early Check on Ovary Cancer," *The New York Times*, June 13, 2007, www.nytimes.com/2007/06/13/health/13cancer.html.

**134—While ultrasound is one of a doctor's few diagnostic tools:** "Ovarian Cancer," *Memorial Sloan Kettering Cancer Center*, 2014, https://www.mskcc.org/cancer-care/types/ovarian.

**134—I meet nanny Susan Gianotti at one of Dr. Leonard's group meetings:** Gianotti, interview, November 12, 2014.

**135—Other than getting pregnant, there's not much a woman can do:** Cancer Research UK, "Ovarian Cancer Risks and Causes," 2014, current guide at: http://www.cancerresearchuk.org/about-cancer/ovarian-cancer/risks-causes.

**135—Drs. Kara Britt and Roger Short proposed:** Britt and Short, "The Plight of Nuns," 2.

**135—Marjorie Greenfield, MD is Chief of General Obstetrics and Gynecology:** Marjorie Greenfield, "Nullipara: Childlessness and Your Health," NotMom Summit, Marriott Hotel, Cleveland, OH, workshop, October 9, 2015.

**137—Jenny Bates doesn't:** Bates, interview, November 25, 2015.

**137—Judy Teufel, after having both her ovaries and her breasts removed:** Teufel, interview, November 7, 2014.

**138—Unspayed cats and dogs get breast, uterine, and ovarian cancers:** The Humane Society of the United States, "Why You Should Spay/Neuter Your Pet," http://www.humanesociety. org/issues/pet_overpopulation/facts/why_spay_neuter.html.

**138—But chimpanzees and other primates don't get these cancers:** Amber Moore, "Humans More Likely to Develop Cancer Than Chimps Thanks to DNA Modifications," *Medical Daily*, August 24, 2012, http://www.medicaldaily.com/humans-more-likely-develop-cancer-chimps-thanks-dna-modifications-242142.

## CHAPTER 8. SPIRIT MOVES
**140—But what's the difference between religion and spirituality:** Jon C. Stuckey, in Robab Latifnejad Roudsari, Helen T. Allan, and Pam A. Smith, "Looking at Infertility through the Lens of Religion and Spirituality: A Review of the Literature," *Human Fertility*, vol. 10, no. 3 (September 2007): 142, https://www.ncbi.nlm.nih.gov/pubmed/17786646.

**140—Growing up as part of the only Jewish family in small-town North Carolina:** Beth Rosenberg, in recorded telephone interview with the author, April 5, 2017.

**142—In its 2014 Religious Landscape Study:** Pew Research Center, "America's Changing Religious Landscape," Religion & Public Life, May 12, 2015, www.pewforum.org/2015/05/12/americas-changing-religious-landscape/.

**144—Brenda Niblock has read the Bible dozens of times:** Brenda Niblock, in recorded personal interview with the author, March 8, 2017.

**146—Julia McQuillan, PhD of the University of Nebraska:** Julia McQuillan, Arthur L. Greil, Karina M. Shreffler, Patricia A. Wonch-Hill, Kari C. Gentzler, John D. Hathcoat, "Does the Reason Matter? Variations in Childlessness Concerns among US Women," *Journal of Marriage and Family*, vol. 74, no. 5 (October 2012): 1166, onlinelibrary.wiley.com/doi/10.1111 /j.1741-3737.2012.01015.x/abstract.

**147—When her family shattered, Marianne Allison fell away:** Marianne Allison, in recorded personal interview with the author, March 24, 2017.

**151—While they were still living with their families of origin:** Abma and Martinez, "Childlessness among Older Women," 1053.

**151—Abma and Martinez's study was cited in an article titled:** Bryce J. Christensen and Robert W. Patterson, "Childless— and Godless," *The Natural Family*, vol. 23, no. 3 (Fall 2009), http: //familyinamerica.org/journals/fall-2009/childless-and-godless /#.Wrl0bpPwbkI.

**152—"I was in a period of deep longing for something meaningful":** Jen Hofmann, in recorded telephone interview with the author, March 21, 2017.

**156—At a morning mass celebrating long-wed couples in 2014:** "Marriage Requires Love That Imitates Christ, Pope Says" (June 2, 2014), https://www.catholicnewsagency.com/ news/marriage-requires-love-that-imitates-christ-pope-says.

**156—I like the first part:** Hanna, interview, June 14, 2017.

**160—Forty-seven-year-old Meg Woodard knew as a preteen:** Meg Woodard, in recorded personal interview with the author, May 21, 2015.

**161—An accident of geography:** Susan Hammer, in recorded personal interview with the author, February 1, 2017.

**163—Anne Wennhold has traveled many roads:** Anne Wennhold, in recorded telephone interview with the author, March 26, 2016.

**165—A team of researchers at Harvard Medical School:** Alice D. Domar, Alan Penzias, Jeffery A. Dusek, Amora Magna, Dalia Merari, Barbara Nielsen, and Debika Paul, "The Stress and Distress of Infertility: Does Religion Help Women Cope?" *Sexuality, Reproduction & Menopause* vol. 3, no. 2 (October 2005): 47, www.infona.pl/resource/bwmeta1.element.elsevier-2e1b17e2-55bf-31b2-9a90-ffb2911ed4ba.

**166—In their review of academic literature on religion:** Roudsari, "Looking at Infertility," 142.

**166—Another study mentioned in their review captured the dilemma:** Roudsari, "Looking at Infertility," 144.

**168—Another finding of Dr. McQuillan's research:** McQuillan, "Does the Reason Matter?" 1175.

## CHAPTER 9. ELDER ORPHANS
**171—There's even a name for what we may someday become:** North Shore–Long Island Jewish Health System, "Aging Baby

Boomers, Childless and Unmarried, at Risk of Becoming 'Elder Orphans'," *ScienceDaily*, (May 15, 2015), https://www.science daily.com/releases/2015/05/150515083532.htm.

**171—"Aging seniors face all sorts of uncertainties":** Susan B. Garland, "Childless Seniors Need to Build a Safety Net," *Kiplinger's Retirement Report*, (July 2015), 2, www.kiplinger.com/article/retirement/T023-C000-S004-childless-seniors-need-to-build-a-safety-net.html.

**172—Fiasco. Phone calls ricochet between a small island:** Tex Gieling, in a recorded personal interview with the author, June 25, 2015.

**176—There's a crucial way station between independence and interdependence:** Keren Brown Wilson, in a recorded personal interview with the author, June 26, 2016.

**176—In his bestselling book *Being Mortal*:** Atul Gawande, *Being Mortal: Medicine and What Matters in the End* (New York: Metropolitan Books, Henry Holt and Company, 2014), 22.

**178—One not-for-profit community service system:** Village to Village Network, FAQs, http://www.vtvnetwork.org/content.aspx?page_id=274&club_id=691012.

**178—Beacon Hill Village in the Boston area:** Beacon Hill Village, "About Beacon Hill Village," http://www.beaconhillvillage.org/content.aspx?page_id=22&club_id=332658&module_id=75811.

**179—Keren Brown Wilson is a proponent of congregate care living:** Brown Wilson, interview, June 26, 2016.

**179—In 1983 she and her husband built a simple residential facility:** Tracy Ready, "Assisted Living in America" trailer, *You Tube*, May 23, 2010, https://www.youtube.com/watch?v=wXEq2Yu-vik.

**180—After over sixty years living in her childhood home:** Dunwoodie, interview, August 25, 2015.

**183—According to the Alzheimer's Association:** Alzheimer's Association, "Women and Alzheimer's Disease," Fact Sheet, March 2014, https://www.alz.org/documents_custom/2014_facts_figures_fact_sheet_women.pdf.

**183—A future with dementia for those without children:** Alzheimer's Association, "Stages of Alzheimer's," www.alz.org/alzheimers_disease_stages_of_alzheimers.asp.

**183—A woman who calls herself Naomi Gregory knows she needs help:** Naomi Gregory, *pseudonym*, in a recorded telephone interview with the author, May 14, 2015.

**186—Her assessment is holistic and examines:** Mary Jo Saavedra, *Eldercare 101*, www.eldercare101book.com.

**186—The initial assessment takes about two hours:** Mary Jo Saavedra, in a recorded telephone interview with the author, May 9, 2016.

**188—Planning for our potential future care can be daunting:** Leslie Scism, "Long-Term-Care Insurance, Is It Worth It?" *Wall Street Journal*, May 1, 2015, www.wsj.com/articles/long-term-care-insurance-is-it-worth-it-1430488733.

**189—Paying for care without going broke can be challenging:** "Insights from Genworth's 2015 Cost of Care Survey," April 13, 2016. Genworth's Cost of Care Survey, https://www. genworth.com/dam/Americas/US/PDFs/Consumer/corporate /130568_040115_gnw.pdf.

**189—When Susan Ross was in her midforties:** Susan Ross, in a recorded telephone interview with the author, May 3, 2015.

**192—Three days after doctors told Karen Steinmetz she had terminal cancer:** Kristin Steinmetz, in a recorded telephone interview with the author, March 31, 2016.

**195—More than half of Americans age fifty-five to sixty-four don't have wills:** Richard Eisenberg, "Americans' Ostrich Approach to Estate Planning," *Forbes/Personal Finance*, April 9, 2014, www.forbes.com/sites/nextavenue/2014/04/09/ americans-ostrich-approach-to-estate-planning/#7eecb5795217.

**195—"The prevailing attitude is you really don't talk about aging":** Wennhold, interview, March 26, 2016.

**197—It's my job to tell them what I want:** "Welcome to the Conversation Project Starter Kit" 2016, https://theconversation-project.org/starter-kits/.

## CHAPTER 10. WHAT WE LEAVE BEHIND

**199—In 2013 *Time Magazine* ran a cover story:** Lauren Sandler, "The Childfree Life: When Having It All Means Not Having Children," *Time Magazine*, August 12, 2013, 39–45, time.com/241/having-it-all-without-having-children/.

**200—Using data from 1996 to 2004:** Michael Hurd, "Intervivos Giving by Older People in the United States: Who Received Financial Gifts from the Childless?" *Ageing & Society*, vol. 29, no. 8 (November 2009): 1214, www.cambridge.org/core/journals/ageing-and-society/article/intervivos-giving-by-older-people-in-the-united-states-who-received-financial-gifts-from-the-childless/6D4C4CD30289D09A3B6BBBF98F05A317.

**201—Kristin Steinmetz touched every item stacked in her grandmother's house:** Steinmetz, interview, March 31, 2016.

**202—According to one study, childless Americans over age fifty:** Russell N. James, III, "American Charitable Bequest Demographics (1992-2012)," 33, http://www.pgdc.com/pdf/american-charitable-bequest-demographics-1.pdf.

**202—Another study says the sharp spike in charitable estate planning:** Frank Adloff, "What Encourages Charitable Giving and Philanthropy?" *Ageing & Society*, vol. 29, no. 8 (October 15, 2009): 1185–1205, https://www.cambridge.org/core/journals/ageing-and-society/article/what-encourages-charitable-giving-and-philanthropy/9755393D5A78A702340D808C34C3D2B6.

**202—Gathered around a conference table on a rainy spring afternoon:** Debbie Fischer and Kate Kaufmann, "Non-Motherhood in a World of Giving," Oregon Community Foundation workshop, April 24, 2014.

**203—With assets over $1.6 billion:** Oregon Community Foundation, "2015 Annual Report."

**204—"Establishing a foundation is attractive for childless people":** Adloff, "What Encourages Charitable Giving," 1185.

**205—After examining the demographics of American charitable bequests:** James, "American Charitable Bequest Demographics," 33.

**205—Italian researchers Marco Albertini and Martin Kohli point out:** Marco Albertini and Martin Kohli, "What Childless Older People Give: Is the Generational Link Broken?" *Ageing & Society,* vol. 29, no. 8 (2009): 1272, cadmus.eui.eu/handle/1814/13764.

**205—According to the New York–based Foundation Center:** Foundation Center, "Foundation Stats—Aggregate Fiscal Data of Foundations in the US," 2013, http://data.foundationcenter.org/#/foundations/all/nationwide/total/list/2013.

**205—Here's lifelong Dayton resident Jane Dunwoodie's advice:** Dunwoodie, interview, August 25, 2015.

**207—Deb Fischer figured out a way to educate the next generation:** Fischer, interview, April 23, 2015.

**210—Real estate plays a big role in Tex Gieling's philanthropic plans:** Gieling, interview, June 25, 2015.

**212—While Tex's giving thwarts future construction:** Katen, interview, May 2, 2015.

**213—Marie Erickson found her legacy in both business and family:** Erickson, interview, June 18, 2015.

**215—Trying to make sense of it all:** Sigafoos, interview, May 27, 2015.

**216—For eighty-four-year-old Jane Zembaty:** Zembaty, interview, October 12, 2015.

**217—Conservatively estimated, a mother invests:** Kim Parker and Wendy Wang, "Modern Parenthood: Roles of Moms and Dads Converge As They Balance Work and Family," *Pew Research Center*, March 14, 2013: 27, http://www.pewsocialtrends.org/2013/03/14/modern-parenthood-roles-of-moms-and-dads-converge-as-they-balance-work-and-family/.

**218—Malcolm Gladwell, in his best-selling book:** Malcolm Gladwell, *Outliers: The Story of Success* (New York: Little, Brown & Company, 2008), 43–44.

## AFTERWORD. DO YOU HAVE KIDS?

**225—In an article he wrote for *The American Scholar*:** Christopher Clausen, "Childfree in Toyland," *The American Scholar*, vol. 71 (Winter 2002): 113, https://www.unz.com/print/AmScholar-2002q1-00111/Contents/.

**226—Clausen goes on to describe a time:** Clausen, "Childfree in Toyland," 116.

**230—In April 2016 Hillary Frank, co-producer of the podcast:** Hillary Frank, "Terry Gross on Not Having Kids," *The Longest Shortest Time*, podcast episode 79, April 20, 2016, https://longestshortesttime.com/episode-79-terry-gross-on-not-having-kids/.

**232—The Cassandra Company has tracked emerging trends in youth:** Gabriella Berman, "Cassandra Report Finds Parenthood Is No Longer an Essential Element of Adulthood for Millennials," *Deep Focus*, October 20, 2015, http://www.marketwired.com/press-release/cassandra-report-finds-parenthood-is-no-longer-essential-element-adulthood-millennials-2065471.htm.

**233—Yet many parents seem to have a stockpile of responses:** Urban Dictionary, Definition 2, https://www.urbandictionary.com/define.php?term=Bingo.

**237—A 2017 study by Annalucia Bays of Virginia Commonwealth University:** Annalucia Bays, "Perceptions, Emotions, and Behaviors toward Women Based on Parental Status," *Sex Roles*, vol. 76, no. 3–4 (February 2017): 148, https://link.springer.com/article/10.1007/s11199-016-0655-5.

**237—The same year another study, this one out of:** Leslie Ashburn-Nardo, "Parenthood as a Moral Imperative? Moral Outrage and the Stigmatization of Voluntarily Childfree Men and Women," *Sex Roles*, vol. 76, no. 5–6 (March 2017): 398, https://link.springer.com/article/10.1007/s11199-016-0606-1.

**238—Malone Wright, age sixty, is a spunky professional communicator:** "About Us," TheNotMom.com website, https://www.thenotmom.com/aboutus.

**238—She isn't interested in further polarizing or distancing women:** Karen Malone Wright, in a recorded telephone interview with the author, March 20, 2017.

# ACKNOWLEDGMENTS

**W**hat started as a walk on the beach has since snowballed into hundreds of conversations in meeting rooms and private homes, on trains, busses, and airplanes. I appreciate and am grateful for the candor and trust involved in every story shared. Let's keep talking.

My agent, April Eberhardt, is a savvy business partner, tenacious advocate, and unfailingly supportive friend. The never-ending synchronicities that continue to bring us together are astonishing. Thank you for your enthusiastic commitment to bringing my work to fruition.

Brooke Warner, Cait Levin, and Elke Barter at She Writes Press transformed a stack of worded pages into a publication that's aesthetically pleasing, well-championed, and broadly distributed. May they thrive by promoting women's voices based on the merits of our work.

Without the support of my writing community, these pages would surely have joined other partial manuscripts stored in musty boxes. I am grateful for enduring connections through the now defunct and sorely missed Northwest Institute of Literary Arts. Larry Cheek, my MFA advisor, taught me the power of clean, simple writing and convinced me I was up to the task of crafting a good book. Ana Maria Spagna urged me to be courageous in telling my own story.

These brilliant readers inspired me to write better and go deeper: Lauren Back, Jenny Bates, Jo Scott-Coe, Charlotte Dixon, Heather Durham, Tim Flynn, Leslie Hill, Cynthia Jones, Cameron Kelly, Sue Anne Linde, Caroline Purchase, Sarah Shepherd, Avril Stewart, and Nick Wagner. You propelled me forward through rocky times. Profound thanks to you all.

The Sterling Writer's Room at Portland's exquisite Central Library is an incubator of inspiration and the best place I know to generate word count. I deeply appreciate having access to this beautiful workspace I now consider my second home.

Marilyn Fischer, retired philosophy professor and wonderful friend, opened doors into her vast university community, stimulated my thinking, and cheered me through the writing process. I appreciate our companionship walking parallel publishing paths.

I was honored to be featured speaker at the University of Dayton's Colloquium on Women's and Gender Studies early in my research cycle and again as my work neared completion. Thanks to Directors V. Denise James and Rebecca Whisnaut and their staff for their support and for facilitating interactions with faculty, staff, and students.

Karen Malone Wright launched the first NotMom Summit in Cleveland at a most opportune time. May her work creating community continue, because it's sorely needed. I am grateful to her, Laura Lavoie, and all those who attended the NotMom Summits in 2015 and 2017.

I'm awed by the love and support of so many dear to me, especially Michael and Patty Green, Elizabeth Hale, Ian Heitz, Suzanne Lee, Susan Marrant, Debra Pearce-McCall, Lindsey Schultz, Elizabeth Shypertt, Susan Tull, and my amazing book group. Thank you.

# ACKNOWLEDGMENTS

Many thanks to the young women and men who confirm this work is vital to envisioning the various paths their lives might follow, especially Annamieka Hopps Davidson, Kelly Nardo, and Kristen Genzano.

Finally, I am indebted to my strategic team, Deb Fischer, Elsa Stavney, and Eric Vines, who grasped the importance of this project when I was still intimidated by its very idea. Thanks for asking of me more than I ever thought possible.

# ABOUT THE AUTHOR

Kate Kaufmann first got an inkling of how different life as a non-mom could be after she and her ex abandoned infertility treatments, quit their corporate jobs, and moved from an excellent suburban school district to a rural community in Oregon to raise sheep. Everyone in the country seemed to have kids. So began her quest for defining her identity as a woman without children in a culture high on family.

Since 2012 Kate has talked intimately about the topic with hundreds of women ranging in age from twenty-four to ninety-one and advocates for better understanding of the childless/childfree demographic in classrooms, on panels, and before professional groups, among them the University of Dayton, AARP, and the Oregon Community Foundation.

Kate has an MFA in creative writing and a professional background in corporate staffing, training, and consulting. Her writing has appeared most recently in the *Washington Post*. She lives in Portland, Oregon.

katekaufmann.com

*Author photo © Jerome Hart Photography*

# SELECTED TITLES FROM SHE WRITES PRESS

She Writes Press is an independent publishing company founded to serve women writers everywhere. Visit us at www.shewritespress.com.

*Americashire: A Field Guide to a Marriage* by Jennifer Richardson. $15.95, 978-1-938314-30-8. A couple's decision about whether or not to have a child plays out against the backdrop of their new home in the English countryside.

*Godmother: An Unexpected Journey, Perfect Timing, and Small Miracles* by Odile Atthalin. $16.95, 978-1-63152-172-0. After thirty years of traveling the world, Odile Atthalin—a French intellectual from a well-to-do family in Paris—ends up in Berkeley, CA, where synchronicities abound and ultimately give her everything she has been looking for, including the gift of becoming a godmother.

*Stepmother: A Memoir* by Marianne Lile. $16.95, 978-1-63152-089-1. Lile describes the complexities of the stepmom position, in a family and in the community, and shares her experience wearing a tag that is often misunderstood and weighed down by the numerous myths in society.

*Stop Giving it Away: How to Stop Self-Sacrificing and Start Claiming Your Space, Power, and Happiness* by Cherilynn Veland. $16.95, 978-1-63152-958-0. An empowering guide designed to help women break free from the trappings of the needs, wants, and whims of other people—and the self-imposed limitations that are keeping them from happiness.

*Think Better. Live Better. 5 Steps to Create the Life You Deserve* by Francine Huss. $16.95, 978-1-938314-66-7. With the help of this guide, readers will learn to cultivate more creative thoughts, realign their mindset, and gain a new perspective on life.

*Note to Self: A Seven-Step Path to Gratitude and Growth* by Laurie Buchanan. $16.95, 978-1-63152-113-3. Transforming intention into action, Note to Self equips you to shed your baggage, bridging the gap between where you are and where you want to be—body, mind, and spirit—and empowering you to step into joy-filled living now!

31901064512397